U-BOAT

• versus •

AIRCRAFT

NORMAN FRANKS &
ERIC ZIMMERMAN

GRUB STREET · LONDON

Published by
Grub Street
The Basement
10 Chivalry Road
London SW11 1HT

Maps by Graeme Andrew

British Library Cataloguing in Publication Data
Franks, Norman L. R. (Norman Leslie Robert), 1940-
  U-boat versus aircraft: the dramatic story behind U-boat
  claims in gun action with aircraft in World War II
  1. Anti-submarine warfare – History 2. World War, 1939-1945 – Naval operations
  – Submarine 3. World War, 1939-1945 – Naval operations, German
  4. World War, 1939-1945 – Aerial operations, British 5. World War, 1939-1945 –
  Aerial operations, American 6. World War, 1939-1945 – Aerial operations, Canadian
  I. Title II. Zimmerman, Eric
  940.5'4516
ISBN 1-902304-02-2

Typeset by Pearl Graphics, Hemel Hempstead

Printed and bound in Great Britain by
Biddles Ltd, Guildford and King's Lynn

CONTENTS

ACKNOWLEDGEMENTS

Help has come from many sources. In no specific order, they are, Allison Duffield, of the Imperial War Museum, Mrs Pat Brame, Mrs Frances Ryan, Mrs A Sharpe, David Lees, researcher and U-boat historian, Air Commodore J A Holmes DFC, 190 Squadron, Richard Thomas, 206 and 86 Squadrons, John J Scott 58 Squadron, John Mills, 210 Squadron, Mike Seymour, 210 Squadron historian, R E 'Bob' Dobson, 210 Squadron, Bill Balderson, 210 Squadron, J Dawson, 210 Squadron, Peter W Lewis, 53 Squadron Assn; Mervyn T C Francis, 10 OTU; Herr Rudi Wieser, U-763.Graham Day and Alan Thomas at the Air Historical Branch, MoD, London; Department of the [US] Navy, Naval Historical Center, Washington Navy Yard, USA; Canadian National Archives, Public Records Office, Kew, Surrey, R M Coppock (NHB/MoD ret'd), Walter Cloots, U-boat researcher, Alex Niestlé, U-boat historian and author, Wolfgang Freese, Edward Rumpf, U-boat researcher. Friends and fellow authors Barrett Tillman and Ray Sturtivant. Keith Rennles. A sincere thank you to one and all.

Special thanks are due to Frans Beckers, whose tireless work in scanning and translating the various U-boat war diaries resulted in most of the KTB extracts which are featured abundantly in this book.

And of course, to our ladies, Heather and Linda.

INTRODUCTION

World War Two could be said to be made up of a number of different, almost independent, wars each contributing to the whole. This was certainly so with the anti-U-boat war fought on and below the world's oceans. The lion's share of this conflict was fought in the vast grey wastes of the Atlantic where Britain's life line of supplies from Canada and America was severely threatened by the German submarines.

Britain and her Allies fought a desperate war here, her Navy and Air Force trying to protect the merchant seamen sailing the ships that were bringing not only food but materials of war to a beleaguered Britain as she stood alone against an occupied Europe, dominated by Hitler's victorious forces.

The menace – and this oft-used word is most suitable – was Germany's U-boats. They had proved a formidable foe during WW1 and were now even more of a threat, for in this war they operated from captured French ports along the Bay of Biscay, from where they could easily sail out into the North or South Atlantic, to roam far and wide. They were able to travel to the American and Canadian east coasts, south-west to the seas off South America, down the African coast, round the Cape of Good Hope and into the Indian Ocean. They were also able to penetrate into the Mediterranean, although the Straits of Gibraltar often caused the U-boat crews many problems.

Once at sea in the later stages of the war, the U-boats could be supplied at sea with fuel, torpedoes and food, extending the duration of their patrols without the need to return to their ports. With the inherent dangers of crossing and re-crossing the Bay of Biscay, where Royal Navy ships and Royal Air Force, and later American, aeroplanes searched for them, to stay out re-supplied was a bonus not to be missed.

The anti-U-boat war has been the subject of numerous books but not specifically aimed at telling the stories of those aircraft which, meeting determined U-boat captains and crews, fought it out in gun actions, and paid the price, of either being shot down or damaged.

In the early war years what became the norm by mid-1942, was slow to progress but quickly did so from then on. RAF Coastal Command had not been created to fight a war out in the Atlantic. While its activities, it was thought, would be confined to the coastal areas around the British Isles and particularly the North Sea, things changed dramatically with the fall of Norway and then the fall of France. Patrolling U-boats, that would ordinarily have had to sally forth from and return to their north German ports, had the world's oceans opened up to them once ports such as Lorient, La Pallice, Bordeaux, St Nazaire and Brest became available.

Coastal Command had few long-range aircraft other than the Sunderland and Catalina. Most were twin-engined aeroplanes such as the Whitley, Hudson and Anson. The Vickers Wellington came later and helped, but it was not until the Halifax, Liberator and Fortress land-planes came along to assist the flying boats that things began to improve for the flyers and get worse for the German submariners.

America's entry into the war in late 1941 also helped to suppress U-boat activities with its airforce and naval aviation aircraft added to which came both British and American escort carriers that operated out in the Atlantic. With improved radar and weaponry, the anti-U-boat war was gradually won, but during the years of 1942-44 the struggle was immense.

The sea is vast, ask any Coastal or Naval pilot or crew member who has searched it hour after hour, day after day, week after week. Weather does not help observation and the Atlantic is rarely calm and placid. Each whitecap could be the 'feather' of a periscope, each rain squall could hide a surfaced submarine, each cloud shadow could help to conceal these deadly craft that in any event were relatively small, didn't have the vast superstructures of ships, or smoking funnels to watch for.

In the early period of the conflict, submarine commanders instinctively crash-dived at the first sign of aircraft. Because of this, most Coastal Command aircraft did not carry much in the way of forward-firing nose guns. Without proper radar, or any radar, the chances of finding a U-boat on the surface was pure luck, and the German look-outs had a vested interest in seeing the aeroplane first; their lives depended on it.

Once radar – ASV – was improved, things became a lot easier for the searching aircrew, and this coupled with the break-through in reading German radio traffic, meant that Coastal Command aircraft could at least be sent to areas where known U-boats were sailing. As U-boats had to rise to the surface in order to 'breathe' and re-charge their batteries, they were often on the surface. They could also travel faster on the sea than beneath it. It was at these times they became vulnerable, and of course, were extremely vulnerable whilst crash-diving. If an aircraft could sneak up in cloud or rain, and get within striking distance before the look-outs spotted the approaching danger, crash-diving gave all the advantages to the attacker.

Gradually, it seemed sensible, or even expedient, to remain on the surface if surprised, and fight back with their armament. At least they had a chance or putting off the attacking aeroplane, perhaps un-nerving the man who would be releasing the bombs or depth-charges down on them into making an error, or at best destroy the aeroplane altogether.

To this end, U-boat anti-aircraft gunners were specifically trained. It was their sole purpose to shoot down the aeroplanes that hurtled towards them, and as most were only 50 or 100 feet up, they were large targets. However, nerve had to be held on both sides. Those U-boat gunners knew it was the aeroplane or them more often than not. And even if they survived the attack and a sinking, not many survivors would be rescued. Way out in the Atlantic nobody came to pull you out of a cold, often freezing sea.

What follows, then, are some of the stories where aircraft and U-boats met on the high seas, and where the boats either stayed on the surface by choice or necessity in an attempt to fend off an attacker, and where their fire brought down or damaged the assailant, even if, in the final event, the boat too was lost.

It is a well known fact that some Coastal Command crews never even saw a U-boat while others saw several. Those that fought those boats which remained on the surface to fight back, and those in the boats, however, will not forget their encounters.

Norman Franks, London, England.
Eric Zimmerman, Calgary, Canada.

Books such as this can never be 100 percent accurate or complete for numerous reasons. However, the authors would like to receive any additional information, feedback, comments etc, on the events covered. Anyone wishing to do so, please write to Eric Zimmerman at 151 Applebrook Circle SE, Calgary, Alberta, Canada, T2A 7T3. Thank you.

CHAPTER ONE

OVER THE ENDLESS SEA

Actions that make up the bulk of this book were few and far between in the early period of the war. There may well have been the odd exchange of gunfire, but as far as is known, there were no aircraft shot down by U-boats. At least, no U-boats made any claims, and if any aircraft was shot down unknown to the U-boat crew, Coastal Command didn't know of it either.

Claims by U-boat crews, as we shall see, were also made where no actual aircraft were lost, but it has to be remembered that a U-boat crew had limited horizons. An aircraft seemingly heading away, low on the sea, with smoke coming from an engine, might easily be thought to have gone in, whereas the pilot would struggle to remain airborne, and finally make it back to land. The fact that the aeroplane is later written-off due to its battle damage, or the crew has suffered casualties, fatal or otherwise, is not taken into account from the U-boat's standpoint, but nevertheless, is a factor.

In fact the first recorded and documented action between an aircraft and a submarine which resulted in the aeroplane's loss, did not occur until 1 August 1941, almost two years after the war began. Even then it was an Italian submarine, the *Delfino*, commanded by Alberto Avogardo di Cerrione, and the action took place not in the Atlantic, but in the Mediterranean.

No. 204 Group RAF had a report of a submarine somewhere in the Gulf of Sollum, along the coast east of Tobruk since 29 July, and an anti-sub hunt was organised, with a Sunderland of No. 230 Squadron, RAF, from Aboukir Bay, Egypt, and three RN destroyers. The danger was that the submarine could intercept shipping reinforcing the garrison at Tobruk, hence the search. The 230 Squadron crew were:

F/L E Brand	Pilot	Sgt G E Starkey
P/O E E Dennis	2nd pilot	Sgt J I Mell
P/O R M East	Nav	Sgt R Horsburgh
F/O R E Packington		Sgt E Shoosmith
Sgt W H Yates		Sgt S E Gould
Sgt W M White RAAF		LAC G E Cooper (No.103 MU)

The Sunderland – L2166, coded 'U' and named *Perak* was already a veteran. Nine months earlier, captained by Flight Lieutenant P H Alington, L2166 had attacked and sunk the Italian submarine *Gondar* off Alexandria. The second pilot/navigator had been Flying Officer E Brand, who now, as a Flight Lieutenant, commanded L2166.

Engert Brand's crew spotted the submarine and went straight into the attack, but the Italians were not surprised and began to defend themselves. It was 37 minutes to midnight in position 32°12´ North 24°46´ East (positions in future will merely be noted as 3212/2446). Gun flashes greeted the Sunderland crew and machine-gun fire hit the huge flying boat repeatedly. Brand came on steadily, finally releasing a stick of six depth charges (D/Cs), the explosions from which gave the boat a severe shaking but did no permanent damage.

The Italian gunners now saw the Sunderland on fire and then it dipped and crashed into the sea. There had been no time for the Sunderland crew to get off any radio message, or at least none was received by base. The location of the destroyers is uncertain, but they were certainly not in the immediate vicinity because the submarine did not dive, but headed in the direction of the crash site where they were able to rescue four of the Sunderland's crew, including Brand. The others were Flying Officer Packington, and Sergeants White and Yates. The other eight were lost. In fact the crew consisted of 11 men, but there was a twelfth on board, LAC G E Cooper, attached from No.103 MU.

The twelve men remained missing until 15 September, on which date a message was received from a German broadcast that an Italian submarine had shot down a Sunderland on 1 August, and the crew had been taken prisoner. Sadly the 'crew' only consisted of four survivors.

* * *

It was another Italian submarine that claimed an aircraft shot down on Armistice Day 1941 (11 November). The *Tazzoli* commanded by Carlo Fecia di Cossato, claimed being attacked by a Blenheim in the Bay of Biscay, off the mouth of the Gironde River, and received credit for a victory. Unfortunately there is no record of any Blenheim being lost, and it was not the usual sort of aircraft that would be operating in the area. Only weather recce Blenheims might be here, and none reported an action with a submarine.

The nearest one can get is Hudson 'D' of 53 Squadron on an anti-sub sweep. The crew sighted a submarine in position 4850/1120 at 1315 hours, which is way out in the Bay and nowhere near the Gironde. They attacked with D/Cs as the boat dived, but made no mention of any gunfire from the boat. However, this aircraft in fact attacked U-203 in Grid BE63. Therefore, with the lack of Italian information it is impossible to identify the aircraft 'lost'.

Fleet Air Arm Action

Just ten days following America's and Japan's entry into the war, U-131, commanded by Korvettenkapitän Arend Baumann, was located by an aircraft from the escort carrier HMS *Audacity*, part of the escort to a Gibraltar-Britain convoy HG76. The time was 1330 hours, in German Grid reference DH3349, west-south-west of Gibraltar. An 802 Squadron Martlet of the Fleet Air Arm, flown by Sub Lieutenant George R P Fletcher spotted the boat and came in low and fast for a strafing run but was met by a hail of flak which blasted the fighter into the sea, killing its pilot.

Only minutes later U-131 herself was destroyed, sunk by surface escorts from the convoy, Commander F J Walker's sloop HMS *Stork*, and the destroyers *Blankney*, *Exmooor* and *Stanley*, with the corvette *Penstemon*. *Penstemon* picked up the submarine on her asdic and made a depth-charge attack. Then U-131 surfaced and was seen making off at speed, but gunfire from the warships holed the pressure hull, forcing Baumann to scuttle. He and all his crew were rescued.

HMS *Audacity* was the first of a long line of escort carriers and the full story of convoy HG76 depicts one of the more famous convoy actions of WW2.

Fatal Detachment – 15/7/42

No.159 Squadron was formed as a heavy bomber unit at the beginning of 1942, equipped with the American Consolidated Liberator, destined for the Middle East. However, before it became established, the Squadron was posted out to the Far East. During the move, in the early summer, a detachment of aircraft remained in Palestine, some of which were used on anti-submarine duties. On one such sortie, a Squadron Liberator II is believed to have come across U-561, commanded by Kapitänleutnant Robert Bartels. At least, there is certainly no other obvious candidate.

Details of exactly what occurred from the RAF side are sparse, simply because the aircraft failed to return. Nor apparently did it report the discovery of the U-boat to its base, or if it did, that message did not get through, for as far as the RAF were concerned, Liberator AL566 did not return. This is surprising, because while the submarine crew reported two attacks, over an hour apart, there is every indication that there was only this one Liberator involved. The identification of the B24 was also complicated because the U-boat crew saw the high-winged four-engined aircraft with its large fuselage as a flying boat – noting that is was probably a Sunderland.

The first attack came at 2207 hours in German Grid CP8259 – east-north-east of Port Said in the Eastern Mediterranean. The aircraft was spotted by its navigation lights and as it closed in it was met by 20 mm gunfire, the gunners claiming hits. As it went over the boat further flak was sent up and the aircraft banked away to port, the sub crash-dived. No bombs were dropped.

However, the Liberator crew must have remained in the area for the next hour, and one explanation of why no sighting report was received, was that it had indeed been hit and its radio knocked out. In the event, U-561 surfaced just over an hour later in the same location, and at 2315 a 'flying-boat' was observed on a parallel course, at a height of 30-40 metres.

With his patience rewarded, the Lib pilot brought his aircraft round and four flares were dropped as a head-on approach became obvious to the German gunners. They opened fire and immediately saw their shells strike home. Smoke began to stream from the aircraft which was seen to jettison its bombs, but the aircraft continued to come on, its gunners strafing the boat despite the flames and, as the U-boat crew described it, with the aircraft starting to break up. Two large objects detached themselves from the machine – possibly men baling out – that were seen to fall slowly to the sea. Moments later the aircraft itself plunged burning into the waves and broke apart. If the action described was indeed that which involved this B24 and U-561, then the gallant but luckless RAF crew had been:

W/O W S Pottie	Pilot	P/O G Mallaby	AG
Sgt H E Birk RAAF	2nd pilot	P/O H Liesk	AG
W/O W S Miller	Observer	F/S J S A Hodge	AG
Sgt M C Fell	AG		

Only one body from the crew was recovered, that of Sergeant Hilary Eldred Birk from Croyden, New South Wales, washed ashore some time later and buried at Benghazi.

Whitley Attachment

With the Battle of the Atlantic really hotting up, Bomber Command was often asked for help with aircraft and crews. 'Bomber' Harris, C-in-C Bomber Command had his own problems but whenever he could he did loan squadrons to Coastal for short periods, and also No. 10 Operational Training Unit (OTU). The latter were made up of crews in the final stages of their training before posting to an operational bomber squadron. What better way of completing this training than operating over the Bay of Biscay where their piloting and navigational skills could be put to good use? (As they were only given Whitleys to fly, some of the crews might comment differently on this *better reason*!)

However, one unit that was attached was No.77 Squadron, commencing May 1942. The detachment, to RAF Chivenor, was to end in October 1942 but shortly before this date, they had a last minute rush of excitement. On 2 September, Whitley 'H' (Z9515) was out on a Strike against shipping, having taken off in the early hours. Its crew consisted of:

P/O A Cassie	Pilot	Sgt T McMahon
Sgt C E Johnson		Sgt A R Chapman
Sgt P G Everett		

Some hours later RAF St Eval picked up a feint SOS but it quickly faded out. H/77 failed to return.

They had come across U-256, commanded by Kapitänleutnant Odo Loewe, whose lookout men identified the aircraft as a Wellington. U-356's KTB (*Kriegstagebuch* – Daily War Diary) recorded:

> "Aircraft attacking, distance 800-1,000 metres. Flak. [It] Attacks from the port side. Flak hits observed on aircraft cupola [cockpit]. Strafing from the aircraft, 2-3 bombs dropped which fall 10-20 metres astern. Heavy damage. The aircraft was a Vickers Wellington. Aircraft disappears out of sight at a very low altitude, smoke is pouring from the port motor. There is damage to the U-boat's upper deck, possibly from the aircraft's propeller on its overpass."

The attack was timed at 0830 hours in German Grid BF5490. The Germans obviously thought the damage was from the aircraft as it went over rather than from the exploding bombs, which indicated a VERY LOW approach, and perhaps the pilots had already been hit by the flak fire and were beginning to lose control. Whether the smoking engine was a result of flak or of the striking of the U-boat must be speculation. Searches were made for the Whitley crew but with a very feint and curtailed SOS, their position was unknown. If they survived a crash-landing, they did not survive long enough to be rescued. A Whitley, unlike some aircraft, did not fly very far on one engine.

The next day, Whitley 'P' of 77 Squadron sank U-705 west of Ushant with the loss of its entire 45-man crew. The same day, V/77 attacked U-660 which survived unscathed. Returning to Bomber Command, 77 Squadron began converting to Halifax four-engined bombers.

"465"

RAF Coastal Command was made up of squadrons of several nationalities quite apart from British. Canadian, Australian, Polish, Czech and Norwegian squadrons all took their part in the anti-submarine war. On 21 September 1942, a Norwegian crew found themselves on the wrong side of a U-boat's anti-aircraft fire.

No.330 Norwegian Squadron consisted of two Flights, 'B' based at Reykjavik, Iceland, and 'A' Flight at Oban and Sullom Voe. The Iceland Flight had Northrop N3s and Catalina flying boats, 'A' Flight just Catalinas. The Iceland Flight also used Akureyri, an inlet on the north of the island.

On 21 Sepember 1942, Catalina III 'Z' (FP525) of 330 Squadron, operating from Akureyri, Iceland, was flying air escort for convoy QP14 (Russia-Britain). Flying astern of the ships at 1114 hours, the Norwegians spotted U-606 (Kapitänleutnant Dietrich von der Esch) on the surface, trying to catch the convoy. The Germans gave their position as Grid

AB4176, north-east of Jan Mayen Island and the KTB extract records:

> "Aircraft, Consolidated, at a distance of 1,500 metres, it releases a smoke float. When the distance is 800 metres – flak. At 200 metres we see four bombs released. The aircraft crosses over [us]. Smoke stream pouring out of the port-side motor. [It] flies away in the direction of two smoke clouds on the horizon, gradually losing height. Disappears out of sight."

The Catalina had made a run as the submarine remained on the surface, opening up with flak fire. The Norwegian wireless operator sent off a '465' signal ('am in action with a U-boat'), and like so many other 465 messages, it was followed by an ominous silence.

The U-boat scored hits on the petrol tanks and two of the crew were wounded. Lieutenant C J A Stansburg pressed home his attack despite the gunfire and released four D/Cs but they caused no serious damage. It was quite another story for the Catalina, and damage was so severe that Stansburg had no choice but to make a forced landing near the convoy. Everyone got clear before the flying boat sank, and they were all rescued by the destroyer *Marne*. U-606 was lost on 22 February 1943 under the command of another captain, during an attack on convoy ON166.

Unfortunately the crew of FP525 is not recorded in the squadron diary but the following men were the usual crew of Lieutenant Stansburg and are listed here for information. Some, if not all, were involved in the above action:

Lt C J A Stansburg	Pilot	Kvm Laerum	WOP
S/Lt Aas	2nd pilot	1404 I W Johansen	FME
S/Lt P Devold	Nav	1695 Hansen	FME
Kvm Hilmar	WOP	639 Søensen	FMA
Kvm Bjerkseth	WOP		

Gibraltar Hudsons

Britain's Gibraltar air-based aircraft saw much action in the mid-war years, operating not only east into the western Mediterranean, but also west and north-west into the Atlantic and southern Bay of Biscay area. There were several twin-engined squadrons here, flying both Wellingtons and Hudsons – 48, 233, 459, 500, 608, and later 172 and 179 Squadrons.

Their first loss to submarine gunfire came on 1 November 1942, a period of intense activity because of *Operation Torch*, the Allied landings in Algeria, due to begin on the 8th. There was much shipping in the area off southern and south-western Spain. U-565 under the command of Kapitänleutnant Wilhelm Franken was attacked twice by Hudsons on the 1st, 233 Squadron being the RAF unit involved.

The first attack came in German Grid CH5977, which is located in the western Mediterranean, south of the Balearic Islands (now the popular holiday locations of Majorca and Ibiza), at 1250. The alarm was sounded as an aircraft was spotted, followed by a crash-dive. The Germans estimated the aircraft was at a height of 30 metres as it released a bomb which exploded near the bows, which caused severe damage, forcing U-565 back to surface. As the gunners clambered onto the bridge, the aircraft was seen coming round for another run from the port side, its bomb doors still open. The gunners opened fire, scoring hits on the approaching machine. This time it went over at 150 metres but no bombs came down. A third approach, this time from the starboard side, was again countered by flak and more hits were observed. Obviously damaged, it banked away and disappeared.

The aircraft was a Hudson III, V9169, on an anti-submarine sweep. It had taken off one minute past 9 am, shortly after another Hudson, AE591, had left, both on a Sweep to the east. At 1139, V9169 had altered course to investigate a suspicious object which turned out to be the conning tower of a U-boat. The Hudson crew were:

F/S S Woodward	Pilot	Sgt L Hudson
Sgt G Tempest		Sgt R Tetley

(Sgt L *Hudson* is not a typing error!)

Seven minutes after turning, Woodward was diving from 2,000 feet to 150 feet, the navigator noting the position as 3735/0138. The boat was diving and as the aircraft went over, four D/Cs tumbled down, falling 75 yards ahead and slightly starboard of the swirl left by the crash-dive.

No sooner had the Hudson began to circle than the U-boat reappeared and Woodward went in again, to attack with an anti-submarine bomb. However, the aircraft was hit in the tailplane and the bomb fell 30 yards off to starboard, despite the U-boat crew saying nothing was dropped. With more damage on the next approach, Woodward was having trouble with his controls and with an obviously determined U-boat crew fighting back, wisely decided to head for home.

Meantime, the other Hudson, alerted by the radio call from Woodward's crew, had come to the spot. The boat recorded that it was still in the same Grid position, and although no actual time is recorded, has to be within minutes of the first Hudson departing. The Germans identified another Hudson, this time AE591, its crew being:

Sgt D H Jenkins	Pilot	F/S C Smith
F/O P G Attenborough		P/O A V J Bettridge

The German gun crews watched as the Hudson passed by, then turned, coming in to make a strafing and bomb run. The gunners opened fire and as the Hudson went over it dropped three bombs which fell 20-40 metres off the starboard side of the boat, but no further damage was sustained. However, the gunners had scored again. They watched as the Hudson banked, its port engine streaming fire and smoke. Their blood up, the gunners continued to hammer the burning aircraft which became enveloped in flames before diving into the sea 500 metres away. None of the four-man crew survived.

The guns fell silent. Within minutes the gunners had fought off two attacks, shot down one aircraft and damaged another. There was relief and congratulations amongst them and the men below decks who knew only too well how close they had come to death or injury. U-565 in fact would survive this and other patrols in the Med, until finally damaged beyond repair by an American air raid while in a Greek port in September 1944, and scuttled with depth charges.

Trinidad Hudson

The next loss was another Hudson, but this time the action took place on the other side of the Atlantic. 53 Squadron RAF had left the dull British shores in June 1942 for the sunny climes of the Caribbean, after a short stay in the United States. Based at Waller Field, Trinidad, its aircraft, painted white, had been fitted with Yagi radar aerials. The shipping off the eastern seaboard of the Americas were having a grim time from U-boat attacks, especially tankers bringing crude oil from South America and southern USA, northwards.

Hudson 'L' (V9253) on a *Bauxite* A/S patrol, caught U-505 on the surface south-east of Trinidad – Grid E012 – on 10 November, attacking out of low cloud to achieve total surprise. Four D/Cs were dropped, one of which made a direct hit and exploded on contact. The U-boat gunners had just started to fire, but undoubtedly it was the force of the explosion that caused the Hudson to be blown out of the sky, crashing into the sea with the loss of its five-man crew (the fifth man was an American Navy seaman flying along as an observer).

The boat was lucky to have survived but nevertheless, she suffered heavy damage and had two crewmen badly injured. U-505 broke off her patrol and limped back to Lorient, arriving on 12 December. So at least the RAF crew had stopped her war cruise but at the cost of their own lives:

F/S R R Sillcock RAAF	Pilot	Sgt W Skinner	WOP/AG
Sgt P G Nelson RNZAF	Nav	Sgt T R Millar	WOP/AG
Seaman 1c H L Brew USN (passenger)			

Hudson Mayhem

The attack upon U-595 (Kapitänleutnant Jürgen Quaet-Faslem) on 14 November 1942 by two Hudsons of 608 Squadron RAF, was covered in some detail in my book *Search, Find and Kill* pages 216-218 (Norman Franks, published by Grub Street in 1995).

Briefly, the Hudsons, operating from Tafaraouri, Oran following the invasion of Algeria, had found U-595 and there followed several attacks, each fended off by gunfire from the submarine. Seriously damaged and unable to dive, Hudsons of 500 Squadron then began to attack her. Three of the Hudsons were hit and damaged by the flak gunners, those of 'X' (W/C D Spotswood DFC) hit in the fuel tank, starboard engine and aileron, forcing him to break off; 'F' (F/O H M S Green) hit as it went over, its D/Cs failing to drop and then 'K' (F/O G A B Lord) hit in the port front fuel tank and starboard engine. Despite the damage, Hudson 'F' came in again only to be hit in the wings, while signal cartridges were ignited in the cockpit, forcing the pilot to withdraw.

Still unable to dive and knowing all was lost, Quaet-Faslem headed his boat for the beach near Tenes. Grounding his boat the crew passed into French hands but shortly afterwards became prisoners of American ground forces. Despite the severe damage to three Hudsons, no aircrew were hurt.

The next day came the famous incident to Hudson 'S' of 500 Squadron, piloted by Flying Officer M A Ensor. During an attack on U-259 (KL Klaus Köpke), north of Algiers, one of his depth charges exploded on contact just like 53 Squadron's had done off Trinidad. The Hudson was severely damaged and became almost uncontrollable, forcing Mick Ensor to order a bale out. Only Ensor and one of his crew survived, rescued by the sloops *Erne* and *Leith*.

Leigh Light Action
There is no doubt that the introduction of the Leigh Light, used by Coastal Command aircraft to illuminate surfaced U-boats travelling at night, was a major turning point in the anti-U-boat war. Pioneered by Wellingtons of 172 Squadron and particularly by Squadron Leader Jeaff Greswell (later Wing Commander and CO of 179 Squadron, and a future Air Commodore CB CBE DSO DFC) who made the first Leigh Light attack against the Italian submarine *Luigi Torelli* on the night of 4 June 1942, Coastal now had the means of not only finding boats in darkness with radar, but then putting them in the *spotlight*!

U-boats, because of the intense operations of Coastal Command over the Bay of Biscay in daylight, had taken to crossing the Bay at night whenever possible and on the surface for speedy running. Thinking themselves immune to attack, even if detected on radar, crews had a shock when night almost turned to day as a Leigh Light-equipped aeroplane flying towards the radar blip, suddenly turned on its Light, hurtling towards them from out of the darkness with bomb doors open.

By late 1942, Leigh Light Wellingtons dominated the night sky over the Bay, but it was still a better option for the boats to try crossing in or out of their French Bay ports at night rather than in daylight. Now, however, at least the boat's gunners were ready for the blinding light that heralded an aircraft attack. But as the Light was usually only switched on at the last moment – for obvious reasons – it meant that the depth charges would be falling about their ears within seconds. It was yet another hazard for the U-boat men to face, and many failed to survive the encounter.

* * *

Two days after Christmas 1942, 27 December, Flight Lieutenant Comfort of 179 Squadron was on patrol in the early hours, having taken off at 2240 the previous night – Boxing Day to the British. He was at 2,000 feet below a cloud base of 3,000 feet over a calm sea with good visibility, course 260 degrees. It was around 4 am in the morning but still some way short of dawn. The man taking his turn on the radar picked up a contact at $4^1/_2$ miles. (Because of the secret nature of the RAF's ASV radar, it was always referred to as the Special Equipment – or S/E). The Germans, in turn, had developed *Metox*, a device that could sense airborne radar and thus be warned of an approaching aeroplane. To counter this, the RAF crews would fly for a period with their radar off, only switching it on for a quick scan and if nothing appeared, they would switch it off again.

Comfort turned his Wellington (LA971 'T') and lost height to 400 feet as he was homed in. Just short of the target the Leigh Light went on, illuminating a submerging U-boat in position 3722/0125, but by the time the Wellington was over it, it had gone down well before the release point. Obviously the boat had sensed the radar, or in the calm conditions, alert lookouts had either seen or heard the aeroplane. Comfort now adopted the usual 'baiting tactics' – flying off some distance before coming back, hoping the sub had resurfaced.

After half an hour they were back, making a square search but at 0536 decided to continue the patrol, but then they returned once again at first light. At 0726 radar picked up a blip at $4^1/_2$ miles, Comfort once again losing height but at half a mile as the Light came on, it only illuminated an empty sea. He circled and another contact appeared to the west. Comfort turned in the direction and at $3^1/_2$ miles they picked up visually a surfaced U-boat in position 3729/0120.

They attacked up-track and at half a mile the U-boat began firing, immediately scoring hits on the port engine and starting a fire in the aircraft. Evasive action was taken before attacking from the boat's port quarter, releasing four D/Cs from 100 feet. Not till the Wellington passed over and the rear gunner was able to commence firing did the U-boat's fire stop. He also saw the D/Cs explode 50 yards on the boat's port beam, but they had to break off because of the damage to the aircraft. They sent out an SOS and jettisoned all loose equipment and finally made it to Tafaraoui, near Oran and safety, rather than try to make Gibraltar. So, while the aircraft had survived, damage to it had undoubtedly saved the U-boat from any second attack. Just as with the damaging of a U-boat, where it was forced to abort its cruise, so a damaged aircraft was judged a 'success' if it wasn't able follow up an attack. The RAF crew had been:

F/L A H Comfort	Pilot	Sgt Nichols	WOP/AG
P/O Feltes	2nd pilot	Sgt Johnson	WOP/AG
F/O McHardy	Nav	Sgt Hotson	WOP/AG

Despite Comfort's crew noting that the boat had Italian paintwork, she was in fact U-73. Her captain – Oberleutnant Horst Deckert – reported being attacked at 0715 in Grid CH82, although the aircraft type was described as a Beaufort.

U-73's KTB recorded the following:

> (1st encounter) "Grid CH8252, 0715 hours. Bristol Beaufort, attack distance 5,000 metres, flak, aircraft veers off, at a distance of only 50 metres we have a view of its belly. Several flak hits on the fuselage. Aircraft heads towards the coast [and] at a distance of 800 metres it jettisons its bombs. Disappears from sight."
>
> (2nd encounter) "0817 hours. Lockheed Hudson. Attack. Height 30 metres. Aircraft comes in strafing from a distance of 2,000 metres. At 800 metres we open fire with flak. Several hits on the aircraft. Four bombs 80-250 metres from the boat, light damage. Aircraft turns off and flies towards the African coast."

An interesting development came from this attack. As mentioned earlier, it had not been deemed all that necessary for Coastal aircraft to have any forward armament, although certain aircraft were designed to have forward guns and used them. However, a comment following this incident was that: 'Use of flak against searchlight aircraft brings the necessity for early provision of front guns.' From this, Air Vice-Marshal Albert Durston AFC (Coastal Command HQ) gave an interim OK for the provision of fixed front guns, with effect from 15 January 1943, but noted that what was urgently needed was for moveable (at least 30 degrees of arc) guns as soon as possible.

A Hudson of 500 Squadron had been the U-boat's second antagonist, and its crew found U-73 an hour later and made an attack, but this time the aircraft was brought down by flak. The Squadron had sent out half a dozen aircraft during the early part of the morning, one – AM689 'M' – ordered to hunt for a submarine reported on the surface.

Pilot Officer J Pugh and his three-man crew headed for the area, and began the search. They were on the eighth leg of a square search before they found it at 0812 hours, about 50 miles from the nearest land. It was fully surfaced, heading west in position 3729/0120.

Pugh attacked immediately, being met by gunfire, which struck home 150 yards from the target. One cannon shell hit forward of the starboard side of the cockpit, the shell entering the radio set and filling the Hudson with smoke and a shower of insulating wool from the side of the fuselage. Another shell hit the starboard engine and wing, the engine stopping as the aircraft was right over the boat. All four D/Cs went down across the boat's stern as the sub began going down. As tracer shells were still visible after this, it appears that some of the guncrew had remained at their posts as the boat went down. U-73 received some damage.

The Hudson became difficult to handle. The port engine was opened fully but with only 2,000 revs obtained, Pugh had difficulty in keeping straight, the machine turning to starboard. Height was gradually lost and he had to order the crew to prepare for ditching, but only the rear gunner heard the order. Three minutes after the attack the Hudson hit the sea. The wireless operator was at his set, the navigator standing behind the empty co-pilot's seat, the latter being thrown forward down into the nose of the aircraft.

Water soon began to rush into the nose compartment and Pugh ordered the rear gunner to release the dinghy. Pugh's emergency hatch had opened on impact and he saw the dinghy – upside down – float past, so climbed out and rescued it, dragging it back to the sinking aeroplane. Meantime the other two had helped the navigator to the port wing as the Hudson began to sink. It finally went under as the four men clambered into the dinghy.

The navigator had an injured hand which was bandaged and then they began paddling southwards. Half an hour later they sighted land and just before 10 am an aircraft flew over. The men fired off cartridge flares but they were not seen. Another aircraft on the horizon didn't spot anything of them either. Despite the paddling, the dinghy was drifting to the west and at 1115, a whale began investigating them!

Another aircraft at 1148 saw their flares and began circling, but they lost sight of it just after mid-day in a rain shower. A 608 Squadron Hudson found them again and then aircraft 'U' of 500 Squadron appeared and dropped rations. At 2.15 in the afternoon a Walrus amphibian was spotted heading for them and after beating up the dinghy, landed and took off the injured navigator and Flight Sergeant Emberson. Hudsons of 500 and 608 Squadrons continued to circle the dinghy until the Walrus returned to make its second pick-up, taking Pugh and Flight Sergeant Wilkins to safety at Algiers. The Navy Walrus was crewed by Sub-Lieutenant Neil Fuller and Sub-Lieutenant Stan Laurie of 700 Squadron. Pugh and Wilkins later returned to base at Blida, with Broomfield and Emberson being admitted to a hospital in Algiers. John Pugh was later to receive a DFC and Wilkins the DFM.

No.500 Squadron lost another Hudson this same morning, piloted by Flying Officer Varian, making a sweep over the area between Sardinia and the Balearic Islands. There was no clue as to their loss.

U-73 had quite a successful war until sunk in December 1943. She sank seven ships plus the aircraft carrier HMS *Eagle* during Operation *Pedestal* on 11 August 1942 – the famous supply convoy to Malta. U-73 was on her 17th patrol when lost to US destroyers.

| P/O J R Pugh | Pilot | F/S Emberson | WOP/AG |
| Sgt Broomfield | Nav | F/S A E Wilkins | WOP/AG |

CHAPTER TWO

STAYING UP

Surprise, Surprise!
As mentioned in the Introduction, it is a well known and well stated fact that some crews of anti-U-boat aircraft might fly a whole tour of operations covering many long hours without ever sighting their prey. The fact that their presence helped keep U-boats below the surface and therefore slowed them down while using valuable fuel for undersea travel cannot be over-emphasised. It all helped.

Other crews, of course, saw any number of submarines and even had more than one attack, successful or otherwise. Occasionally, by sheer chance, a crew would encounter a submarine – both parties being taken by surprise. One example occurred on 1 March 1943 out in the Atlantic.

Flying Officer N Barson and his 59 Squadron crew were flying in a Fortress II (FL463 'D') on patrol, cruising along at 2,000 feet under 8/10ths cloud, base 3,000 feet, over a moderate sea with visibility between 12 to 15 miles. In area 4700/1800, the airman manning and observing from the beam gun position suddenly spotted the U-boat some one to two miles away to starboard.

The Fortress had left base at 0750 that morning, and now, at 47 minutes past mid-day, it was on its last leg of the patrol. The crew were convinced that the submarine had just that moment decided to surface when it was seen. Barson, flying due east on a 90° course immediately put the Fort into a diving turn to the right in order to be up-sun, whilst losing height rapidly. Coming in on the boat's port bow, he released seven D/Cs from 60-80 feet while she was still fully surfaced. There were six men seen on the U-boat, four of whom were in the conning tower, the other two on the aft deck – not the best place to find oneself at moments such as these.

As the aircraft approached, the submarine opened up with red and blue tracer and continued to fire a few seconds after the attack. This diminished somewhat as the rear gunner began firing down as his guns came to bear. He also saw the D/Cs explode on the far side of the boat, mostly overshooting. However, the Fortress had been hit, which had not helped the aiming, sustaining damage to the hydraulic system, causing oil to start squirting into the cockpit and navigator's compartments. The throttle control of No.4 engine was shot away and the auto-pilot knocked out. There was other damage too, and smoke began to fill the aircraft somewhat alarmingly for several moments.

The U-boat appeared to have 'lost way' and after flying off to collect his thoughts and assess the damage, Barson returned, no more than a minute later but by this time the boat had crash-dived, leaving only the D/C scum to mark the spot. Barson dropped a marker but the crew saw no more of their recent opponent. So this was a case in which accurate flak-fire gave the U-boat captain those precious seconds to get his men back down the hatches and his boat under the sea before the aircraft returned.

The submarine was Oberleutnant Karl-Jürgen Wächter's U-223 on her first patrol during which she had sunk two ships. The captain reported an attack and fighting back with flak but suffering light damage. The actual KTB entry noted:

> "Grid BE5554, 1242 hours, attack by four-engined Boeing, distance 1,000 metres. Flak forces the aircraft to veer off with the result that the bombs fall well off to starboard. Crash dive."

Note that there was no claim of hits by U-233, only that she had successfully used flak to repulse an attack. The Fortress crew:

F/O N Barson	Pilot	F/S J L Lees
F/O C E Blair		Sgt J R Pilon
P/O H R Longmuir	Nav	Sgt A J Bailey
P/O W S Massina		

Second Time Unlucky

One crew that saw more than one U-boat were unlucky. Flying Officer G D Lundon of 172 Squadron not only found a U-boat on 19 February 1943, but managed to sink her. She was U-268, a type VIIC, making her way to a Bay port following her first war cruise after leaving Kiel in January. Lundon's Leigh Light attack sent her straight to the bottom with comparative ease and no fuss.

However, on 4 March, in the same Wellington VIII (MP505 'B') and with exactly the same crew, he came across U-333, commanded by Oberleutnant zur See Werner Schwaff, in German Grid BF5897 – in the Bay. She was outbound on her sixth war cruise. The German crew later admitted to being surprised by the attack, timed at 2131 hours, in darkness. When the Leigh Light bathed them in its powerful beam, the gunners reacted quickly and the Wimpy was set on fire as it flew over U-333 and moments later it crashed into the sea. There were no survivors from:

F/O G D Lundon	Pilot	F/O N Bernett	WOP/AG
P/O J D Prideaux	2nd pilot	Sgt C H Smith	WOP/AG

| F/O G B Alred | Nav | Sgt D M McLeod | WOP/AG |

U-333 was known as a lucky boat. Lundon had released four D/Cs in his attack and two of them acually hit the boat. One of these bounced away causing only minor damage while the other broke up on impact and failed to explode. The boat's KTB noted:

> "Air attack; two-engined land-based aircraft with Leigh Light. Flak. Hits on the aircraft. Fire on aircraft burning heavily as it crosses over. Flies on for about 200 metres and crashes into the sea, burning on the surface for about two minutes. Four bombs were released causing light damage. 2136 hours – dived."

Also significant in the action was that Oberleutnant Schwaff alterted BdU (U-boat HQ) that U-333 had had no warning from its *Metox* radar search receiver. Admiral Karl Dönitz, legendary commander of Germany's U-boat arm, speculated whether this might be due to the introduction of centimetric radar and in fact the Wellington was equipped with ASV Mark III. This latest radar operating on a wavelength of 9.7 cm. could not be detected by *Metox*, so an advantage had swung in favour of the attackers.

We shall meet U-333 again later in this book, when commanded by Peter Cremer.

Surface Actions

Although no formal orders had yet been made for U-boat crews to remain surfaced and fight off air attacks as yet, individual submarine commanders had, as mentioned earlier, decided it was perhaps safer to do so in certain circumstances. On 22 March 1943, Kapitänleutnant Manfred Kinzel, commanding U-338, a type VIIC, returning from a successful Atlantic patrol, was attacked on the outer fringes of the Bay (Grid BE6139) at 0958 hours. She had already suffered damage from a 220 Squadron Fortress on the 19th and was making her way home. Her new attacker was a four-engined Halifax, normally a bomber but now adapted for long-range sorties with Coastal Command, helping to bridge the Atlantic Gap – that area in the mid-Atlantic until now out of reach of aircraft from either Britain, Iceland or America.

The Halifax was 'B' of 502 Squadron, which had taken off at 0655 for a convoy escort, but it did not reach the ships. It was crewed by:

P/O L J McCulloch	Pilot	Sgt P Schmigelsky RCAF	
Sgt J Shepherd		Sgt S Ellam	
F/S J H Henderson RAAF		Sgt H C Taylor RAAF	
Sgt F Hope		F/O A J Stuart	passenger

The log book of U-338 indicates a surprise attack, leaving no time to dive. Guns were manned and opened fire on a four-engined aircraft. A stick of bombs came down at them, one falling near the bow but the boat suffered no serious damage. Kinzel's flak gunners observed hits on a starboard engine and the fuselage. The aircraft began trailing smoke and then plunged into the sea. The boat later nosed her way to the area of the crash, and rescued the sole survivor, Flight Sergeant Taylor, who was taken to St Nazaire and into captivity. Flying Officer Stuart, along for the ride, was a navigator from No.1 (Observer) Advanced Flying Unit. The boat's KTB recorded:

> "Attack by a four-engined bomber. No time to dive. Flak. Four bombs, one of which lands near the bow. Hits on the aircraft, starboard outer motor and hull. The aircraft emits a thin smoke-stream and plunges into the sea. One prisoner, an Australian mechanic. The other six crewmen were not seen. Type, Halifax."

Kinzel and his command were believed lost on 20 September 1943, sunk in action with corvette HMCS *Drumheller* on convoy escort to ON202/ONS18, south-west of Iceland with the loss of all 51 crew members.

On 5 April U-438 (KL Heinrich Heinsohn) claimed shooting down an aircraft while outbound in the Bay (Grid BE34). Although the claim is listed in the KTB of BdU there are no further details, and no apparent RAF loss, either by 15 or 19 Groups of Coastal Command. Nor are there any action reports. One Whitley did see a U-boat but that was not in the same area. Perhaps a case of expectation overtaking fact.

*   *   *

There were two Australian Sunderland squadrons within Coastal Command, both of which saw considerable action during WW2, 10 Squadron RAAF and 461 Squadron RAAF. On 18 April 1943, Sunderland III 'E' of 10 Squadron (DV969) set off on patrol at 5 am to fly over the *Derange* area of the Bay. Coastal Command set specific patrol areas during the war, known by their code names of *Derange, Percussion, Seaslug* and *Musketry*.

Flying Officer E H Farmer, from Queensland, flew out at 3,500 feet, 1,000 feet above a minimal cloud layer of just 1/10th. The sea was calm with visibility 12-15 miles, visibility which enabled the crew to spot a submarine eight miles off in position 4657/1110, at 0855 hours. Just as well, for they had their S/E switched off.

Farmer dived to attack but broke off at 1,000 yards, flying at 500 feet, when it became obvious that the U-boat was making no attempt to dive. Up till this point most boats would have started to crash-dive, so Farmer became wary. He circled at a distance of two miles, climbing back to 2,300 feet, then, at 0910, Farmer made an approach with the sun behind them, up the U-boat's track, releasing two 250lb GP bombs from 1,600 feet. The boat was still on the surface and blazing away with its AA armament, but the

Sunderland was not hit and climbed away after the attack. The Australians replied from nose and upper turret guns.

As Farmer came round again, the flak started again, this time hitting the flying boat three times in the nose and starboard wing. The man manning the nose gun and the 2nd WOP were both hit by shell splinters. Six D/Cs went down which exploded astern of the submarine, and pulling out from the attack, Farmer commenced a wide circuit. Returning two minutes later the boat had gone. The boat commander had seen the opportunity of diving, and had taken it probably guessing the Sunderland had exausted its bombs and depth-charges. LAC Greatz was one of the wounded, a splinter hitting him above the left eye; probably he was at the nose gun. The other crewman wounded is not mentioned in the squadron diary but was presumably Sergeant P L Johnson. The crew consisted of:

F/O E H Farmer	Captain	Sgt C W Ramsey	1st WOP
F/O K L Ridings	1st pilot	Sgt P L Johnson	2nd WOP
F/O P A Edwards	2nd pilot	Sgt H E Knights	Rigger
P/O G R Eastwood	Nav	Sgt N E Burbidge	R/Gunner
Sgt W Slater	1st Fitter	Sgt P Stanton	Armourer
LAC W P Greatz	2nd Fitter	Sgt O A Gibbs	WAG(u/t)

Their target had been U-634 – commanded by Oberleutnant Eberhard Dahlhaus – who reported an attack by a Sunderland in Grid BF4444 at 0900. She was not damaged but claimed hits on the flying boat. Her KTB records:

> "Too late to dive. Flak. Two bombs on port side, 30 metres astern of the boat. Second attack, six bombs to starboard, 70 metres astern. Strafing from the aircraft's rear gunner scored hits on the conning tower and bridge. Flak, hits on the aircraft observed. After a second attack, crash dive."

According to the Official RAAF History, this action heralded a fundamental change in German tactics, the U-boat remaining on the surface and opposing the Sunderland with several gun runs. It was a portent of things to come.

Conspicuous Gallantry Medal
Back in the Mediterranean meantime, 500 Squadron were again in action on the night of 23/24 April 1943. Warrant Officer Ronald Obee, in Hudson 'N' (AM781), operating from Tafaraoui, was patrolling off Oran in approximate position 3610/0030 and made a radar contact at 2309, having already made two sweeps of the area. After dropping from 3,000 feet to 200 feet to investigate, a surfaced U-boat was sighted and an attack run immediately begun. However, the U-boat was not caught napping.

During the approach accurate flak fire was met when just 60 yards away which at first went over the starboard wing. Flight Sergeant Curruthers at the front gun began return fire, but then a shell hit the aircraft and exploded in the cockpit. Obee was hit in the abdomen and his clothes were set alight. Afterwards it was assumed that he had died almost immediately but initially it was thought he was only unconscious. As Flight Sergeant Kempster controlled the aircraft, saving it from an initial crash, Obee's body was taken from the seat and Sergeant A F Blackwell closed the bomb doors before taking over the controls, flying the Hudson back to base.

Having arrived above the airfield, Blackwell ordered the other two men to bale out as he was not sure he could land the Hudson safely. Knowing now that their pilot was dead, Blackwell, once the other two had departed, headed the Hudson out to sea, then baled out himself, the machine later crashing on a salt lake. Arthur Blackwell was awarded the Conspicuous Gallantry Medal, while Alfred Sidney Kempster received the DFM.

After the war it was thought the attack was against U-602 as it had been sunk but no depth-charges had been released. Later it was discovered that U-453, commanded by Kapitänleutnant Egon-Reiner, Freiherr von Schlippenbach, reported being attacked at 0016 hours on the 24th, in Grid CH8241, claiming a twin-engined aircraft shot down. The KTB recorded:

"0012 hours – light flare. Two-engined aircraft crosses over at 500 metres. No attack. Disappears. 0016 hours, attack aircraft is positioning its lights. Now appears that there is a second aircraft. The first aircraft shows its lights to prevent a collision. Height 200 metres. When at a distance of 500 metres, flak. Hits on aircraft – strafing. Aircraft emits a dark smoke-stream, seen thanks to the light of a flare. 0020 hours – flare extinguished. Forward of the starboard side a parachute is seen. A man hangs on. Boat turns in the direction to pick him up. He disappears out of sight when landing in the sea. Type of aircraft: Handley Page Hampden, two-engined."

As far as is known there was no second aircraft and the parachute seen is a bit of a mystery unless it was a parachute flare that was inadvertently released but did not ignite, and the German crew were misled by size and distance.

W/O R Obee	Pilot	F/S A S Kempster	WOP/AG**
Sgt A F Blackwell RAAF	Nav *	F/S C R Curruthers	WOP/AG
F/S K Weatheritt			

* British, joined RAAF whilst living in Australia. ** Kempster had been involved in the attack on U-595 on 14 November 1942.

* * *

On the first day of May 1943, Flight Sergeant P W Phillips, flying

Wellington 'N' of 172 Squadron, located a U-boat seven minutes after midnight over the Bay. Investigating a S/E contact in position 4445/1157, a very surprised U-boat was revealed in the Leigh Light. An immediate attack obtained a good straddle with six D/Cs which fell right across the target, but as the Wellington went over the submarine the crew felt a distinct shudder. Looking back the boat was swamped with foam from the explosions, this being clearly visible for several minutes.

Nothing more was seen so the patrol was resumed but an hour later the crew discovered that they had been hit, and there was a problem with some of the hydraulics. Still unknown, however, was that the AA fire had also caused damage to the port wheel tyre, but they became acutely aware of it as Phillips landed back at base at Predannack. The Wellington crashed as soon as the damaged wheel touched the runway, but happily there were no injuries to the crew.

Their antagonist had been U-613, commanded by Kapitänleutnant Helmut Köppe, the only boat to report a Leigh Light assisted attack on this date, Grid BE9638, at 0013 hours. The boat crash-dived moments later without damage.

Sgt P W Phillips	Pilot	Sgt A A Turner	WOP/AG
Sgt N J Harris	2nd pilot	Sgt W H Ware	WOP/AG
Sgt H A Bate	Nav	Sgt G W Duncan	WOP/AG

Leading from the Front

Wing Commander W E Oulton commanded No.58 Squadon, but was not content to lead from the ground. He often took a crew out on anti-sub patrols and had some measure of success in mid-1943. He had attacked a submarine on 5 May, had a gun-duel with another on the 7th, sank U-266 on the 15th, then shared in sinking U-563 on the 31st.

The action on 7 May was against U-214, commanded by Kapitänleutnant Günter Reeder, after he had already encountered one boat earlier. Wilf Oulton headed out on a Derange sortie at 0435 hours and at 0655 his second pilot, Pilot Officer Jones, sighted a U-boat on the starboard bow and dropping down to 300 feet, they attacked with six D/Cs in their Halifax HR745 'S'. The D/Cs went down 10-15 seconds after the boat had crash-dived and nothing else was seen. This had been U-306.

At 1015, flying just above broken cloud, at 4,000 feet or so, the watchful Jones saw another boat. Using cloud cover Oulton headed for it and when they broke into a clear patch at 3,000 feet, the boat was four miles ahead. As the Halifax came in the boat opened fire – this one was not crash-diving.

The gunners' aim was good. Hits were scored on the leading edge of the starboard wing between the engines, damaging the super-charger control, constant speed control unit, wing tank and with some slight damage to the outer starboard engine's cowling. The navigator began to return fire with the VGO gun as Oulton continued the approach although the starboard outer was beginning to sound distinctly rough. Their remaining three D/Cs went down at 1019, and the boat finally dived, leaving what appeared to be a body on the surface. One of the boat's crew was thought to have been hit by the navigator's fire and as they roared over the conning tower, had seen one man leaning backwards with his mouth wide open.

From the boat's KTB we know that the attack occurred in German Grid BF44 at 1014 hours. The submarine's captain, Kapitänleutnant Günter Reeder, was seriously wounded in the attack. Time and position leave no doubt that U-214 was the target. Perhaps it was Reeder the Liberator crew had seen leaning back, open-mouthed?

W/C W E Oulton DFC	Pilot	Sgt F G Andrews	WOP/AG
P/O W H A Jones	2nd pilot	Sgt A J Hoey	WOP/AG
F/O B S Gibson	Nav	Sgt W M Graham	WOP/AG
Sgt S Webster	Eng		

U-228 (KL Erwin Christopherson) was also attacked at this time and claimed a possible victory. The boat's KTB noted:

"1050 hours, Grid BF7245. Aircraft approaching from 200 degrees, height 500 metres, distance 4-5,000 metres. Full speed, action stations. When aircraft is still 2,000 metres off, open fire with MG C38, causing aircraft to break off and circle the boat at 1,500 metres distance. During this time the boat keeps up continual fire. Bootsmaat Bauer and Bootsmaat Görtz stay cool and fire well. During the changing of a magazine the aircraft turns in for an attack from the bow. Turn hard to port, aircraft is strafing and releases six bombs from 25 metres height. All fall to starboard, the two closest 20-25 metres off; the boat is given a severe shaking, especially near the stern. Aircraft passes over the boat at a very low height strafing from the rear cupola. Our defense fire is good, the aircraft does not approach again, turns off at 1,000 metres, at an estimated 100 metres height. Several hits are observed on the port side, aft section and smoke is also seen. At 1055, crash dive as it is not clear if there will be another approach. No further bombs, perhaps the aircraft was shot down, at least damaged. Type Avro Lancaster."

Their victim was almost certainly a Halifax of 58 Squadron, HR792 'A'. This aircraft had taken off on a Derange 1 patrol at 0510 hours and a signal to them had been acknowledged at 0614 – then nothing. Their ETA back home was slated for 1400, but hours came and went. Obviously U-228's gunners must have scored heavily and the Halifax had crashed after the boat had dived. The Halifax crew were:

| Sgt N F Robertson RAAF | Pilot | Sgt R G Bridge | WOP/AG |

Sgt R Brickles	2nd pilot	Sgt W Mapley	WOP/AG
Sgt L A Fisher	Nav	Sgt L T Brett	WOP/AG
Sgt J M Randall	Eng		

U-228's gunners Bauer and Görtz were to make another claim on 8 July but they were off target on that occasion (see Chapter 3 and Appendix).

A Double Kill – Almost

Oberleutnant zur See Herbert Engel's U-666 scored two 'victories' over the Bay of Biscay on 9 May 1943. Outward bound, the boat was found and attacked by a Halifax of 58 Squadron (HR743 'N'), flown by Flight Sergeant J A Hoather in position Grid BE6988. James Hoather had just been awarded the DFM for locating a German merchant vessel escorted by four destroyers the previous month. He remained in the area to shadow the ships despite attacks by land-based fighters. The award was Gazetted on 11 May, two days after his death.

On the 9th, Hoather found his target was staying up to fight and he did not drop any D/Cs on his first run. Coming round for a second attack the U-boat's gunners scored several hits, damaging one of the port engines which began to trail smoke. In trying to bank yet again (or the pilot or the controls had also been hit), the Halifax crashed into the sea with the loss of all eight men on board. U-666's crew made their claim at 1028, although they said it was a Sunderland, but no Sunderlands were lost this date. The boat's KTB recorded:

> "Sunderland. Flak. Sunderland passes down the starboard side of the boat, strafing. Then at 2,000 metres the aircraft banks for a second attack on the port side. Flak. Sunderland passes astern of the boat and receives six hits in port motor. Aircraft again attempts to attack by banking to port but loses height and crashes in the sea 500 metres from the boat. The wreckage vanishes immediately under the water."

F/S J A Hoather DFM	Pilot	Sgt E Ramjohn
Sgt T E Hamley		Sgt A Simpson
F/L L R Ott		Sgt H S Butler
Sgt J Summerville		Sgt R Y Herd

Just over two hours later, U-666 was located again, this time in Grid BE6979. Once again she stayed on the surface and fought back, the gunners claiming hits on an attacking Whitley, and although it was not seen to be shot down, was claimed as a probable. The KTB record:

> "Aircraft type Whitley 2-engined. Flak, strafing from the aircraft. Aircraft receives flak hits and emits a smoke stream. At a distance of 300 metres it ditches its bombs and flies away. Crash dive."

In fact it was a Whitley of No.10 OTU, the Bomber Command OTU loaned to Coastal. Aircraft 'C' (BD278) had taken off at 0732 hours, passed Bishop's Rock – a focal point and a good check on position for aircraft heading for the Bay – at 0817. At 1054 they investigated two Spanish trawlers, and at 1225 sighted and attacked a U-boat with D/Cs and machine-gun fire. The aircraft was hit in the tail by the boat's gunners and the pilot wisely headed for home, landing back at 1600.

Sgt A J Savage	Pilot	Sgt M Hampson
P/O R N Searle		Sgt I G Davies
Sgt F J Baker		Sgt D W Milliken

New Coastal Command Directive

The fact that U-boats were staying up to fight was not lost on Coastal Command, and this is borne out by the events of 13 May. Sunderland 'G' of 423 Squadron RCAF, flown by Flight Lieutenant Johnnie Musgrave, was sent off just before midnight on the 12th to escort convoy HX237 which consisted of 43 ships and eight escort vessels.

Meeting the convoy at 8 am, the SNO (Senior Naval Officer) sent them off on a 'Viper' patrol at 0815 and just 15 minutes later they spotted a fully surfaced U-boat as they flew at 10,000 feet. The boat was ten miles from the convoy in position 4845/2215, north-north-east of the Azores.

Taking advantage of cloud, Musgrave made his approach and then dived. The boat seemed to be taken by surprise but at one mile she began to fire at the approaching flying boat. Seeing that the U-boat captain had no intention of diving, Musgrave broke off the approach and called the convoy commander.

Musgrave kept in touch with the boat while the SNO despatched a corvette, aircraft and submarine exchanging fire for 20 minutes, during which time one cannon shell hit the fuselage but did no serious damage. The air gunners fired around 2,000 rounds during the contest.

Finally the corvette came within gun range and began to fire, at which time the sub finally dived. It came at a moment when Musgrave was not in a good position. He immediately went in but because the boat was already down, only selected two D/Cs which went into the water ahead of the swirl.

A Swordfish then arrived from an escort carrier, and dropped smoke floats and then the corvette – HMCS *Drumheller* – arrived and began to depth-charge the area, while Musgrave returned to the convoy prior to returning home.

The U-boat had been U-753, commanded by Korvettenkäpitan Alfred Manhardt von Mannstein. The attentions of her attackers, the corvette being joined by the frigate *Lagon*, finally sank her with her 47-man crew. She was one of three U-boats lost to this convoy's escorts. Better luck with the one 20 mm shell that hit the Lib and von Mannstein may have been able to crash-dive earlier and get away.

Musgrave's commanding officer later made a report comment on the actions of his pilot, confirming that he had been '... obeying the latest Coastal Command Instructions and calling the convoy escort which was only ten miles away.' Therefore we can see that Coastal Command HQ was not encouraging aircraft to attack a boat which was staying up to fight if there was an alternative. In this case convoy escort ships were nearby, while in the Bay of Biscay, there would soon be directives to shadow and call up help from other aircraft rather than attack, and they would later be augmented by escort groups of fast frigates and corvettes being on hand to support aircraft which had located U-boats.

F/L J Musgrave	Pilot	Sgt A L D Welch
F/L R W Thompson	2nd pilot	Sgt E J Carden
F/O N V Martin	Nav	Sgt J Vaughan
F/S A Hayden		Sgt C A Maul

Another CGM

On the afternoon of 16 May, Sergeant J S Powell of 224 Squadron was piloting Liberator FL948 – M-Mother – on a patrol from St Eval on a Derange sortie to the Bay. Through binoculars he spotted a submarine on the surface and headed in from her port beam. The time was 1450, the position 4631/0930. Jim Powell recalled in 1985:

'It must be remembered that until the spring of 1943, every U-boat sighted in the Bay, crash-dived at once. We had in fact been briefed to expect their new tactic of staying up to fight it out, but never having experienced this we made an immediate 'standard' attack when we spotted a surfaced U-boat on our port bow at 4-5 miles.

'Turn and dive and level out at about 50 feet – when the waves really do seem to touch the props – bomb doors open, thumb on the bomb tit on the wheel, but .... it didn't crash-dive but engaged us with cannon and machine gun fire as we ran in. We were hit several times but the one that did the damage was a shell from the deck gun that burst between the port-inner and the cockpit.

'The explosion blew me sideways and inadvertently I pressed the tit, so our first stick undershot and I pulled out and up while our turret guns peppered away at the U-boat and at least one of the deck-gun crew went down and overboard.

'As I was weighing up the pro's and con's of a different approach the damned U-boat crash-dived, so we went in hell-for-leather and dropped our second stick across the wake. We circled for some time but saw no trace of a hit. I was still pretty dizzy and probably a bit concussed from the hit, but "Lennie" West my co-pilot took over for a while and after checking there was no material damage I decided to carry on with the patrol.

'One sighting was usually about a month's ration but about 20 minutes later we saw another U-boat steaming away on the surface. It too stayed on top as we closed, and then circled as all our guns were brought to bear and they hammered back at us. But then I thought we'd pull a bluff – standard approach and bomb doors open – and it crash-dived to avoid our non-existent depth-charges. Our guns gave it a real pasting as it went down but again no positive results.

'Within half an hour our totally disbelieving eyes spotted a *third* U-boat and this one adopted exactly the same tactics, exchanging fire while we circled, and crash-diving as soon as we made our mock D/C attack.

'In the context of our hectic couple of hours, it must be remembered that while our main job was of course to kill U-boats, it was nearly as important to make them dive; to keep them down, to use up their batteries and fuel and to constantly remind their crews that crossing the Bay was an unendingly nerve-racking business these days.'

Jim Powell brought his damaged B24 home safely and for his determination this day, he received the Conspicuous Gallantry Medal.

F/S J S Powell	Pilot	F/S R Haynes
F/S L West	2nd pilot	Sgt H Krampp
Sgt J Spark	Nav	Sgt J R Whitman
F/S W H Flavell		

The first submarine had been U-648, commanded by Oberleutnant zur See Peter-Arthur Stahl – a boat which features prominently in this book. Stahl reported an attack by a four-engined aircraft in Grid BF4461 at 1455 hours. It was met with flak fire and hits were claimed. Six bombs had fallen, followed by four more after the boat had crash-dived. U-648 was having a busy day, having already been attacked by Whitley E/10 OTU.

No. 10 OTU in the Wars

In mid-May 1943 the underpowered Whitleys of 10 OTU were taking a pounding. On the 17th, Whitley 'J' (Z9438) took off from St Eval at 1148 hours and failed to return. Also lost this date was Whitley 'P' (BD260) that went off a couple of hours earlier. These were ten-hour patrols – a long time over water for a twin-engined aeroplane that wasn't trusted to get far if one packed up. 'P' ran into Ju88s of KG/40 at mid-day and was shot down, the crew being rescued by a Spanish trawler and landed at Vigo.

Whitley 'J' met U-648, commanded by Oberleutnant zur See Peter-Arthur Stahl, inbound, at 1424 hours in Grid BF4553. They faced the attack with flak fire, claiming a twin-engined aircraft shot into the sea after it had released four D/Cs, which caused no damage to the boat. The crews of 'J' was:

Sgt J H Casstles	Pilot	Sgt J L Hamilton	WOP/AG
Sgt R K Tewfik	2nd pilot	Sgt R E L Johnson	WOP/AG
Sgt G D Evans	Nav	Sgt D Seigal	WOP/AG

U-648 was another submarine which was to have further successes over aircraft, recorded later in this book.

* * *

Five days later, the 22nd, U-103 – Kapitänleutnant Gustav-Adolf Janssen – was located by Whitley 'N' (Z9440) of 10 OTU. The trainee crew had left St Eval at 1035, passing Bishop's Rock at 1124. Patrolling at 4,500 feet they sighted and attacked the submarine with machine-gun fire at 1448. They came in over a moderate sea, a bit bumpy with occasional fine rain but with visibility of 10-15 miles.

The boat remained surfaced and fought back, shells kicking up the water near the approaching bomber and then one exploded directly under the nose. The bomb-aimer was knocked off his seat and lost the bomb-release toggle. He yelled to the pilot to drop the bombs but was not heard in all the excitement.

After tracking over the boat the rear gunner opened up on the conning tower scoring hits and he thought he saw one man knocked overboard. Given a breathing space the boat went down. U-103 later reported an attack by a Halifax (aircraft identification was never a strong point with U-boat crews) in Grid BF47 – north-west of Cape Finisterre, and without doubt her gunfire saved them from being straddled with depth-charges. N/10 OTU returned safely to base at 2015 with only slight damage and no crew injuries. Both sides had been lucky. And so had officers from the SS *Fort Concord*, sunk by U-boats attacking convoy HX237 on 18 May and picked up by U-103!

F/S D W Brookes	Pilot	P/O J T Saunders	WOP/AG
F/S H Reid	2nd pilot	Sgt K G Sewell	WOP/AG
Sgt J H Walton	Nav		

Tactics Change

It was now more than evident that German U-boat commanders had changed their tactics. This was due in no small measure to the success of the Leigh Light aircraft that made crossing the Bay of Biscay far more dangerous in the hours of darkness. Dönitz, attempting to solve the problem, had ordered crossing at night to cease, and that unless a boat could dive long before an aircraft came at them, they were to stay on the surface and fight back.

The reasoning was alright, it gave better chances of seeing aircraft during daylight and there was a better chance of doing damage to an attacker as it came in low and steady, which would either destroy the aircraft, or at least put it off from making a good attack. What the Admiral did not appreciate fully, or if he did, he decided to see how things actually worked out, was the arithmetic involved. In other words, loss of aircraft versus loss of U-boats.

Air Marshal Sir John Slessor CB DSO MC, AOC-in-C Coastal Command wanted to kill U-boats and wasn't too worried how he did it. He knew only too well the damage these submarines were doing to convoys. Quite apart from food for Britain, there would at some stage be an invasion of Europe coming along and men and munitions needed to be brought from abroad if that was going to succeed. If the Germans were now going to stay on the surface and fight, that was fine with him. It meant that even if he lost an aircraft in the attack, it was worth it to kill a U-boat. He had more aircraft than Dönitz had U-boats.

Dönitz, of course, now thought that his *Metox* detection gear was helping the attackers. *Metox* did give off radiation and the Germans believed the Allies had equipment which could detect this emission. This was not the case! This became another red-herring which Dönitz and his staff spent much time and research to resolve. It was true that radiation from *Metox* could be picked up by aircraft with suitable sensors from some 30 miles away but it was the Germans themselves who proved this. So this was not how Allied airmen were finding U-boats, rather it was the ASV Mark III, the first centimetric radar, which was making the difference. (Helped too, of course, by the Allies' success with Enigma and being able to decipher or interpret certain radio traffic.)

Once Dönitz had put his new 'stay up and fight' tactic in place, Coastal Command, never slow to be innovative, began to swamp the Bay, knowing that until the Germans realised their mistake, its crews had a greater chance of finding boats on the surface. It was one thing to know through 'Enigma' that there were boats there, quite another to have them stay in sight and not dive. It wasn't very long before Dönitz was being forced to send out boats in groups for mutual protection. One boat was more vulnerable to attack, but with three or even five boats, combined defensive fire had to help. That again might prove true, but it nevertheless played into Slessor's hand; there were more boats to attack.

This escalation in the Bay air war made it necessary for Coastal crews not to attack at once any group of boats they found, but to circle out of range of their guns and call up other aircraft that were in the area. (There were generally several around.) Attacks by several aircraft would divide the enemy's fire and give a better chance of sinkings. U-boat armament improved, and for a brief period the Germans devised a plan to give some boats especially heavy armament which would give an attacking aircraft a very rude awakening.

The Aircraft Flak Trap

U-441, commanded by Kapitänleutnant Klaus Götz von Hartmann, was one of those boats which carried additional AA guns and was fitted out as an 'aircraft trap'. The purpose of the boat was to invite attacks by aircraft and then shoot them down with her heavier armament. BdU's hope was that heavy losses in aircraft would discourage the Allied airmen from pushing home their attacks with the vigour they had been showing recently.

On 24 May 1943, Sunderland 'L' of 228 Squadron (EJ139) was the first to spot U-441 prowling about in the Bay. As was the usual practice, the pilot immediately headed in, its depth-charges run out in readiness. During the run in the Sunderland was hit heavily but the crew managed to drop their D/Cs before staggering off. Some sources indicate the flying boat was finished off by Ju88s but this is not backed-up by U-441's KTB record, which states that the aircraft crashed into the sea with an explosion and fire just 300 metres from the boat.

The boat's KTB also noted the time as 2050, in Grid BF4948, and that the attack caused serious damage, with a bad leak and a reduction in her steering ability. One crewman had also been wounded so the patrol was abandoned.

Despite this the Germans were encouraged by this result, but during the action a weld had failed on the after quadruple 20 mm gun mount which had rendered it inoperable. It was felt that if this had not happened, the flying boat would never have completed its run and therefore damage would not have been sustained. The RAF crew who all perished were:

F/O H J Debnam	Pilot	F/S B Crossland
F/O C L Houedard		Sgt L Whatley
F/O A H Pelham-Clinton		Sgt E French
F/O W C Haylock		Sgt W Easson
F/S F W Capes	Nav	Sgt A Sales
F/S R Cooper		

U-441's repairs were pushed through in order for the boat to repeat the experiment but, unluckily, with disastrous results. On her second cruise as an 'aircraft trap' she encountered Beaufighters of 248 Squadron on 12 July 1943 and barely survived an action that savaged her and decimated her crew – ten killed, 13 wounded. All the officers were killed or wounded, including the wounding of Hartmann. The senior man, the ship's doctor, Paul Pfaffinger, took over, recovered the wounded and got U-441 home, for which he received the Deutsche Kreuz. It was bad luck that they had encountered nimble hard-hitting Beaus rather than the hoped-for lumbering Coastal aircraft. However, this resulted in the abandonment of the 'trap' experiment, which might otherwise have given Coastal Command aircraft a bit of a problem.

* * *

Hudsons were still working hard down in the Mediterranean. On 26 May 1943, a crew of 500 Squadron were on a night patrol, commencing at 0215 am, and picked up a S/E contact at 14 miles which turned out to be a small boat. At 0622, while at 1,500 feet, another S/E contact, at eight miles, turned into a fully surfaced U-boat four minutes later. Emerging from cloud as they descended, they found the sub right below them, in position 3607/0303. They had located U-755, the boat later confirming the attack by signal. The Hudson attacked, dropping three D/Cs from stern to bow but in the poor light only one explosion was seen, and that was 50 yards astern.

During the run-in the boat had opened fire, and the aircraft blazed away in return. However, flak hit the port engine. Climbing away, the Hudson came in for a dive-bombing attack, releasing two anti-submarine bombs, one being seen to explode just five yards off the boat's port beam near the conning tower. A second dive-bombing attack sent one bomb down at 0620, exploding 20 yards astern.

By this time smoke was streaming from the damaged port engine, which forced the pilot to break off the action and return to base. The crew had been:

S/L H G Holmes DFC*   Pilot   F/O L E Short DFC RAAF
F/O K T Busch   Sgt R C Follers

* Squadron Leader Huntley Gordon Holmes had been involved in an attack on another U-boat on 14 November 1942, and shooting down an enemy aircraft, for which he and Lionel Edward Short had received DFCs.

* * *

U-755, a type VIIC, under the command of Kapitänleutnant Walter Göing, was 13 miles north of Alboran Island in the Western Mediterranean. Although she survived this attack, one crewman had been killed and two wounded, as well as serious damage being caused which forced her to abort her cruise. She reported the attack, noting the Grid reference as CH75. However, U-755 failed to make base, being sunk by a 608 Squadron Hudson on 28 May.

* * *

A 224 Squadron Liberator, on escort to convoy SL129, had an encounter with U-594 (KL Friedrich Mumm) on 27 May 1943, the U-boat claiming to have damaged it, in Grid BE6558. (The crew also thought it was a Lancaster.) This was quite correct, for the Lib ('T') piloted by Flight Sergeant J S Edwards was slightly damaged in the No.2 port engine nacelle during an exchange of gunfire, which also put holes in the undercarriage and nose. Edwards' first attack, around 2200 hours, was abortive as the D/Cs failed to release. His second attack saw six D/Cs go down but they overshot astern. The Lib crew had been escorting convoy SL129, and the encounter took place in position 4645/1330.

F/S J S Edwards	Pilot	Sgt S H White RCAF
Sgt G C Browning		Sgt J McMahon
Sgt J R Villis		F/S N E Lord
Sgt S K Price		Sgt F Wilkinson

The next day U-594 again had an encounter with an aircraft. Halifax 'H' of 502 Squadron, (F/O A J Davey) this time in Grid BE6467 (outer Bay) at 1530. Again they identified the attacker as an Avro Lancaster, and also claimed damaging it, however, despite an exchange of gunfire, the aircraft was not hit. When finally the Halifax pilot got into a position to attack, the boat had dived. A 600 lb anti-submarine bomb was dropped on the swirl but without result.

Iceland-Faeroes Gap

There were many sorties by various squadrons from Shetland and Orkney during the mid-war years, it being strategically placed for aircraft to cover the Iceland-Faeroes Gap. This was the area U-boats travelled though when coming from Germany, and or via-Norway, prior to making base in a Biscay port, or heading south to the Mediterranean.

On 30 May, Kapitänleutnant Heinrich Schröteler was taking his U-667 through this area, later reporting an aircraft attack whilst in Grid AE91. Catalina 'V' of 190 Squadron (FP183) had located them, having left Sullom Voe (Shetlands) at 0857 that morning. It was well over six hours later that the encounter took place, the Catalina crew sighting a surfaced U-boat at 1540, nine miles away, from 1,200 feet.

The pilot headed down as the boat began violent evasive action to starboard while men on the conning tower began firing. The aircraft released six D/Cs, the nearest falling 30 yards or so astern. No doubt there was some concern before the drop due to the flying boat taking hits, the hull being hit, the port engine and propeller being damaged, while the second pilot was hit in the head by a shell splinter.

Having released their D/Cs there was little else to do but watch as the U-boat proceeded on her way, the Catalina disengaging the area an hour later as finally the boat began to submerge. Jack Holmes was the Flight Commander and generally flew with different crews, so that on this day, Cecil White was the actual skipper. Jack Holmes DFC & Bar, who retired as an Air Commodore in 1967, recalls:

'On 29 May 1943 we were flying at around 4,000 feet in the Iceland-Faeroes Gap. F/O White was in the first pilot's (left hand) seat with Sergeant Wood in the right hand seat. I was in the nav/radio cabin, probably discussing patrol patterns with the navigator. I was called to the flight deck to examine a possible U-boat sighting. Some four to five miles ahead there was a small tuft of spray on the surface – almost certainly a U-boat. White put the aircraft into a high-speed dive to catch the U-boat before she could submerge. Clearly that was never its intention as tracer began to whip past the cockpit.

'At about 400 yards from the target a large bang and explosion sent pieces of shrapnel whining around the cockpit in a haze of dust. White received a cut on the head but pressed on, attempting to maintain a traverse on the U-boat, which swept across in a tight turn to port so that our stick of depth-charges exploded slightly astern.

'Our port engine had been hit and the rpm raced up the clock probably because of damage to the constant speed unit. Our hull had also been holed by the cannon shell(s).

'The U-boat continued on the surface; we hoped that she had been damaged but there was little evidence of it. Some fire was exchanged at long range and the U-boat soon submerged. It was sickening to think that she would probably go on to sink Allied shipping.

'During the attack I had been standing braced between the first and second pilots and didn't get off absolutely scot free. A piece of shrapnel cut through my flying boot and nicked by big toe making a cut all of a half-inch long! How lucky we were compared with the experience of John Cruickshank, of our squadron, and his crew. (see 17 July 1944)

'We returned to Sullom Voe without further trouble. A shore party was waiting to whisk us up the slipway before too much of the Voe flooded through Schröteler's hole in the hull.'

S/L J A Holmes	Captain	Sgt H R T Hill
F/O C B White	Pilot	Sgt R D Row
Sgt G J Wood	2nd pilot	Sgt J Brown
P/O D R Wetmore		Sgt S Cliff
Sgt R J Anning		Sgt S G Arcas

U-459 in Trouble

Korvettenkapitän Georg von Wilamowitz-Möllendorf, commander of U-459, was inbound on 30 May but failed to make it unseen across the Bay. Whitley 'N' (Z9440) of 10 OTU found him in what the German crew later noted as Grid BF7122 shortly after noon.

The Whitley had left its base at 0940 am and the first anyone knew of a problem was when they heard an SOS call from the aircraft at 1220, although there was only a report of 'engine trouble'. Base did not know that this was due to flak fire from a U-boat – U459.

The U-boat look-outs had seen what they tentatively identified as a four-engined Lancaster, although there is a very obvious difference between that aircraft and a twin-engined Whitley! The KTB noted two runs by the attacker, four bombs being dropped on each run. During the second run flak hits were observed on the centre of the machine, followed by an explosion. The last they saw of it was as it staggered away, losing height.

At 1255 base received another SOS from the Whitley, saying that 'immediate assistance was required.' Quite where they thought it was going to come from is anyone's guess. Their position was given as 4648/0900 but by this time it seems certain that the crew knew they were not going to make it back to Cornwall on one engine so they prepared to ditch. This they did north-west of Cape Finisterre, and all survived. Some time later the six men were rescued by a Spanish fishing boat, the first stage of becoming prisoners of war.

Sgt L O Slade	Pilot	Sgt G F Dimmock
Sgt W J Wood		P/O R A Russell
Sgt W F Wicks		Sgt G W Vines

Within moments of the Whitley's second attack, Liberator 'G' of 224 Squadron (F/L M J Elworthy) arrived on the scene, actually seeing the smoking Whitley making off. Both the boat's KTB and the Liberator's crew report confirm three attacks and a total of ten D/Cs, in position 4430/1030, at 1222 hours. Flak from the U-boat must have helped put off accurate attacks as the boat suffered no damage, but the gunfire certainly knocked some lumps off the Liberator. Unfortunately Elworthy's crew is not listed in the Squadron records.

* * *

The last action of May was again on the 30th. Catalina 'G' (FP264) of 210 Squadron, piloted by F/L D W Eadie, had been flying a morning Bay patrol and had sighted a surfaced U-boat at 0955, in position 4700/1400. During the approach the Catalina was hit in the bow by flak fire which killed one crewman manning the front gun (Sgt H Roper an FMA/AG) and wounded two others. Eadie nevertheless carried on and his D/Cs appeared to straddle the boat which slowed down. The Catalina pilot did not hang around because of the wounded aboard, and headed straight for home. In the event the hull was so badly holed that the flying boat sank on landing, although everyone of the crew got out safely. FP101 was later salvaged and served with 13 OTU until written off in a crash on 7 August 1943. Later, David William Eadie received the DFC and Sergeant James Alexander Dick the DFM, the latter for staying at his post on the radar and not letting the others know how serious his wound was until they reached Pembroke Dock.

Dick and Harold Sharp both worked on damaged equipment, and Sharp gave a rough course to the pilot, then blocked a hole in the bow with Roper's body which had been wrapped in an engine cover. Sharp then helped repair the radar, realising then that they were close to Brest, so quickly changed course for base. On reaching Pembroke Dock, G-George immediately began to sink on landing. Harold Sharp was thrown through one of the side blisters and dragged under but was rescued by one of the harbour boats.

There is nothing in German records to match this attack and the obvious assumption has to be that the boat did not return so that there is no KTB, and also that the boat did not report the action prior to its loss. A limited check shows that the boat could have been U-418, Oberleutnant zur See Gerhard Lange, which was sunk by a Beaufighter of 236 Squadron on 1 June, flown by Flying Officer M C Bateman, in position 4705/0855.

This boat was inbound and could certainly have covered the distance between the two positions in the 48 hours plus between attacks. Otherwise it might have been an Italian boat, records of which have not been scanned.

F/L D W Eadie	Pilot	Sgt J A Dick	2nd WOP/AG *
Sgt A G Leigh	2nd pilot/	Sgt W L Stubbs	Nav? *
F/S H Sharp	Eng	Sgt S C Parsloe	WOP/AG
Sgt C Cooper	2nd Eng	Sgt L Walker	
Sgt H Roper	FMA/AG +	Sgt O'Connor	

+ killed; * wounded

Hudsons Try for U-535

Iceland-based 269 Squadron's Hudsons had several encounters with U-boats during its period operating from there and in early June 1943, met Kapitänleutnant Helmut Ellmenreich's U-535, a type IX C-40 submarine.

She had left Kiel for the North Atlantic on 25 May, but on 8 June was found and attacked by Sergeant R B Couchman and crew of 269, near convoy SC132. In the attack which followed, the Hudson's D/Cs caused damage to the boat, while the German gunners near-missed the aircraft with their gunfire. Once clear of danger, Couchman watched as the sub began to go round in circles, trailing oil, but after 18 minutes she submerged, leaving a long trail of oil two-and-half miles long. Couchman returned to the spot half an hour later but there was no sign of the sub or the oil slick.

Next on the scene was Hudson 'H' of 269, which had been sent off from Reykjavik at 1412 hours with the express purpose of continuing, if possible, the attack on the U-boat. As luck would have it, U-535 had resurfaced and the RAF crew saw her when just half a mile away and immediately dived to attack.

As they came in cannon shells were bursting to starboard, as well as close tracer fire. There was no indication of being hit, but as the Hudson tracked over the sub, the D/Cs failed to release. Flying Officer J A Turnbull, no doubt cursing, turned to make a second attack with his front, belly and side guns, while trying to get the D/Cs to release. This time U-535's guns were on target. Shells slammed into the Hudson with hits in both wings, two rounds going through the nose, one through the starboard propeller and two more in the tailplane. Even the radar caught a bullet, the missile going right through the cathode-ray tube.

Turnbull pulled off, his D/Cs still stubbornly staying-put. It had to be frustrating that the moment men train and then wait for is finally thwarted by a mechanical problem, although there is just a chance a stray bullet had hit something vital.

Half an hour later an American PBY from VP 84 arrived on the scene, Turnbull warning its crew that the boat was staying up to fight and had already damaged their aircraft. Perhaps wisely, the PBY headed away but returned later to continue shadowing the sub as Turnbull decided his D/Cs were just not going to leave the aircraft, so left.

| F/O J A Turnbull | Pilot | Sgt N K Lamberth * | WOP/AG |
| Sgt R J Anderson | Nav | Sgt A S Gee * | WOP/AG |

* (Unfortunately the Squadron Form 541 does not record WOP/AGs during this period but Lamberth and Gee were usually in Turnbull's crew at this time.)

U-535 later headed towards the Azores to act as a tanker. Later, heading for a Bay port she and other boats were attacked by a Liberator of 53 Squadron, U-535 being sunk with all hands (see Chapter Three).

CHAPTER THREE

SURFACE ACTIONS

A Kill, a Sad Loss and a Rescue

By mid-1943 Coastal Command crews were fully aware of the German's 'stay up and fight' policy, and the losses in aircraft and crews were on the increase. On 11 June a Fortress of 206 Squadron from RAF Benbecula (FA704 'R'), met U-417 (Oberleutnant zur See Wolfgang Schreiner) in the Northern Transit Area (the Iceland-Faeroes Gap), and the boat put up such a determined flak barrage that the Fortress was severely damaged with hits through its nose compartment, cockpit, mainplanes, bomb bays and rear turret.

Despite this, the pilot, Wing Commander R B Thomson – the CO of 206 Squadron – completed his run and dropped his D/Cs to such good effect that U-417 was destroyed, position 6320/1030. Several crew men were seen in the water, but few survived for very long in this cold area.

Meantime, the Fortress had ditched, and sank within 90 seconds. The eight-man crew clambered into one dinghy but lost all their supplies. They were in the dinghy for three days before rescue by a 190 Squadron Catalina, having had to watch shortly beforehand the sad attempt by an American Catalina from VP-84 (P-3) to land and pick them up. It ended in disaster, crashing into the waves.

Nine of the crew were left floating around in two life rafts. Five days later just one survivor of this group was rescued, the others having died of exposure. For this gallant attempt the American DFC was recommended posthumously to the captain of the flying boat, Douglas S Vieira and the co-pilot, Phillip A Bodinet, with Air Medals going to the others. The survivor, Lionel F Pelletier, was recommended for the Navy and Marine Corps Medal, which he subsequently received.

Lt D S Vieira USNR	Pilot	AMM1c L W Provon USN
Lt P A Bodinet USNR	2nd pilot	ARM2c J E Peoples USN
Lt F Kleinbrink USNR	Nav	ARM3cV6 C H Baker USNR
ACMM(AA) F A Cernak USN		AOM3c O A Chaney USN
ARM1c L F Pelletier USN		

The 190 Squadron crew were captained by Jack Holmes DFC who, as we read in the previous chapter, had attacked U-667 back on 30 May. Thomson was a future Air Vice-Marshal CB DSO DFC, and his crew comprised:

W/C R B Thomson	Pilot	Sgt R Owens
F/S A F Chisnall	2nd pilot	Sgt R A Senior
F/O J F Clarke	Nav	Sgt F Sweetlove
F/O J L Humphries	1st WOP	F/L A R D Barrett
		(Stn Arm't Officer)

The day following Thomson's shoot down, the 12th, U-645, commanded by Oberleutnant zur See Otto Ferro, in the outer Bay area, was attacked by what he reported were two Liberators. Both aircraft were engaged by flak fire and claimed as damaged.

The first attack came well north of the Azores, Grid BD3666 at 1300 hours. The aircraft crossed over them and released five bombs (D/Cs), the closest exploding 15 metres astern causing slight damage. Further attempts to close with the boat were held off by accurate flak over the next 40 minutes or so, with further hits on the machine. It finally flew off north-east trailing smoke.

The Liberator was from 86 Squadron, flown by a veteran Coastal pilot, Flying Officer C W Burcher (FL932 'H') from RAF Aldergrove. The crew were flying an anti-submarine patrol in support of convoy TA48, having taken off at 0555 that morning. At 1300 hours, in position 4850/2500, they had spotted the U-boat and attacked, sweeping in across the conning tower from the starboard bow, releasing depth-charges which appeared mostly to overshoot. Heavy flak was experienced from a boat that was obviously staying on the surface.

Cyril Burcher circled to make a head-on attack with guns, but turns by the U-boat made it difficult. Two attacks were made, exchanging gunfire, and at 1333 Burcher flew off to inform the convoy of the presence of a submarine. When he returned 20 minutes later, the boat had gone down. There was no record of any damage, at least not serious enough to note, to the Liberator. Burcher and crew had sunk U632 on 6 April, and would sink U-643 on 8 October.

F/O C W Burcher	Pilot	Sgt J Pheasey	WOP/AG
DFC RAAF		Sgt J E Parrott	WOP/AG
F/S J Lloyd	2nd pilot	Sgt R E Crump	WOP/AG
F/S A D Payne	Nav		
F/O S C Cox DFM	Eng		

The second attack U-645 experienced came at 1615 hours, Grid BE1415. The U-boat later reported several strafing attacks and finally an approach which ended with five D/Cs being dropped which fell 50-100 metres to starboard. Again flak hits were observed on the aircraft, and as it flew off the boat crash-dived at 1633.

Once again it was an 86 Squadron Liberator (FK226 'G') flown by F/O A C I Samuel. It had left base at 0945, again to help escort TA48. The crew spied the U-boat's conning tower at 1621 in position 4815/2510 at a distance of $2^1/_2$ miles whilst flying at 1,500 feet. As they came in they met intense AA fire, so Samuel pulled off to circle, hoping for a head-on attack but the boat's manoeuvres prevented this. After ten minutes of exchanging gunfire, Samuel closed in and attacked, weaving as he did so, whilst his front gunner blazed away.

He raced in over the boat at 90 degrees from her starboard beam forward of the conning tower and released his D/Cs. The aircraft was badly hit, and one of the WOP/AGs – Flying Officer J W James – standing by the open bomb doors was killed. Another shell exploded inside the fuselage causing a fire, but this was quickly extinguished by the crew. With damage to a fuel tank and the bomb bay, Samuel headed for home without delay.

Thus had U-645 survived two attacks by Libs of 86 Squadron, fending both off with accurate AA fire, causing damage to at least one of them and killing a crew member. What's more, Samuel too was an experienced Coastal hand, for he had attacked and sunk U-169 back on 27 March, and except for his co-pilot, with the same crew.

F/O A C I Samuel	Pilot	F/S R Hopkins	WOP/AG
Sgt W P Hollick	2nd pilot	F/O J W James	WOP/AG
F/O C Goodyear	Nav	F/S E G Butler	WOP/AG
F/S A S Bunney	Eng	Sgt C Cutler	WOP/AG

Group Sailings Begin

In order to help his boats cross the dangerous Bay of Biscay, Dönitz now ordered group sailings of three to five submarines at a time. It was hoped their combined fire would help protect them from air attack, and if a chance to dive came, at least one boat could remain active on the surface while the others went below the waves.

One of the first group sailings began on 11 June, with U-564 and U-185 sailing from Bordeaux and meeting up with U-134 and U-653 from La Pallice, and U-358 from St Nazaire. The group was sighted the next day but night fell before other aircraft could be brought to the area of the shadowing aircraft. That night the boats travelled submerged (because of the danger from Leigh Light aircraft) and surfaced the next day.

By the evening of the 13th, the group had reached position 4430/1500, some 250 miles off Cape Finisterre, and had safely traversed the Musketry search area and were virtually through the *Seaslug* area. The German skippers must have been congratulating themselves on their achievement, and also being satisfied that their combined strength earlier had thwarted any attempt at air attack.

However, they were then seen by a searching Sunderland from 228 Squadron, whose pilot, Flying Officer L B Lee, decided on an immediate attack on such tempting targets, and went straight in in the face of daunting odds. It was too much to hope that he might survive. Hit several times on the way in, he nevertheless dropped his D/Cs across U-564, but the Sunderland never pulled away from its run and crashed into the sea with the loss of its entire 11-man crew.

The surviving KTBs all put the action in Grid BE9498 at about 1859 hours. All five boats remained surfaced and shared the credit for the downed Sunderland. Leonard Lee's heroic attack was not in vain, U-564 suffered serious damage and had to abort its patrol. U-185 was detached from the group to act as escort. These two boats were to have a further, and for U-564 (Hans Fiedler) a final, encounter with Coastal Command.

F/O L B Lee	Pilot	Sgt R Shaw
F/O D F Hill		Sgt R Smith
P/O G Lough		Sgt J Fraser
F/O A K McDougal		Sgt A Carmichael
F/O R J Agur		Sgt D Davies
Sgt V Goldstone		

As the two submarines headed home, obviously the news was out that Lee had attacked something and so Coastal aircraft were looking for boats on the 14th. As Kapitänleutnant August Maus escorted the damaged U-564, a destroyer escort had also been sent out from Royan to relieve him and take the cripple into Bordeaux. Coastal stopped all that.

A Whitley V of 10 OTU (BD220 'G') piloted by an Australian, Sergeant A J Benson, found the pair in position 4417/1025 at 1439 and began shadowing them as instructed, while carrying out homing procedure. However, no other aircraft turned up and time was running out for Benson and his crew. He requested permission from base to make an attack, which was approved at 1645, just after a Hampden of 415 RCAF Squadron arrived on scene.

U-564 was the ideal target, being unable to dive or to take much in the way of evasive action. However, during Benson's run-in both boat's opened fire and the Whitley was hit, but it did not prevent the D/Cs going down. This further punishment was the end for U-564 and she sank quickly, at 1730, and U-185's crew were only able to rescue a total of 18 of her crew, including Fiedler.

Meantime, Arthur 'Buzz' Benson was in trouble. His hydraulics had been hit and his starboard engine was causing concern. As he headed towards home, he later had to report his engine u/s, and as already mentioned, Whitley aircraft did not get far on one. In due time he had to ditch and was later rescued by French fishermen, who, being unable to return them to England for fear of reprisals to their families, had to take them back to their fishing port and into captivity. Once it became known that his attack had sunk U-564, Benson was awarded the DFM, the announcement being made while in prison camp. (The full story of this action can be seen in the Appendix to my book *Search, Find and Kill*. NF)

U-185 later made rendezvous with the destroyers (Z24 and Z25) and handed over the survivors. A flight of Ju88 fighters also sent out to give escort, ran into the Hampden, which they shot down.

Mosquitos versus a Group

Another group of five boats had sailed in mid-June, U-68, U-155, U-159, U-415 and U-634. Out over the Bay on a fighter patrol on the morning of 14 June – looking for KG40's Ju88C long-range fighters – was a section of four Mosquitos, three from 307 Polish Squadron, the fourth from 410 Squadron RCAF. They would not ordinarily have been required to attack a U-boat if they spotted one, for it needed a bit more than 20 mm cannon to sink one, but the challenge was just too tempting.

Squadron Leader S Szablowski and his navigator, Sergeant H Gajewski (HJ648 'B') was leading and ordered the aircraft into line astern at 0930 over position 4450/0850. He went down, making the second boat his first target and saw his cannon fire striking all around the conning tower. Raising his sights, he then began to rake the third boat, but then flak from all the boats hit the Mossie's port engine which promptly stopped. The second Mosquito came in but its guns refused to fire and the pilot had to break away.

The aircraft were 500 miles from home and with one badly damaged, discretion seemed the better part of valour – and orders – so they headed back, Szablowski making a successful belly landing at Predannack. However, his cannon fire had inflicted casualties on both U-68 (Oberleutnant Albert Lauzemis) – one killed and three wounded including the captain, and U-155 (Oberleutnant Johannes Altmeier) with five wounded, forcing both to abort and return to Lorient, thereby stopping their patrols. There is no record of the Squadron Leader being reprimanded, and hopefully he wasn't for he had achieved a good result.

* * *

This same 14 June, another Group of boats – U-600, U-615 and U-257 – were also out crossing the Bay, having sailed from La Pallice. These submarines had already been harrassed by Coastal aircraft earlier in the day and now other aircraft were hunting them.

It is not totally clear what actions occurred; a Fortress of 220 Squadron (FK212 'V') is often noted as being shot down by the boats but it was downed by Ju88s. Another source indicated Sunderland JM687 of 228 Squadron (F/O S White) then Pilot Officer Orr of No.10 OTU, followed later by Sergeant Manson of the same unit, the latter out of D/Cs so could only exchange gunfire with the boats. Pilot Officer J W Hermiston of 547 Squadron was also driven off by gunfire. In the event, we cannot say with any certainty which, if any, aircraft this boat's crew claimed. One of those little mysteries for which we hope an answer will appear, even if it comes following the publication of this book.

Two days later U-600 was again the centre of attention, this time from a 59 Squadron Liberator V (FL973 'V'), piloted by Flying Officer E E Allen. Under a 10/10ths cloud layer, flying at 1,500 feet above a moderate sea, with visibility seven miles, a radar contact was made at 13 miles. Changing course Allen began to lose height, using a small cloud bank as cover. The time was just after 0900.

Passing through this, Allen and crew then sighted the three fully surfaced boats at three miles, sailing along in Vic formation in position 4322/1413. Allen thundered in, going initially for the starboard sub but at 1,200 yards the flak began to reach for them. Allen changed course for the centre boat which he no doubt felt had less room to manoeuvre, but met a concentrated hail of AA fire from all three boats, which scored four hits on the Lib. This knocked out most of the instruments but not before six D/Cs went down, falling 50 yards from the boat's port side. As they flew over the rear gunner blazed away, killing one of the conning tower crewmen, then Allen circled $2^1/2$ miles off, contemplating whether they would have to ditch. However, a quick inspection found only the electronics u/s, the four engines purring sweetly, so Allen came round for a second run, but the boats were starting to submerge. Allen dropped his remaining D/Cs on the fast disappearing starboard boat, which fell just ahead of the swirl, but no results were seen or claimed. With the damage, and now out of depth-charges, Allen left the scene. Once again, flak fire had saved the situation, forcing the RAF crew to misjudge the attack, and then, while examining the damage, giving the opposition time to get below the waves.

F/O E E Allen RCAF	Pilot	Sgt J M Taylor
P/O W J Thomas	2nd pilot	P/O H G Barton
F/O G W Laforme	Nav	F/O G W Fletcher
P/O A W Henry		

U-600's KTB noted:

> "1615 hours, BF7272 – attack by two-engined aircraft. Strafing, three bombs, height 30 metres. One bomb explodes 20-30 metres from fore part of the boat, the second near bow and the third to starboard. One man wounded. Strafing. Flak. Boat turns to port because the rudder is blocked. We fire off a red Verey Light. Other boat is not in sight.
>
> "1631 hours – FT [radio message] concerning the attack. Damage repaired; U-257 rejoins the group.
>
> "1735 hours, BF7195 – Same aircraft again in sight. [not clear if same aircraft or the same **type** of aeroplane]. Attacks the group.

Strafing, no bombs, flak from the three boats. Hits on the aircraft. Cross over with smoke pouring from port motor. Aircraft receives hits from our 2 cm flak at a distance of 50-100 metres. Explosion on the aircraft, plunges into the sea. Aircraft had already disintegrated before it hit the water. Disappears entirely under water."

U-615 did not return from this patrol, being sunk on 7 August in the Caribbean, but the KTBs of the other two boats confirm the action, noted as being in Grid BE96 at 0916.

No.10 OTU Again

Two Whitleys from 10 OTU found a submarine on 20th June, thought to be the Italian boat *Barbarigo*, commanded by Tenenti di vascello Umberto De Julio. The boat was outbound, heading across the Bay, in position 4528/0931 at 1637. The two aircraft, 'J', Pilot Officer Orr, and 'L' (LA814), Sergeant H Martin, came in from the north, Orr making the first sighting at ten miles. Orr dropped his D/Cs but they undershot, the only damage being inflicted being a severe strafing by the rear gunner.

Martin followed moments later, as the boat slewed round 90 degrees, presenting her stern to the approaching bomber. Orr and his crew, as they turned to the right to begin to circle, could not make out any gunfire from the boat, but fire she did. Martin's Whitley went over the boat, releasing its D/Cs but these too fell short. As it began to climb slightly, smoke could be seen trailing from it and moments later it crashed into the sea, taking its six-man crew with it.

Having survived the attacks, the submarine dived. The *Barbarigo* had sailed from Bordeaux on 16 June for the Far East, but did not survive the cruise, being lost to unknown causes. There is no immediate suggestion that 10 OTU inflicted any damage, but one never knows; perhaps something had gone amiss which contributed to the boat's later loss.

P/O H Martin	Pilot	Sgt R W Warhurst
P/O C M Bingham		P/O A B C Durnell
Sgt W I Ettle		P/O F W Tomlins

Reports Match

On many occasions when historians try to match up reports of actions from both sides, some comment or observations differ, but it is satisfying on those other occasions when everything fits. Such a fit confirms the actions of U-518, commanded by Kapitänleutnant Friedrich-Wilhelm Wissmann, and the crew of Sunderland 'T' of No.10 Squadron RAAF.

The submarine, on her third war cruise, had been severely damaged on 27 June 1943 (three days after leaving Lorient) by another Sunderland, this time aircraft 'P' (W6005) of 201 Squadron (F/O B E H Layne RNZAF), and was limping back to France. At 11.15 am on the morning of 30 June, the

Australian Sunderland crew found her in position 4453/0821 and as the aircraft came at her was met by heavy flak but was not hit. The pilot – Flight Lieutenant H W Skinner – considering the height too great did not make a drop but circled in preparation for a second run. This time he came in at 150 feet but his D/Cs overshot by 50 yards so the boat escaped further damage.

However, the aircraft did not. Met by further concentrated fire the Sunderland's wings and rear portion of the hull were hit. Severe damage was inflicted to the rear turret, mortally wounding the 20-year-old gunner, Flight Sergeant J S Burnham; the port elevator was also clobbered. Skinner had no choice but to break off and head immediately for home.

U-518 reported the attack in Grid BF76 at 1105, with an initial run by a Sunderland which did not drop anything but was met by flak fire, then a second attack in which five bombs were dropped and were avoided, and which was also met by flak. The aircraft had then departed.

F/L H W Skinner	Pilot	F/S J S Burnham	AG
F/O V D Collins	2nd pilot	F/S O A Gibbs*	WOP/AG
P/O R R Swinson	3rd pilot	Sgt A R Aldridge	Fitter
F/O W H Hill	Nav	Sgt N H Orford	Armourer
Sgt W Slater*	Engineer	F/S K M Meldrum	WOP/AG
Sgt W P Greatz*	Fitter	Sgt P L Johnson*	WOP/AG

*See also page 24.

However, on 3 July, another boat, U-628, commanded by Kapitänleutnant Heinrich Hasenschar, was not so successful. Attacked by a Liberator from 224 Squadron (FL963 'L') in position 4411/0845 at 1405 hours, the boat was destroyed by two attacks. In the initial run the first ever 35 lb anti-submarine bombs were used, followed by a stick of four D/Cs on the second.

On board the aircraft was an armament specialist, who came along to see what effect the new bombs would have, always provided a target was found. Luckily for him one was and the bombs, dropped in a stick of 18, were released. Flak from the submarine hit and damaged the Liberator in the starboard wing, fin and rudder and holed a fuel tank.

The passenger, seeing survivors from the stricken boat in the water was then seen to be taking off his Mae West to throw to the men in the water, but it was suggested to him that he might need it himself if the damage proved serious. However, they made it back to St Eval without difficulty. There were, of course, no survivors from U-628, all 49 crew members being lost. The Liberator pilot received the DSO, while Eddie Cheek, a veteran WOP/AG, received the DFM.

S/L P J Cundy DFC	Pilot	F/S E S Cheek	WOP/AG
P/O E Allen	2nd pilot	F/S I A Graham	WOP/AG
F/S C Owen	Eng	Sgt D Doncaster	AG
F/O R W King	Nav	Sgt A H Graham	AG
Lt-Col Farrant	Passenger		

The American Anti-U-boat Squadrons in Action
By now the Americans had joined in the Battle of the Atlantic and the fight
against the U-boats. Equipped with four-engined B24 (designated PB4Y by
the US Navy) Liberators, they, like their RAF counterparts, were able to
range far and wide, and had units based not only in England but in
Morocco, covering the Bay, Straits of Gibraltar, and the south-western
Spanish coast area.

One such aircraft from the latter, the base at Port Lyauty, French
Morocco, had one of its aircraft fail to return on 3 July, captained by 1st
Lieutenant H W Fraser of the US 1st A/S Squadron. The unit was part of
the 480th A/S Group (until mid-June, part of the 2037th A/S Group). He
and his crew must have met Oberleutnant Gerhard Thäter's U-466, and
Oberleutnant Heinz Förster's U-359, sailing in company, outbound, to the
west of Oporto, Portugal. They had sailed from La Pallice and St Nazaire
respectively on 29 June.

Both boat crews identified the attacker as a Liberator which dropped a
stick of three bombs on U-466 without causing any damage. The boats
remained surfaced, scored hits on the bomber and believed they had shot it
down. The B-24's last reported position was about 4000/1500, which falls
in the German Grid adjacent to CF39 where the two U-boats noted the
action. All ten men aboard the Liberator were lost.

U-466's KTB noted:

> "CF3921. Martin bomber approaching from behind the boat. Both
> boats open fire with flak, when the aircraft was at a distance of 800
> metres. Strafing from the aircraft. Three bombs fall between the
> boats. At 1826 hours both boats crash-dive."

Heinz Förster had seen hits on the aircraft and had observed a parachute
before his boat dived.

* * *

Two days later an RAF Liberator from 53 Squadron sank U-535 – Kapitänleutnant Helmut Ellmenreich – one of three boats heading back to France
having completed duty as emergency tankers for other U-boats in the
vicinity of the Azores.

At 1655 hours on this 5 July, the three boats were just off the north-west
coast of Spain, near Cape Vilano (Grid BF78), in formation, with U-536
leading, U-535 on her port quarter and U-170 astern. At this moment, the
53 Squadron aircraft was returning from a sortie made in conjunction with
ships of the 2nd Escort Group (commanded by the legendary Captain F J
Walker). This Group, and similar ones, spent time in the outer-Bay area
scouring the seas for inbound or outbound U-boats, relying also on Coastal
Command aircraft locating them before calling them in for the hunt. This
was a further development of the anti-submarine war. Rather than a

sighting by an aircraft having to wait for other aircraft who may, or may not be, in the general area, the sloops or destroyers of the RN Groups were generally around and provided the U-boats were not too near land, where they could be under threat from land-based German aircraft, they soon raced to the scene of any would-be action.

On this occasion, however, the ships were too far away, so the Liberator pilot decided to attack alone, being also down on his fuel. In the first attack smart evasive tactics by the boats plus heavy AA fire, threw the attack off. A second approach was carried out in which U-536 was strafed but on this run the D/Cs hung-up so again the Lib crew were frustrated.

Down below, Kapitänleutnant Rolf Schauenburg (U-536), the senior officer, had had enough and signalled the others to dive while the aircraft was circling. Possibly U-535 did not catch sight of the signal – a red flag – for while U-536 and U-170 both pulled the plug, U-535 remained on the surface and faced the next attack alone. Accurate gunfire from the boat scored hits on the Lib (BZ751 'G') but the aircraft placed eight D/Cs across her, just abaft the conning tower. Having taken hits in the wings, fuselage and tailplane, as well as having a crew member wounded, the Lib departed the scene immediately and reached home.

U-535, however, went down. The other two boats heard the explosions and surfaced after dark – five hours later – and searched in vain for survivors. U-535 had carried down her entire crew of 55 souls. One has to wonder if U-535 had delayed slightly in order to give cover to the other two boats, but in any event, the action cost them dear.

The whole engagement had initially been in accordance with BdU's new doctrine, formulated as a result of the fight between U-758 and the American VC-9 Squadron on 8 June (see Chapter Four), much in line with Dönitz's own thinking as mentioned earlier. The 53 Squadron crew were:

F/S W Anderson RNZAF Pilot	F/S G H Sheeran
Sgt G B Tomlinson	Sgt C Coley
W/O I C Bradshaw	Sgt W R Robinson
Sgt R N Lord	

Over-claim
U-228 made a claim for an aircraft shot down on 8 July, as noted in her KTB:

"1940 hours, Grid 4233. Flying boat at 150 degrees, 400 metres height, distance 2,000 metres. Probably descended quickly from a great height since it appeared suddenly and visibility is good. Full speed, and all weapons open fire repelling the approach. Type 'Catalina', underside brightly painted. With violent course changes and full speed we manoeuvre to keep the flying boat behind us at a distance of about 400 metres and 200 in height. Flying boat opens fire from front and side hatches. Our own fire is very effective,

BtsMts Bauer and Görtz (again) are the shooters. Several hits in bow and stern sections observed. Suddenly the flying boat went over in a steep approach, turned off sharply and crossed over. Uncertain if another approach will follow – 1945 hours, crash-dive. Through accurate flak, an approach and therefore bomb release was prevented; the aircraft was probably downed."

Well, it wasn't! Nor was it hit. The Catalina was aircraft 'G' of 210 Squadron, one of the aircraft detached at Gibraltar. Flying Officer D H Clarke and crew had sighted a U-boat's wake at 1745 hours and then the boat itself at 6-8 miles, in position 4202/1410. The crew did not have its radar switched on.

Clarke lost height and manoeuvred to get up-sun and attacked down track, releasing six D/Cs from 40-50 feet, ten seconds after the boat had crash-dived, although its stern was still visible under the water.

Continuing the patrol, Clarke was at 3,000 feet at 1943 hours when U-228 was spotted, fully surfaced, some five miles away. Without D/Cs, Clarke still headed in for a strafing run, his gunners firing 240 rounds of machine-gun fire, scoring hits on the conning tower and along the whole length of the hull. The boat had replied with cannon but without success, and crash-dived ten minutes later.

So this is an example of a boat's crew believing they had hit their antagonist, and that their defensive fire had prevented a depth-charge attack. In fact no hits were scored on the Catalina, and the reason for a lack of depth-charges was that the flying boat had already dropped them two hours earlier on another submarine. (U-641, K L Horst Rendtel.)

U-Boat 1 – Catalina 0

On 9 July 1943, a Catalina of 210 Squadron (FP155 'F') was on patrol west of Lisbon, and at 1135 hours the crew spotted a surfaced U-boat in position 3830/1402. The pilot, using cloud cover, made an attacking approach, having also manoeuvred to put the sun behind him, and finally broke cloud at 2,500 feet, four miles off. At 1,500 yards the submarine's gunners began to open fire scoring hits on the port side of the flying boat; the wings, a fuel tank, port engine and the hull were all hit. The nose gunner was wounded but the pilot continued the attack.

The aircraft opened up with its own guns at 300 yards and then released a stick of D/Cs as it passed over the starboard bow of the boat at 50 feet. D/Cs on the port side hung-up due to flak damage and the three that went down from the starboard side were not observed further because of smoke in the cockpit. The Catalina, now on fire, curved round to port and ditched just minutes later and everyone got out before it sank within three minutes. Jerry Dawson was later to write this account of the episode, based from his recollections and the report by Denis Ryan which later went into an edition of 'Coastal Command Review':

'About two hours after take off a wireless message was received instructing the captain to search for a damaged U-boat in a position 200-250 miles west of Lisbon, so on reaching Cape St Vincent the aircraft turned on to a north-westerly course for the new search area.

'About 1345 hours when the aircraft was some 250 miles west of Lisbon, a U-boat was sighted a few miles away on the port bow travelling at full speed on the surface and on a course crossing the Catalina's at right angles. The alarm horn blared, the Rigger dashed to the front gun and the blister guns were swung out. The Captain launched his attack in a shallow dive weaving the aircraft from side to side in evasive action. The first burst of tracer shells from the U-boat passed by harmlessly to starboard. The enemy gunner then corrected his aim; the aircraft flew into a hail of fire and was hit repeatedly, but the attack was pressed home. Unfortunately, only the three depth-charges under the starboard wing released, and although these exploded, the effect on the U-boat could not be seen.

'The attack completed, the Catalina was in a bad state. The navigator's and engineer's compartments were ablaze, the port engine was on fire and coughing badly, while black smoke and escaping petrol streamed astern. The hull was pierced in several places and there was a gaping hole just inboard of the pitot head, presumably responsible for the ASI not registering and the three port D/Cs not releasing.

'The Captain feathered the port airscrew while the second pilot attacked the fire with extinguishers but to no avail. Attempts to jettison the D/Cs failed. The fire was obviously gaining, as the cockpit was filling with smoke, so the Captain decided to alight immediately. As the aircraft turned to starboard into a wind of about 20 knots, the pilot stalled her in with floats up. After one bounce the aircraft settled nicely with the port wing tip in the water.

'Petrol was pouring on the sea from the port engine and igniting and there were signs that the fire would spread to the starboard side, so there was a danger of the D/Cs exploding. A hurried evacuation of the aircraft was imperative. The Captain and three crew members jumped into the sea from the bow cockpit while the rest of the crew pushed the dinghies out through the starboard blister, it being too dangerous to inflate these alongside the burning aircraft. Unfortunately, flames and choking smoke in the bunk compartment made retrieval of the wireless and emergency packs impossible.

'Six of the crew had jumped into the sea from the starboard blister, those nearest the Captain assisting him to get the H-type (circular) dinghy out of its valise and inflated after a few minutes struggling. Seven men then scrambled in. The Rigger – a strong swimmer – was seen heading towards a second dinghy, an American Air Cruiser with oars, which after a minute or two he reached and inflated, then rowed towards the first dinghy. Three crew members then transferred to it so that there were now four men in each. Everyone used his shoes to bale until both dinghies were tolerably dry. The dinghies were then tied together.

'Sadly, two of the crew were missing. The second wireless operator had been wounded and although helped into the water complete with Mae West, neither he nor the navigator made the dinghies. After about ten minutes the Catalina blew up with a soft 'crump' and the wreckage sank, leaving only a patch of burning petrol.

'The dinghies contained topping-up pumps, two knives, three Fluorescene blocks, pliers, helio mirrors and a patching outfit. The crew's pockets yielded three two-ounce chocolate bars, an orange and two steel shaving mirrors.

'We had force landed some 250 miles west of the Tagus, but Ryan knew that a fairly concentrated air effort was in progress and that we were not far off a shipping route. The wind was from the NNE which was unhelpful, but there was always the hope it would go round to the west. We reckoned we could last for a week without aid; perhaps ten days for the fitter ones. Most of us were OK, only the flight engineer had a tiny sliver of metal in his thigh and the Captain's knuckles were slightly burned.

'All our watches had stopped, but at 2000 hours we estimated, a Catalina was seen approaching from the east at 3,000 feet but it passed about five miles to the north and disappeared in cloud. We had not been due to return until 0200 on the 10th, so the prospects of a search the following day kept up our spirits.

'We spent a cold night, with sleep impossible, so the dawn was very welcome. The sun got up and the majority of us dozed, to be awakened by the sound of an aircraft. It proved to be a Liberator flying west, but our efforts to attract its attention were unavailing. Towards nightfall a Catalina was seen some 20 miles to the south but it came no nearer. That night was rough and the dinghies parted but after much shouting and whistle blowing they were secured again.

'Another Catalina was sighted the next afternoon and a Fluorescene block was immediately trailed. Although a vivid green streak stretched back some 300 yards from the dinghies it failed to attract the attention of the aircraft which passed about seven miles to the north.

'Over 48 hours had passed since anyone had had anything to drink, but strangely enough, nobody felt thirsty. Nevertheless, it was decided to divide the orange for the evening meal and it was cut into eight pieces by the Captain. Efforts were made to catch fish with improvised tackle, but these were unsuccessful.

'About six in the evening of the fourth day someone let out a startling exclamation! "There's a ship!" As the dinghies lifted on a trough we all saw two ships, an escort vessel and a merchant ship on a parallel course seven miles away. The crew's luck had turned.

'The sun was out and so the helio and shaving mirrors were brought into play immediately. These attracted the attention of the escort vessel, although a 63-year-old quartermaster on the merchant ship, the SS *Port Fairy* had already seen the dinghies with the naked eye. Meantime the dinghies were cut apart, and the oared Air Cruiser made full speed to intercept. No Oxford rowing blue ever made a greater effort than the Rigger who was the oarsman. Everything possible was being waved, mirrors flashed and whistles blown. The suspense was very difficult to bear until there was no doubt that the dinghies had been seen.

'HM Frigate *Swale* halted while the Rigger calmly rowed alongside the boarding net. The frigate then steamed slowly towards the other dinghy. Everyone succeeded in climbing aboard unaided and then found to his surprise that his legs gave way. After effects were not severe apart from considerable breathlessness with the exertion for the first 24 hours, rashes due to sitting in damp clothes, sunburn and individual injuries sustained in the action.

'Our voyage in the dinghies had taken us 100 miles in a southerly direction, and we were later landed safely at Casablanca.'

Denis Ryan later received the DFC and Sergeant James Lawrence Doyle the DFM. Ted Aldenton, the slightly wounded engineer, died as a result of a heart attack on 10 July 1943. By one of those strange coincidences, aboard the *Swale* was the rescued manager of the Buenos Aires branch of Mappin & Webb, whose passenger ship had been torpedoed. As Denis Ryan's father lived in that South American city, he was later able to give Ryan senior a first-hand account of his son's rescue.

The attack was certainly upon U-642 (KL Herbert Brünning), which reported an action with a Catalina in Grid CG4487 at 1340 hours (U-boats were on GST which was two hours ahead of GMT). The KTB reports three bombs and strafing from the aircraft, the sub claiming hits on the machine's hull and engine, but she crash-dived at 1344 before observing the flying boat ditch.

The Catalina had come from Gibraltar. In their later report, the RAF crew said they had picked up the contact at 14 miles when at 5,000 feet. During the attack they noted seeing three German crew members on the deck as they flew over.

F/L D M Ryan	Pilot	F/S J Dawson	WOM/AG
Sgt J I McCrone	2nd pilot	F/S A C Martin DFM	WEM/AG
F/O R L Hunter RCAF	Nav *	Sgt L Yarnell	WOP/AG *
Sgt E S Aldenton	Engineer	Sgt R W Cooper	WOP/AG
Sgt L J Doyle	Rigger	Sgt R W Aubrey	FME/AG
* Lost.			

Another submarine which fought off an attack was that of the American 2nd Anti-Submarine Squadron, part of the 480th A/S Group, piloted by 1st Lieutenant J M Pennoyer. This occurred on 14 July in position 4003/1757, WNW of Lisbon, at 11.15 in the morning, the Liberator operating out of Agadir, French Morocco.

This American crew located Kapitänleutnant Friedrich Deetz's U-757 but met heavy flak as it made an attack run. Hits were scored in the after bomb bay, beneath the fuselage, smashed the No.1 engine and shot out the hydraulic system. Despite the heavy damage the PB4Y made two runs, the first frustrated by the damage, that caused all but one D/C from dropping, and that did not explode. By this time the boat was going down, so a second run was made, releasing six D/Cs on the swirl, but the boat only acknowledged some slight damage.

Pennoyer returned safely to base, without crew casualties, on three engines, and having to get the crew to lower the undercarriage manually as they reached home.

* * *

The 19 and 20 July proved eventful. U-403 reported an attack to BdU upon U-43, the signal stating that the two boats, outbound in company, had been attacked by a Liberator in Grid BE6453 on the night of the 19th. The aircraft had made a strafing run during which it had been hit and probably shot down by flak fire from U-43. The impact and break up of the aircraft had been heard by both boats.

The signal is the only record of the action as both boats were lost with all hands later during their patrol. In some accounts the Liberator is noted as being aircraft 'B' of the 19th Squadron USAAF, but this aircraft was lost on 20 July. In fact it was an 86 Squadron machine, manned by an experienced crew under the command of Flight Lieutenant Willis Roxburgh DFC.

Roxburgh and three others of his crew had teamed up at OTU to fly Hudsons with 206 Squadron in late 1941, and had experienced one U-boat attack on 19 February 1942. They had also taken part in Bomber Command's 1,000 bomber raid on Bremen. They had then gone over to Fortresses, the crew number increasing to eight. This crew sank U-469 on 25 March 1943. Now they were flying a tour with 86 Squadron. However, they were not shot down. What the boat heard was not a crashing aircraft but exploding acoustic torpedoes.

The two U-boats, U-43 (a type IX) and U-403 (type VIIC), commanded respectively by Oberleutnant zur See Hans-Joachim Schwantke and Kapitänleutnant Karl-Franz Heine were sailing on the surface in the outer Bay area. They were spotted by the Liberator V crew (BZ772 'J') who had departed their base at 10.20 that morning on a Seaslug patrol. At 21.25 – some eleven hours from take off – the excitement began.

The U-boat lookouts sighted the danger, reporting later their position as

BE6453, which corresponds with 86 Squadron's calculated 4710/1410. As pre-arranged, U-403 immediately crash-dived, covered by U-43. As the aircraft came in, U-43's gunners began to open fire. Sergeant Richard Thomas, stationed in the Lib's fuselage, recorded:

> 'We were feeling confident as we flew out this mid-July morning on another Atlantic patrol. We took off at 10.20 hours knowing that our return to base would be in the early hours of the following day. Gone now were the flights of short duration in the Lockheed Hudson, or the longer trips in the Fortress. Now we were in the air for seventeen to eighteen hours at a stretch, flying round the clock. At the height of the battle over the Bay, from May to July 1943, we had got ourselves into a steady rhythm of being airborne for some fifty hours or so in every five days, spending almost half our waking lives within the confines of the huge Liberator which had now become our home.
>
> 'We had been airborne for around eleven hours when we spotted the U-boats, two of them on the surface, one with its conning tower hatch open. The Liberator swung into the attack, bomb doors open. One submarine began its dive almost immediately, the other remaining on the surface, opening up with its 20 mm cannons. I could hear the rattle of machine-gun fire from our top turret as Ray worked away with the twin Brownings.
>
> 'Our first run was abortive. We were carrying a new weapon, a torpedo with an acoustic homing device in its head, which, for security reasons, was called the Mark 24 mine (code name Fido). It needed to be launched at precisely the right moment if it was to be effective. As Willis Roxburgh pulled the machine round for a second turn I felt the crump as a cannon shell tore through the metal fabric. The force knocked me off my feet. Lying on the floor of the wireless compartment I felt a drip of blood coming from the mid-turret above me. I pulled myself upright, grasping Ray's legs – a sudden dread seized my mind.
>
> 'Are you OK?' I shouted. The answer came faintly.
>
> 'Yes, but something has cut my hand. Blood's spouting everywhere.'
>
> 'Do you want me to take over?'
>
> 'No, there isn't time. We're going in again. The second sub's begun to dive.'
>
> 'Roxburgh released the two special torpedoes as the swirl of the U-boat began to disappear. The first boat must have reached what would normally be a safe depth. The torpedoes hit the water, disappearing into the grey depths with scarcely a splash. In theory they should follow the sound of the popping bubbles caused by the rapid rotation of the submarine's propellers, homing in for the kill.
>
> 'We circled the area in our Liberator, all eyes scanning the sea

below. A disturbance of the surface indicated that some contact must have been made, but there was no tell-tale sign of debris, no oil slick, no solid indication that the attack had been successful. The secret weapon *could* have worked. There was no certain way of knowing if it had. Finally we broke away from the scene of attack to continue our patrol, as I got the first-aid kit from its storage cabinet and began to dress Ray's gashed hand. Once more the moments of high excitement tapered off the boring routine.'

It is always interesting to compare the results as each side saw it. After the attack, U-403 reported to BdU the attack by a Liberator, which made a strafing run on her. This corresponds with the strafing attack during which nothing was dropped from the aeroplane. Whether in the gloom of evening the gunners saw the flash of cannon shell hits will never be known, as both submarines failed to return from their patrols. However, they did claim the Liberator as shot down, actually saying that both boat crews had heard the impact and break up of the aircraft as it hit the water. What they heard, of course, was the explosion of at least one of the two torpedoes, which had either self-detonated, or perhaps had even hit the sea-bed. The disturbance noted by the Liberator's crew was also the torpedo(s) going off, signalling to them a possible success but unconfirmed by any tangible evidence.

Roxburgh and his crew landed back at base at 0335 hours on the 20th. A total air time of 17 hours, 15 minutes. U-43 was lost to air attack on the 30th by a US Navy Avenger aircraft from the USS *Santee*, with the loss of all 55 hands. The Avenger pilot had also dropped a Fido (acoustic torpedo) but this time it had scored. She had been carrying mines to lay off Lagos, which exploded with devastating effect. U-403 lasted till 17 August, sunk by a Hudson from 200 Squadron RAF, in company with a Free French Wellington, south-west of Dakar, again with the loss of all aboard (49).

F/L W Roxburgh DFC	Pilot	F/S R Thomas	WOP/AG
Sgt L R Meech	2nd pilot	F/S R L Simpson	WOP/AG
F/S J Griffiths	Nav	Sgt J K Churchill	WOP/AG
F/S D Eley	WOP/RM	Sgt N Rimmer	WOP/AG

Hold-off Tactics
Also on the 19th, Flight Lieutenant E E Allen of 59 Squadron was once again in action (see earlier, 16 June 1943). Out on a Seaslug Patrol he investigated a radar contact at eight miles and found U-667 (Kapitän-leutnant Heinrich Schröteler) inbound, in position 4515/1640, at 1542 hours.

On the initial approach the Liberator met flak fire and was hit in the port wing and forced to break away. There followed a protracted duel during which the aircraft circled, strafing the violently manoeuvring boat which put up a curtain of gunfire.

Finally two attacks were carried out, one with a D/C release from 3,300 feet which overshot 75 yards and did not appear to explode, the second with two D/Cs from 75 feet which missed ahead of the target. In all the Liberator (FL977 'H') was hit ten times and Flying Officer A W Henry, manning the port waist gun position was hit and badly wounded in the knee. With damage and a wounded man aboard, Allen headed for home.

Why Allen had attacked from such a height was due to the fact that he only had three D/Cs, his other armament being two 600 lb A/S bombs. In attacking first at height he was hoping that the boat would dive because his two bombs were designed to do the maximum damage below the surface. Unfortunately his 'hold-off' tactics did not work.

From the boat's KTB we can see that at 1540 the Liberator was sighted visually without any electronic detection.

"U-boat remained surfaced and met the initial approach with heavy flak, causing the aircraft to veer off. The aircraft continued to circle, its gunners trading fire with the U-boat. After several feints the aircraft made another approach at 1633. Bombs released but another emergency turn caused the D/Cs to explode ahead and to starboard. During the run several flak hits observed and after circling for a few minutes, aircraft departed at 1650. Boat submerged at 1653. Excellent handling and good shooting had saved the boat."

F/L E E Allen RCAF	Pilot	P/O H G Barton
Sgt H Jones	2nd pilot	F/O G W Fletcher
F/O G W Leforme	Nav	P/O J Parsons
F/O A W Henry	AG	

This action once again showed up the lack of a nose gun in the Liberator, and some other aircraft, so that in gun duels with U-boats that stayed on the surface, the submariners probably realised that a head-on run was less likely to give them too much trouble from machine-gun fire. Coastal Command was still alive to the problem, but seemingly not moved to improve matters with any great urgency.

Elwood Ernest Allen DFC was eventually shot down by a U-boat during an attack on the night of 6/7 June 1944 – a period of intense action in the Channel at the time of D-Day, as we shall read later. We shall also read more about further encounters by U-667 with Coastal Command aircraft.

U-558's Struggle

On 20 July, Kapitänleutnant Günther Krech was bringing his U-558 back home but was found by an American Liberator, 'B', of the 19th A/S Squadron, piloted by Lieutenant H E Dyment, his navigator being Lieutenant Ferrini. They had been airborne from RAF St Eval at 0815 that morning on a Musketry Patrol.

Late morning RAF control received an action report from the Americans that they were about to engage a submarine, giving the position as 4530/0945. The aircraft failed to return but communications intelligence established that the B24 had attacked and dropped D/Cs on a U-boat which in turn had shot down the attacker with its entire ten-man crew.

The loss of this aircraft is often assigned to U-43 but as previously noted, the attack on U-43 occurred on the 19th. In fact B/19 was almost certainly lost in an encounter with the inbound U-558. This boat under her veteran commander had already been attacked twice from the air while approaching Biscay. On the 14th she had been attacked by Wellington 'M' of 179 Squadron off Lisbon, flak having damaged the bomber, whose D/Cs had caused no damage.

On the 17th, Liberator 'P' of 224 Squadron (from Gib), piloted by Wing Commander A E Clouston DFC AFC, 224's CO, had attacked U-558 off Porto (4251/1107), and the boat had fought back and damaged the attacking aeroplane, although in this instance the Lib caused some damage to her.

The Lib's radar had picked up the boat at 18 miles and attacked in poor visibility due to rain squalls. The navigator began firing the .5 nose gun at long range, the boat firing its 20 mm, then other guns. The aircraft was hit more than 30 times, mostly in the wings, engine and fuselage from small calibre guns, and also received damage from bomb fragments! These were from the 24 x 35 lb bombs Clouston released from 300 feet. A second run and the rest of the bombs failed to release. Clouston saw the boat dive leaving oil and he was convinced some of the gunners were still at their posts.

Arthur Clouston (later Air Commodore DSO DFC AFC & Bar) gave an excellent account of this action in his 1954 book *The Dangerous Skies*:

'I put the nose down. From one thousand feet we dived out of cloud and rain into brilliant sunshine. Sea and submarine raced to meet us. We could almost hear the shouts of "Achtung" and the racketing hooter of the sub's "actions stations" alarm.

'Grapes of flak began to blister the sky around us, jolting the sky and shaking the aircraft. We were looking down the barrels of their guns. It was impossible for them to miss at such point-blank range.

'But the stick of depth-charges was away, straddling the submarine, and the Liberator was straining and shuddering as I levelled her up at ten feet, and had to bank violently to avoid hitting the periscope with the port wing. Then the blast from our own high explosives lifted us into the air.

'We came round for a second attack. The submarine was trying to crash-dive, sliding under the water with the gunners still firing. We could see the tense fear in their faces, but still they kept up the barrage, firing at us to the last as the waves drowned them in their seats [*sic*].

'The sea closed over the conning tower; and then the tail rose out of the water, standing up almost vertically for moments that seemed minutes, her propellers threshing the air. At last, slowly, lazily almost, she slipped below for the last time, and the sea began to boil with bubbles of air, and oil, and mud, and debris.

'It had all happened so quickly that it was almost as if it had never been. The tense thrill and exultation of the flight were gone, replaced by a quieter sense of satisfaction and contentment at the success of the attack. For the submarine personnel I could feel no pity, only a detached admiration for their gunners.

'I checked in turn with each of my own crew. We had been peppered with thirty-one holes, but no one had been hit.'

W/C A E Clouston	Pilot	P/O L West
DFC AFC		F/S A Bloomfield
F/O P J McAvoy		Sgt J M Burke
F/L J B Maylam		
F/O J G Greenfield		

Not included in the crew rosta was Captain Hickman. According to Clouston, Hickman was an American airforce officer, an expert in the new centimetric radar that was being tested, and who had flown with them unofficially. Having been diverted to Gibraltar after a patrol, Clouston was on his way back to England when they encountered the U-boat. He was a bit over optimistic as to the result of the attack, but he was not the only one deceived by the assumed results of an encounter.

On the morning of the 20th U-558 sent a message saying she was under attack once again, at 1119 hours in Grid BF7262. The aircraft was claimed as damaged, but more hurt was inflicted on the submarine, and two crewmen were also lost overboard. Her next message came at 1225 from Grid BF7253 – and was her last.

The attacker in this case was another American crew in Liberator, 'F' from the 19th A/S Squadron, as if in revenge for the loss of their comrades earlier. 'F' was captained by Lieutenant C F Gallimeier, his navigator listed as Lieutenant Rosoff, and as he attacked, fire from the boat damaged his port inner engine which cut out. Charles Gallimeier broke off the action but his seven D/Cs had done some damage. No sooner had this action died down than a Halifax of 58 Squadron (DT642 'H' F/L G A Sawtell) headed in and its salvo of D/Cs sent U-558 to the bottom.

Krech, his second lieutenant and three ratings were picked up five days later by the Canadian warship *Athabascan* but the other 41 crewmen perished. U-558 had been on ten war cruises and sunk 20 ships. Her men had fought off five air attacks in a week, shot down one aeroplane and damaged three others.

By strange fate, the four survivors had been found by the veteran Coastal pilot S/L T M Bulloch on the 24th, which brought the rescue ships to them the next day.

CHAPTER FOUR

ESCORT CARRIERS

Ugly, Grubby Little Ships, Lacking Both Speed and Grace[1]
The earlier problem of trying to cover the mid-Atlantic areas with aircraft
was fast being overcome with the introduction of long-range four-engined
aircraft such as the Halifax, Liberator and Fortress. Another logical
progression was the use of aircraft carriers to escort the convoys, thereby
having aircraft around all the time. However, it was not that simple.
Aircraft carriers are huge ships and not built overnight. Those that the
Allies had at the start of 1942 were heavily engaged elsewhere, particularly
now that the war with Japan had begun. Carriers were an important element
in the vast expanse of the Pacific Ocean and the US Navy were naturally
unwilling to send any carriers to the Atlantic.

The British Royal Navy had limited carriers too but the answer came by
producing not large fleet carriers but smaller, quickly-built aircraft carriers,
turned out by American shipyards after America's entry into the war.
Sometimes referred to as *Woolworths* carriers, they nevertheless filled the
immediate gap. They might not be able to carry large numbers of aircraft,
but then a handful used to help defend a convoy was far better than none at
all, or using the MSFU concept. The Merchant Ship Fighter Unit was a
single Hurricane fighter fitted to a launch platform on the bows of the
merchant ship. If danger approached – usually in the form of enemy aircraft
– the fighter could be launched to defend the ships or at least force the
hostile machine away. Once that was completed and/or the fuel ran out, the
fighter had to either ditch, or the pilot had to bale out, hopeful of being
rescued whichever avenue he took. Sometimes he was, sometimes not, but
the fighter was always lost unless some friendly coast was within flying
distance.

The American Escort Carrier really became established in 1943, with
such ships as the *Card*, *Bogue* and *Core*. They carried perhaps just one US
Navy squadron, equipped with two types of aeroplane, the Avenger and the
Wildcat. The Grumman TBM and TBF Avenger was a three-seat torpedo

---

[1] As described by Hugh Popham in his book *Sea Flight* Wm. Kimber 1954. (Popham had
been a fleet pilot, used to the larger carriers!)

bomber used by the Americans in the Pacific and later by the Fleet Air Arm. The Wildcat, the F4F, was a single-seat fighter, later superceded by the F6F Hellcat. The two types generally worked in unison once a U-boat was found, the fighter making a low level strafing attack, to suppress flak and help cover the Avenger's approach, which was adaped to carry both bombs and depth charges. It was also equipped with ASV radar.

On 4 June 1943, the USS *Bogue* and her squadron VC-9, was providing air cover for convoy GUS-7A, south-west of the Azores. Lurking nearby was Kapitänleutnant Horst Rendtel's U-641. Having surfaced, she was sighted by the Avenger pilot Lieutenant (jg) W S Fowler at 1716 hours, five miles from him, position given as 3150/4321. Fowler immediately headed in for an attack but his enthusiastic approach was too fast and he had to abort and go round again. On his second run two D/Cs were released which exploded off the U-boat's starboard side.

At 1728 a second Avenger, piloted by the CO of VC-9, Lieutenant-Commander W M Drane, arrived. The two aircraft then made a co-ordinated run on U-641 which had remained on the surface the whole time, putting up a heavy and accurate flak barrage. Drane dropped four D/Cs which fell on the boat's port quarter and caused some light damage. However, Fowler's aircraft was hit in the engine but remained flying and he was able to return safely to the carrier. At the appearance of a third Avenger, U-641's commander decided it was time he wasn't around and crash-dived to safety.

The U-boat crew wildly identified its attackers as a Curtiss and a Hurricane, the action taking place in Grid DF4221 at 2130 German time. Hits had been claimed on the 'Hurricane', although it was not observed to crash, so only claimed as a probable. (This action has in the past been listed as occuring on the 5th but it was the 4th.)

Pilot	Radioman	Gunner
Lt W S Fowler	ARM2c C J Wojcik	AMM3c H R Buckill
Lt-Cdr W M Drane	ARM1c R F Egger	AMM2c C T McKinley

Four days later VC-9 were in action again, this time against Kapitänleutnant Helmut Manseck and his U-758. The *Bogue* group were now providing distant support for convoy UGS-9, again to the south of the Azores. The convoy had been sighted and reported by U-758 just before it was attacked by carrier aircraft.

First to find the submarine was an Avenger piloted by Lieutenant (jg) L S Bailliett at 1508 hours, in position 2907/3334. Attacking immediately, four bombs exploded around the stern of the sub which was putting up a heavy defensive fire. Bailliett then made a strafing run and then he was relieved by another Avenger, Lieutenant W S Fowler. At 1547 Fowler roared in and carried out an attack with three D/Cs despite being heavily hit on the approach. Shells smashed into the TBM's engine, starboard wing, and bomb bay, also seriously wounding the radioman. Fowler immediately departed the scene and returned safely to the carrier.

A third Avenger, flown by Lieutenant (jg) F D Fodge, now arrived, circling the boat while trading gunfire until supported by an arriving Wildcat piloted by Lieutenant (jg) P Perabo. With the Wildcat carrying out a strafing run, U-758's captain decided it was time to submerge. Two of his 2 cm guns were now out of action, and 11 of his bridge crew had received some degree of wounds.

The boat dived and was attacked after it had submerged by the last Avenger, but the D/Cs did no serious damage. She briefly surfaced again and after trading further gunfire with the Wildcat, dived again and escaped despite being hunted by the destroyer USS *Clemson*. The action was reported by U-758 as being in Grid DG4364, beginning at 1918 hours. Interestingly enough, Manseck identified the attackers as carrier aircraft but the types as Martlets (correct – that is what the British FAA called them), Lysanders (a high-wing, fixed undercarriage RAF liaison aircraft which never operated from carriers) and a (P.51) Mustang!

It was believed that the sub had been attacked by eight aircraft, one of which had been shot down and four damaged. Only one Avenger had been damaged, and U-758 was forced to abort her mission to the Caribbean due to damage and casualties.

The attack also had other consequences. U-758 was the first U-boat to go into action with a quadruple 20-mm gun mount. This good showing against heavy air attack helped to convince BdU that extra AA armament and armour plating would allow U-boats to successfully employ 'fight back' tactics. As related in an earlier chapter, this false belief would carry on throughout the summer of 1943 and lead to numerous aircraft versus U-boat battles which usually ended poorly for the U-boat.[1]

Avengers:

Lt L S Bailliett	ARM3c J H Finch	ACM2c R L Goodwin
Lt W S Fowler	ARM2c C J Wojcik	ARM3c H R Buckill
Lt F D Fodge	ARM3c N J Circle	AMM2c C D Falwell

Wildcat:

Lt P Perabo

* * *

USN Squadron VC-13 was on the USS *Core* in July 1943, and saw action on the 13th. U-487, commanded by Oberleutnant zur See Helmut Metz, was a U-tanker (Milch Cow) – a particularly attractive target for any Allied anti-submarine unit. Having refuelled a number of boats en-route to the Caribbean and South America, she was south-west of the Azores where she

---

(1) See *Conflict over the Bay* by Norman Franks, Wm Kimber & Co, 1986, and scheduled to be re-printed by Grub Street in 1999.

was to act as tanker to Group 'Monsoon' whose destination was the Far East. The carrier was part of the escort to convoy GUS-9 and was searching some 200 miles ahead of the ships.

Thanks to 'Ultra' intelligence the U-boat rendezvous zones were known to the Allies. In accordance with their doctrine the Americans made offensive use of this intelligence and directed the escort carrier *Core* to scout the area. On the afternoon of the 13th a VC-13 Avenger, flown by Lieutenant R P Williams, with Lieutenant (jg) E A Steiger flying a Wildcat, formed the team which made a visual sighting of U-487 at 1521 in position 2715/3418. The pair had been out since just before 1300 and were flying at 7,000 feet, using radar only intermittently whenever cloud conditions and visibility made it necessary. It had been the TBM's gunner that had noticed a white wake about ten miles off the port quarter, Williams turning towards it. Using low lying clouds as cover the aircraft were able to totally surprise the U-boat. A number of the boat's crew were actually sun-bathing as the two aircraft suddenly came diving down on them.

The first pass was un-opposed and Steiger strafed the sub, closely followed by Williams who made a good attack and straddle with four D/Cs. As the two aircraft circled, the boat came to a stop after a tight right-hand circle and oil could be seen around her. U-487 was in obvious trouble but her AA gunners responded quickly and shot down the Wildcat as it attempted a second attack, and Steiger was killed. He had made the attack even though he only had one gun working and was just a few hundred feet from the boat's port quarter when it suddenly swerved to the left, dropped its nose, and plunged into the water about 100 feet off the boat's port bow.

Unfortunately for U-487 this victory gave no respite as in the meantime, Williams had called a sighting report and further aircraft were heading in. Four TBMs were catapulted off the carrier, followed by an F4F-4 flown by Lt-Commander C W Brewer, the CO. Brewer, in fact, arrived just in time to see Steiger's fighter go in, as Williams reported to the carrier that the sub '... had gotten one of our planes.' Brewer said he was making his run to cover the other TBMs who would soon be making their attacks. He loosed off some 1,200 rounds of .50 ammunition, and then another Wildcat which had been out with another search team arrived. The first new TBM came in, piloted by Lieutenant (jg) J F Schoby. His four D/Cs tumbled down from 100 feet, and the explosions hurled the boat into the air and when next seen some 30 feet of her stern protruded from the water at a 45° angle. About five seconds later it slid under the surface. The U-boat eventually sank, leaving only 33 of her crew to be rescued by the destroyer USS *Barker*. Metz was not among them. U-487's loss was only one of a series of disasters that totally blunted the intended strike by Group 'Monsoon' into Far Eastern waters.

Avengers:

Lt R P Williams	ARM1c M C Grinstead	AMM2c M H Paden
Lt J F Schoby	ARM2c A R Martin	ARM3c J A Lavender

Top left: Mick Ensor of 500 Squadron was forced to bale out after attacking U-259 on 15 November 1942. Amidst gunfire, his D/Cs went down and one exploded on contact, damaging the Hudson so badly it had to be abandoned. *(M A Ensor)*

Top right: Lockheed Hudson of 500 Squadron in the Middle East. *(G Jones)*

Bottom: Hudson of Coastal; many U-boat deck crews saw this angle by this well used type.

Top: Whitley of 502 Squadron (Z6651) in 1942. Note ASV aerials. *(G Gray)*

Bottom left: F/S J S Powell, 224 Squadron, won the CGM on 16 May 1943 for his persistence in attacking U-boats.

(J S Powell)

Bottom right: Ray Tewfik, 2nd pilot to Sgt Casstles, 10 OTU, lost attacking U-648, 17 May 1943. *(M T C Francis)*

Top: The crew of EJ139, 228 Squadron, captained by F/O H J Debnam, 2nd from the left, was lost attacking U-441 on 24 May 1943.　　　　*(T Capes via J Evans)*

Middle left: Harold Sharp, 210 Squadron flight engineer, had a narrow escape following an attack on a U-boat on 30 May 1943.　　　　*(Mrs A Sharp)*

Middle right: The eventual rescue of R/206 Squadron, shot down on 11 June 1943 by U-667, which was sunk. The Catalina is from 190 Squadron, which effected a good landing on 14 June.

Left: KL Heinrich Schröteler, U-667, fought off 'V' of 190 Squadron, 30 May

Top left: The dinghy by the nose of the Catalina.

Top right: Thomson's crew in the dinghy.

Above: Peter Cundy and crew sank U-628 on 3 July 1943 but not before the boat's gunners had put shells through the starboard elevator, starboard wing and engine, having to fly home on three engines. L to r: F/O R W King, S/L Cundy, Col Farrant, F/S A H Graham, Sgt D Doncaster, Sgt E S Cheek, F/S I A Graham, F/S C Owen, & F/O E Allen.

(E S Cheek)

Right: Sgt A J 'Buzz' Benson won the DFM for sinking U-564, but not before his Whitley had been damaged and later forced to ditch. His crew were rescued by a French fishing boat which had to take them into captivity.

(A J Benson)

Top: American PBY4T-1 Liberator of Fleet Air Wing 7, RAF Dunkeswell, Devon, 1943. *(USN)*

Middle left: F/L Denis Ryan DFC, 210 Squadron, brought down by U-642 on 9 July 1943. *(Mrs F Ryan)*

Middle right: W Roxburgh and crew had their 86 Squadron Liberator damaged on 19 July 1943 by U-43. The German crew claimed a kill thinking they had heard the aircraft crash, but what they actually heard was an acoustic torpedo hitting the sea bed. L to r: Sgt N Rimmer, F/S J Griffiths, F/S R Thomas, F/L W Roxburgh DFC, F/S R L Simpson, Sgt L R Meech, F/S D Eley, Sgt J K Churchill. *(R Thomas)*

Left: Jerry Dawson, Ryan's WOM/AG on 9 July 1943. *(J Dawson)*

Top left: KL Günther Krech, commander of U-558, shot down an American Liberator of the 19th A/S Squadron on 20 July 1943.

Top right: U-588 under attack on 17 July by W/C A E Clouston DFC AFC, 224 Squadron, but gunfire from the boat damaged the B24.

Middle right: US Navy TBM/ TBF 1D Avenger. *(via B Tillman)*

Middle: 224 Squadron, summer 1943. Clouston is in the centre. The two on his right are S/L Peter Cundy, S/L Billy Wicht and Col Farrant, while on his left are HRH Prince Bernhardt, then Major Charles Sweeny USAAF (with dog) and his brother F/O Robert Sweeny.

Top: A Tarpon 1 (TBF - 1) Avenger. With wheels up, this would be a view U-boat crews would not welcome.   *(via B Tillman)*

Middle left: Avengers and Wildcats on USS *Card* in 1943. The censor has blanked our the radar antennae on the F4F wing. From August to November 1943, this ship's aircraft sank eight U-boats.
(Grumman, via B Tillman)

Middle right: German submarines were not the only enemy for the escort carriers; weather was also a constant problem. Note rolling deck while running through an Atlantic swell.   *(Grumman via B Tillman)*

Bottom: USN aircraft in action over the Atlantic in 1943.   *(B Tillman)*

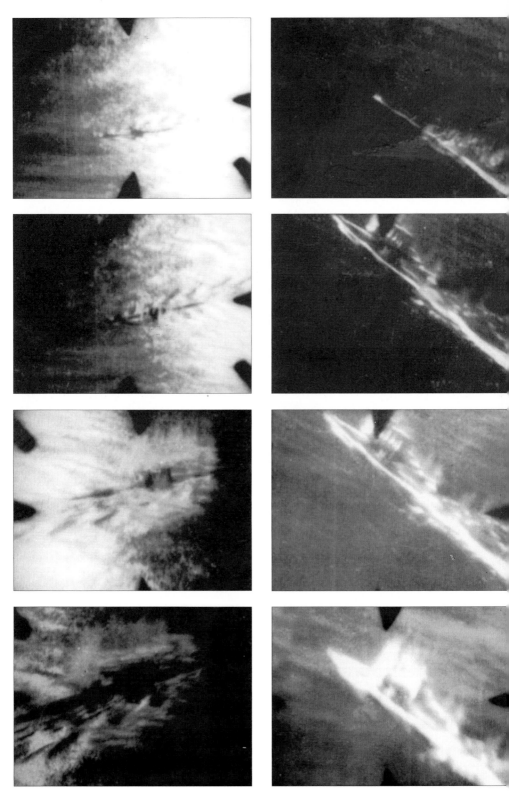

Camera gun sequence by a Bogue aircraft attacking U-758 on 8 June 1943.

(US National Archives

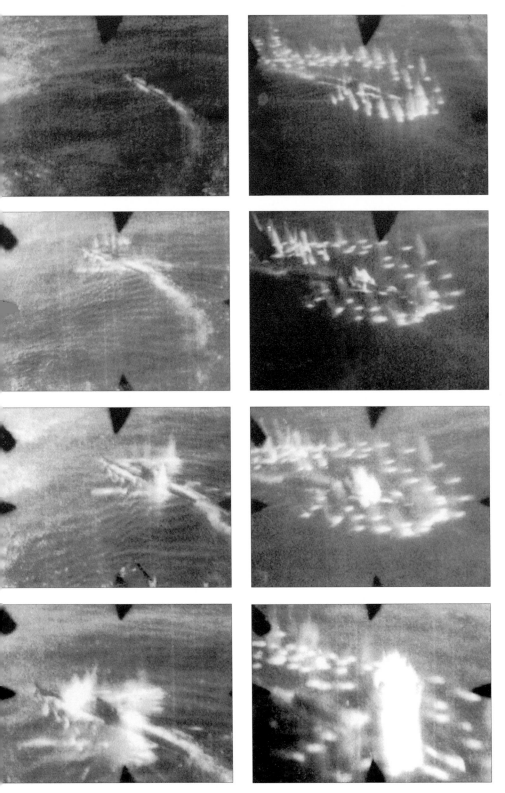

Another camera gun sequence during the action against U-758 on 8 June 1943.

(US National Archives)

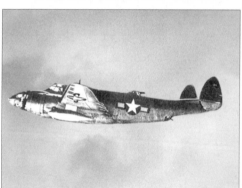

Top left: Hans-Werner Kraus, commander of U-199, damaged by a US Mariner, then sunk by Brazilian aircraft on 24 July 1943, had previously shot down a Mariner on 3 July.

Top right: Heinz Franke (Knight's Cross), commander of U-262. His gunners warded off US aircraft from the Card on 8 August 1943, bringing down both the Avenger and the Wildcat assailing the boat.

Above left: USN Ventura PV-1.

Above right: U-459 (Milch Cow) in mid-Atlantic, 1943.

Right: Hans Hornkohl, commander of U-566, whose epic fight is described in Chapter 8. *(H Hornkohl)*

Top: A Wellington of 172 Squadron, much like the aircraft which crashed into U-459 on 24 July 1943.

Left: Bobby Sweeny and crew had an engine shot out while attacking U-404 on 28 July 1943. Standing: F/O R W King, F/O R V Sweeny, P/O E Allen, F/S I A Graham; kneeling: F/S C Owen, F/S E S Cheek, Sgt A H Graham.

(E S Cheek)

Above: F/O R E Dobson, 53 Squadron, 2nd pilot to W J Irving, whose crew had to make a forced landing in Portugal after being damaged by gunfire from U-boats on 30 July 1943.

(R E Dobson)

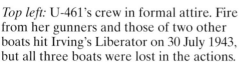

Top left: U-461's crew in formal attire. Fire from her gunners and those of two other boats hit Irving's Liberator on 30 July 1943, but all three boats were lost in the actions.

Top right: F/S E L J 'Peter' Brame, 269 Squadron, on his wedding day in August 1944. Behind him is his best man and WOP/AG, Eddie Beaudry.   *(Mrs P Brame)*

Middle left: Group sailings. Here three U-boats are located; two continue ahead, while one begins a turn to starboard, probably preparatory to diving.

Bottom left: U-489 from 3,000 feet at 0800 hours, 3 August 1943, taken from Peter Brame's Hudson in position 6203/1252.

(via Mrs P Brame)

Bottom right: On 4 August, U-489 was sunk by a 423 Squadron RCAF Sunderland but the flying boat too was hit and crashed Murray Wettlaufer, the second pilot of the Sunderland, was one of the survivors.

(M Wettlaufer)

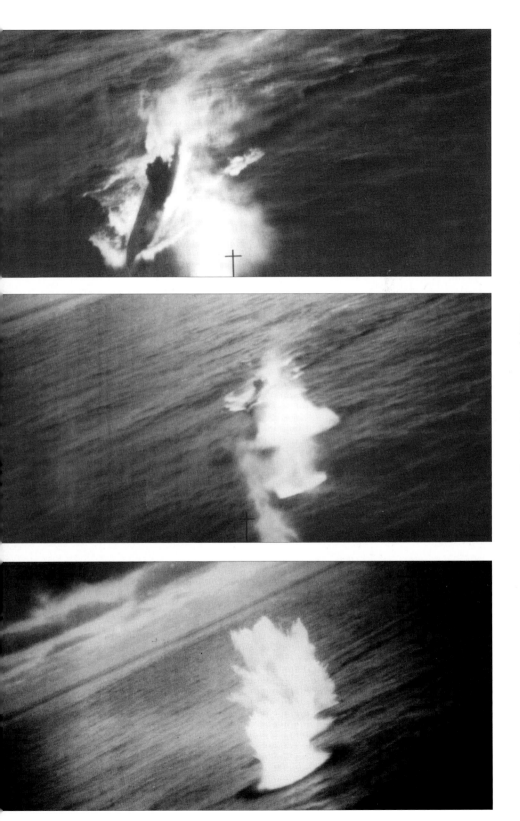

Three pictures of Peter Brame's attack on U-539 on 21 September 1943.

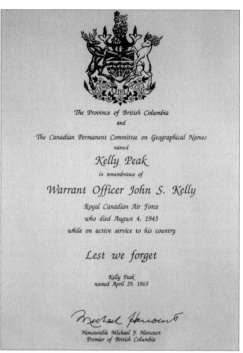

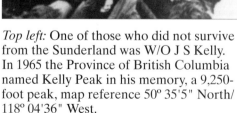

Top left: One of those who did not survive from the Sunderland was W/O J S Kelly. In 1965 the Province of British Columbia named Kelly Peak in his memory, a 9,250-foot peak, map reference 50º 35'5" North/ 118º 04'36" West.

Top right: Eric Hartley and crew, 58 Squadron, in their dinghy after 11 days. They had sunk U-221 on 27 September 1943 but the boat's gunners had got them too.

Middle right: Halifax 'O' (HR744) of 58 Squadron on patrol.

Bottom left: Some of the crew of HMS *Muhattra* helping Hartley's crew aboard on 8 October.

Bottom right: Three 172 Squadron pilots; Eric Hartley before going to 58 Squadron, J L Tweddle and Doug Mumford.

(D A Radburn

Top left: F/L Eric Bland was awarded the DSO for his attack on U-844 on 16 October 1943. Although his Liberator was damaged and had two engines stopped, Bland circled and homed in another aircraft which sank the sub. Bland later had to ditch and two of his crew did not survive.

Top right: Watch officers and gun crew of U-763. Rudi Wieser, who shot down two aircraft on 4 and 5 February 1944 is in the centre, facing camera. *(R Wieser)*

Middle: Inspecting the 20-mm twin guns on U-763; note open breech. *(R Wieser)*

Left: F/L P T Sargent RCAF, 422 Squadron, lost on 16 October 1943. After attacking U-281 and U-448, his Sunderland was badly damaged forcing him to ditch near a British convoy. His harness snagged and he went down with the flying boat.

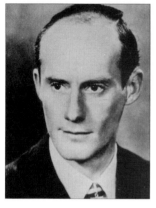

Top left: U-763's commander, KL Ernst
Cordes.   *(R Wieser)*

Top right: U-763 at La Pallice. Note two
kill markings on conning tower.   *(R Wieser)*

Middle left: Oberleutnant Paul Brasack,
commander of U-737, whose gunners
severely damaged a 120 Squadron
Liberator on 6 March 1944.

Above: U-377's armament – a twin 20-mm
gun and quad 20-mm gun.

Right: A U-boat's 37-mm and 20-mm flak guns.

Wildcats:

Lt-Cdr C W Brewer   Lt E H Steiger
Lt J R Brownstein

For Composite Squadron VC-13 this was the first of several successes it had operating from escort carriers of Atlantic Fleet Anti-Submarine Task Groups. It was credited with sinking U-487 and U-67 in July 1943, U-185 and U-84 in August, U-378 in October and U-544 in January 1944. For these actions VC-13 received a Presidential Unit Citation.

Its men were also rewarded. Lt-Commander Charles W Brewer USN, from Tulsa, Oklahoma (but born in Clinton), a graduate from the Naval Academy in 1934 had been on the USS *Ranger* for two years pre-war and after being the exec of VC-13 had taken command in March 1943. He received the Air Medal for his part on 13 July. At 32 years of age he was no young turk, but this didn't stop him. In 1944 he commanded VF-15 with the rank of Commander and saw further action on the carrier *Essex* in the Pacific. He shot down six Japanese aircraft in June 1944 and shared another before he was killed in action on the 19th, the day he scored five of his kills. He had added two DFCs and a Legion of Merit to his decorations and finally a posthumous Navy Cross.

Lieutenant Robert P Williams USNR, of Cardiff, California, received the DFC for his actions on the 13th, and later added a gold star to this for an attack on a U-boat in October 1943. Formally from Snoqualmie, Washington, (although he was born in Pierre, South Dakota) Williams would take command of VC-13 in June 1944. He had earlier served aboard the *Lexington* with VB-2. He had won the Navy Cross during the Battle of the Coral Sea for bombing a Japanese carrier, although his own carrier was lost in that battle. He would be involved in the sinking of three U-boats and the damaging of a fourth for which he received a third DFC and a second Navy Cross.

Lieutenant James F Schoby USNR, from Bode, Iowa, received the DFC. He was killed in a crash on 10 January 1944. DFCs also went to Morris C Grinstead USN, of Letts, Iowa, and Julius R Brownstein USNR from Benton Harbor, Michigan. Earl Steiger USNR, of Buffalo, New York, received a posthumous Navy Cross. An Air Medal went to Melvin H Paden USN, from Salines, California.

* * *

The USS *Card* and Navy squadron VC-1 was the centre of Task Group 21.14 in August 1943. On the 7th an Avenger crew located U-66 and U-117 on the surface and on the 8th, U-262, commanded by Kapitänleutnant Heinz Franke, and U-664, commanded by Kapitänleutnant Adolf Graef, at a supply rendezvous west-north-west of the Azores.

The first two boats were caught by surprise on the surface, the Avenger having closed right in, in position 3800/2100, at 0951 hours. As it happens,

VC-1 had had a run-in with U-66 on the 3rd and her captain had been wounded. She was ordered to make rendezvous with U-117 for assistance and to arrange for a new skipper. This was happening as the USN plane appeared. The Avenger crew noted a clear morning with unlimited visibility with just some slight haze. The TBF-1 was flown by Lieutenant (jg) Ashbury H Sallenger USNR.

It was pretty rare for a team to find two surfaced U-boats, so obviously they had thought themselves safe from air attack. The aircraft were flying at 4,500 feet as Sallenger spotted a large white object which he first took to be a merchant ship but he soon realised it was two submarines close together cruising very slowly and making no waves. At this time they were 82 miles from the Task Group. Sallenger's report says:

'The weather was slightly hazy, there was no cloud cover, and as the submarines were on a course of 220° at a speed of about two knots, I manoeuvred to come out of the sun. They were almost abreast of one another not more than 200 feet apart. There was no indication that fueling operations had been or were going to be conducted. The sides of both submarines were painted white and seemed to be the same size.

'I made the first attack out of the sun with two Mk.47 depth bombs set at 25 feet, selecting the submarine nearest me and slightly astern. I approached at a target angle of 195°, speed 220 knots, releasing at an altitude of 125 feet, plane course 235° T. The submarines were apparently caught unaware and did not open fire with their AA guns till I was about 400 yards away. The fire was very intense from both U-boats, though the plane was not hit.

'The bombs seemed to straddle the U-boat and about three seconds later there were two large explosions, one five to ten feet on the starboard quarter half way between the conning tower 15-20 feet out. I circled sharply to the left gaining altitude while the turret gunner strafed and the radioman took pictures. The attacked submarine immediately began to smoke badly throwing off a dark greyish black smoke. It began making erratic turns in a crazy quilt pattern trailing a heavy oil slick. I had made a preliminary contact report to the ship before the attack and now made another giving the bearing and distance. I then cut off my IFF and climbed to 6,500 feet.

'The undamaged submarine apparently tried to aid the one attacked for about 15 minutes and then started to submerge near the damaged sub. I immediately dived to attack, meeting heavy AA fire from the damaged U-boat. This fire was particularly noticeable because it was necessary to fly directly by the conning tower at 130 knots and 200 feet to drop the Mk. 24 mine[1] about 40 seconds after

---

(1) As previously explained the Mark 24 mine was the cover name for an acoustic homing torpedo, also known as 'Fido'.

the undamaged sub had gone down.

'The mine was dropped on the last seen course of the undamaged sub, 50 yards to the starboard and 150 yards ahead of the swirl. Though I watched carefully, neither I nor my crew saw any results of the mine drop.

'Then I climbed back up to 6,400 feet so the other plane could be vectored to the spot. In about 20 minutes, two TBF-1 and two F4F-4 airplanes arrived and attacked the damaged submarine. Eight minutes before the relieving planes arrived, the damaged submarine made an obvious effort to submerge. For a minute I thought it was gone, but it came back up to a fully surfaced position almost immediately. Watching from my altitude, the sub still on the surface, was strafed unmercifully by the F4F-4s. About five minutes after the depth-bomb attack by the two TBFs, the sub, having been steering a very erratic course, seemed to settle slowly, still smoking. About 30 seconds later, the TBFs dropped their Mk.24 mines, one on either side and ahead of the faint swirl left by the sub. Several minutes later there was another disturbance on the water to starboard and ahead of the last observed position of the U-boat.

'Shortly thereafter, I was recalled to the ship.'

The boat attacked had been U-117, and she was also attacked with D/Cs and 'mines' by other VC-1 Avengers and Wildcats, finally being sunk by one of the Mk.24s with the total loss of her 62-man crew. U-66 survived but was finally sunk on 6 May 1944, her fate sealed by aircraft from the escort carrier Block Island and then by surface action with an American destroyer, but not until a dramatic fire-fight, during which U-66 rammed the destroyer, ended her career.

The very next day, the 8th – a Sunday morning – U-262 and U-664 were found, again by Sallenger, who this time was flying in company with a Wildcat flown by Ensign J F Sprague. The weather this morning was not good, with solid overcast and occasional rain squalls and poor visibility, the two planes ducking in and out of the cloud base. At around 0811 hours they broke cloud at a height of 800 feet and on his port bow Sallenger again spotted two U-boats not more than 1 to $1^1/_2$ miles away, close together but on slightly different courses, their decks awash.

It all happened so fast that Sallenger had not time to advise the carrier of the contact before he made an attack. He signalled to Sprague to attack and the F4F slid under the Avenger and headed for the nearest of the two boats, as Sallenger made his approach from another angle. Sprague made a first class strafing run with his bullets, as Sallenger put it in his report: '.. working over the deck and conning tower methodically.'

With Sallenger little more than half way into his attack, range about 1,000 yards, his TBF was hit by at least one 20 mm explosive shell which came up through the bomb bay into the tunnel compartment. This knocked out his radio, intercom, and other electrical equipment. Later he was to learn the vertical fin and rudder had also taken a hit. He saw the bomb-bay light go out right after the shell hit. The Avenger took several more hits in the tunnel and something began to burn in the bomb bay.

With his electrical system shot out, his bombs would not drop, so he came round for a second run, this time from the starboard quarter. The engine was popping and cutting out during this attack, but Sprague was making further strafing runs, working over the other submarine. On this occasion the AA fire was much heavier and the Avenger was hit again, this time in the left main petrol tank by the wing root, which had about 30 gallons of fuel in it. This immediately burst into flames and then more hits were felt on the aircraft.

Sallenger stayed on his run and dropped two D/Cs manually. He looked back to see if they exploded and was rewarded by two huge water spouts right next to the sub, covering it with water. By now the Avenger's wing was blazing, so Sallenger jettisoned the 'mine' about $1/2$ a mile ahead of the U-boat's course. He then turned into wind and set down on the water with flaps up and bomb doors open as his hydraulics had also been knocked out.

The sea water immediately put out the burning wing fire and he and his gunner got out and secured the dinghy, but then realised that his radioman was missing. Sallenger swam to the other side of the aircraft, dived under and opened the tunnel door. He was half way in the tunnel when the plane started to settle, sinking within 30 seconds of the ditching.

Coming back to the surface, he then saw Sprague heading in for yet another strafing run while they were inflating the dinghy but after that did not recall hearing the Wildcat's engine again. Once in the dinghy they paddled away, and actually went through a large patch of oil that must have been left by one of the U-boats.

Sprague ran out of luck on this run, and with his Wildcat badly hit by flak from U-262, nosed over and crashed into the sea. He did not survive. James Henry O'Hagen Jr, Sallenger's gunner, later reported:

> 'It was about 0730 when Mr Sallenger saw two submarines on the surface. At this time, they seemed to have spotted us. They looked as though they were going to submerge, so Mr Sallenger told me to get ready, that he was going to make his run on them. They opened up fire on us on our first run, hitting the bomb bay, and carrying away the top of the vertical fin and rudder.
>
> 'The shells were all around the plane and it was hard to judge where else we were hit. Our electrical system was shot up and I could not work the turret or get in contact with Mr Sallenger. I called to Downes, our radioman, to ask him to help me turn my turret round as it was stuck. I looked down into the tunnel and he was lying on his face. The radio equipment was on the deck by his feet, the camera by his side smashed up.

'Mr Sallenger came in for his second run to drop the depth bombs that could not be released electrically on the first run, and the return fire was heavier than ever. After we dropped the charge, we pulled away, but we were again hit in the bomb bay tunnel and the port wing gas tank. There was a large hole in the wing, and strips of the turret housing and middle greenhouse [canopy] cover was blasted off. The wing immediately caught on fire. From this point on until we were about 50 feet off the water, I do not remember anything. When I came to, the plane was burning very fast. Mr Sallenger brought it down easily. I got out through the escape hatch in the turret, as Mr Sallenger climbed from the cockpit. We got the life raft and I carried it across the wing. Mr Sallenger tried to get Downes out, but the plane was already under water.

'We inflated the life raft and paddled away from the spot where the plane was, so as to get away from the submarines. A couple of our planes spotted us in the afternoon after we sent up a life raft smoke flare. We were picked up an hour later by one of the destroyers and given first aid.' [USS *Barry*.]

U-262 had suffered some damage during this action and was further damaged the following day by a surface craft D/C attack. Franke turned his spare fuel and supplies over to the other U-boats and returned to base. U-664 carried on with the patrol but this came to an abrupt end. The very next day after the double victory over the *Card*'s aircraft, she had another run-in with VC-1 and this time they sank her.

The carrier had been lucky however, for U-664 had fired torpedoes at her on the evening of the 8th, although she was identified as a tanker. The 'fish' missed their mark and so the U-boat paid the price on the 9th in position 4012/3729.

Avenger:
Lt A H Sallenger   ACRM(A) J D Downes   AMM3c J H O'Hagan
Wildcat:
Ens J F Sprague

* * *

USS *Croatan*

Aircraft from the escort carrier *Croatan* were on patrol on 9 September 1943, and the Avenger piloted by Lieutenant (jg) J W Steere, found a surfaced U-boat 92 miles south-west of the island of Santa Maria, part of the Azores group. Steere immediately shot into cloud and made his approach on radar whilst sending a contact report to the carrier.

Glimpsing the boat through the cloud it showed signs of submerging, so Steere decided to attack before assistance from the ship arrived. As he dropped down into his attack run the U-boat gunners aboard U-214 (Oberleutnant Rupprecht Stock) saw the TBF and opened fire. In the final stages of the approach the aircraft caught a hit in the air intake and bomb bay, but it didn't prevent four D/Cs going down, but results were not seen. Despite the damage, Steere circled and then watched helplessly as U-214 went below.

The boat had been lucky. Its KTB logged the attack in Grid CE9919 at 1525 hours, recording the attack by a Dauntless carrier aircraft with US markings. Two bombs were noted, one of which hit the bridge of the submarine, bounced into the water and then exploded portside, ten metres from the boat, but without causing damage. Stock took his command down at 1532.

The escort carrier *Card* also had an Avenger aircraft damaged during an attack on U-608 on 13 October 1943. Kapitänleutnant Rolf Struckmeier's U-608 was on the surface 600 miles north of the Azores and was found by Avenger 'T9' of VC-9, flown by Lieutenant (jg) H Fryatt.

Diving to attack, the U-boat opened up, its fire passing mainly below the TBF, but shrapnel from one exploding shell cut the hydraulic line for lowering the starboard landing wheel and also the manual release cable. As the Avenger roared over the boat, so it dived. Fryatt released a Mark 24 'mine' but without known results.

Returning to the carrier the damaged undercarriage was going to bring trouble so all other airborne aircraft were landed on first. By this time it was almost dark and things were not helped by a heavy sea running. Fryatt 'pranged' the Avenger onto the deck, smashing into the island and colliding with a parked Avenger; a sailor was also knocked overboard but later recovered. Fryatt and his crew were not harmed and although his aircraft was badly mangled it was later repaired. Aboard a larger carrier it might well have been tipped overboard.

The target boat is sometimes thought to have been U-378, but the KTB of U-608 clearly reports:

> "1858 hours, Grid BD35. Aircraft 800 metres, height 600 metres. Attack. Flak, hits observed on the aircraft, it begins burning. Aircraft released a rocket which hits the water 50 metres in front of the boat. Aircraft type Martlet. Immediately after passing over the boat [we] crash-dived."

There is no report of any smoke coming from the Avenger, so it was more than likely hydraulic fluid streaming from the severed line. The 'rocket' of course, was the acoustic torpedo.

1944

USS *Block Island*

The American escort carrier *Block Island* had VC6 aboard in March 1944 and on the 19th of that month, they found and attacked Oberleutnant Günter Leupold's command, U-1059. Acting on *Ultra* intelligence the carrier group was on Hunter-Killer operations south-west of the Cape Verde Islands.

On the morning of the 19th a patrol team of an Avenger and a Wildcat were on patrol and at 0726 hours, in position 1310/3344, they sighted the submarine. The boat's crew was utterly surprised, many of the crew were actually enjoying a swim! Following the strafing by the Wildcat pilot, Lieutenant (jg) W H Cole, the Avenger, flown by Lieutenant (jg) N T Dowty, planted three D/Cs in a perfect straddle across the stationary U-boat. (Dowty and crew had participated in sinking U-801 two days earlier.)

The fighter made a second strafing run and Dowty banked his TBF for a *coup-de-grâce*. Below, U-1059 was sinking, her captain having been severely wounded, but gamely her gun crews had got into action. Even as the boat sank beneath them the flak gunners scored hits on the approaching Avenger and it plunged into the sea.

The destroyer USS *Corry* later managed to rescue one crewman, Ensign Fitzgerald, from the aircraft but Dowty and the third man were lost. Eight survivors from the U-boat were also picked up including the badly wounded skipper.

Fitzgerald later reported that Dowty had been mortally wounded in the last run but had dropped the last two D/Cs on target, one of which exploded ammunition on the boat, which then rose up before sinking by the stern. Fitzgerald took to his dinghy and found himself amidst the eight German survivors. He helped one wounded man, applying a torniquet to a bad injury, then pushed the sailor back into the sea. He took no chances with the rest either, keeping them at bay with a knife and his .38 pistol until the destroyer arrived.

U-1059 had been on her first cruise, and one can only imagine the feelings of the men swimming in the sea when the aircraft turned up. In the event only one of the men failed to scramble back aboard.

Lt N T Dowty   Ens M E Fitzgerald   ARM1c E W Burton

USS *Solomons*
An Avenger of VC-9 from the escort carrier USS *Solomons* (Task Group 21.12) made an attack on U-860, on her first patrol, commanded by Frigettenkapitän Paul Büchel on 15 June 1944. First sighting of the U-boat was by another Avenger piloted by Ensign George E Edwards Jr USNR (from East St Louis, Illinois) at 1021 hours, 575 miles south of St Helena. A contact report came in from this aircraft noting position 2527/0530, then nothing.

The Avenger's fate was later disclosed by survivors from the submarine after rescue. According to them the Avenger made three runs on U-860 each in the face of heavy flak fire, but on the fourth approach, flak bracketed the attacking TBF-1c and it crashed into the sea. There were no survivors from the three-man crew.

Ens G E Edwards Jr   ARM2c A D Pacyna   AMM2c F Kuszinski Jr

It is thought that U-860 must have been damaged, for she made no attempt to dive on the later approach by four more Avengers sent out by the carrier, with two Wildcats, all from VC-9, led by Lieutenant Commander H M Avery USN in one of the Avengers. As Edwards had not returned, the mission was not only a search for the possible U-boat but also for the missing crew.

Initially neither sub nor dinghy were found, but at 1722 hours Howard Avery, flying at 1,500 feet, sighted a wake 10-12 miles off, and closing in identified a fully surfaced U-boat. At eight miles the submarine began to alter course and as the aircraft closed in, she began to circle, trying to keep her stern towards the attackers, but made no attempt to submerge.

The attack was made in three phases commencing 1746, eight minutes after sunset, and ending at 1753. The first was a co-ordinated strafing and rocket attack by two Avengers and two Wildcats, then another by one Avenger and one Wildcat, and finally a strafing and D/C attack by two Avengers.

One Avenger and two Wildcats had already been out to search but had seen nothing and had returned to the carrier and were about to land when they were sent off to Avery's sighting report area. Arriving at the scene, Avery directed the two Wildcat pilots, Ensigns Wadsworth and McMahon to begin strafing runs on the port and starboard quarters respectively, and Ensign Spear to made a rocket attack in company with the CO's TBF.

Wadsworth began his run from 2,000 feet, pulling out at less than 100 feet directly over the conning tower amidst many bursts of AA fire. His 400 rounds effectively hit the boat's bandstand area. Wadsworth was then ordered to return to the carrier as he was having problems jettisoning a damaged wing tank, which had collected a hit.

McMahon came in from 3,000 feet in a steep dive. In the face of intense AA fire he was able to pepper the deck and conning tower with 200 rounds, pulling out at 500 feet in order to clear the path of the oncoming Avenger. Ensign Spear had commenced his run simultaneously with the Wildcats' runs from 2,000 feet. At 800 yards he began loosing off his rockets in pairs six of which hit slightly ahead of the conning tower. Pulling out, his gunner began firing down at the sub.

Avery came in at the same time, firing six rockets in pairs beginning from 600 yards and these also scored hits. His gunner noted flak exploding right behind their Avenger during the run. In this attack, all four aircraft went over the submarine within ten seconds. The boat appeared to slow down, trailing oil and smoking around the conning tower, but flak was still being directed at the Navy planes.

In the second phase, Lieutenant (jg) Chamberlain, in company with Lieutenant (jg) Weigle and their crews, arrived and Avery directed Weigle, who also carried rockets, to make an attack from the port beam. Ensign McMahon preceded this attack with another strafing run, using up the remainder of his ammunition, pulling out at less than 200 feet. Weigle fired eight rockets in pairs from 600 yards, hitting the U-boat in front of the conning tower. The boat was only just making way and oil still trailed, now in large quantities leaving a greenish-yellow sheen on the surface of the sea.

The final phase was undertaken by Chamberlain, directed now to make a depth-charge attack from the boat's port quarter, while Avery made a strafing run. Disregarding continued flak fire from the sub, Chamberlain headed in and released two D/Cs from less than 50 feet. They landed in front of the conning tower causing a violent explosion which engulfed his TBF and started a fire in the bomb bay and centre cockpit. Chamberlain was able to maintain control and made a 180° turn then made a water landing about 500 yards ahead of the U-boat. Avery meantime had pulled up into a chandelle, enabling his gunner once more to rake the target.

The U-boat was finished. As the aircraft prepared to make further attacks the U-860 began to sink bow first, and then 30-40 survivors could be seen in the water. Darkness now engulfed the scene. Shortly afterwards the destroyers USS *Straub* and *Herzog* arrived on the scene and rescued 21 survivors from the U-boat including her captain, but there was no trace of the downed Avenger crew.

Thus the sinking of U-860 had cost two Avengers lost, and one Wildcat slightly damaged. William Chamberlain had been the very first pilot from an escort carrier to be involved in the sinking of a U-boat back on 22 May 1943, participating in the destruction of U-569, on that occasion VC-9 being on the *Bogue*.

Avengers:

Lt-Cdr H M Avery	ARM2c W J Gorski	AMM1c C D Falwell
Ens M J Spear USNR	ARM3c J Stark	AOM3c J M Chirdon
Lt D E Weigle USNR	ARM2c J H Sullivan	AOM3c C F McPherson
Lt W F Chamberlain USNR	ARM1c J H Finch	AMM2c R G Hennick

Wildcats:
Ens T J Wadsworth USNR
Ens R E McMahon USNR

* * *

The USS *Bogue* had VC-42 serving aboard her in August 1944. On the 14-15th, with fog clearing, the Squadron launched four Avengers at 1410 hours to conduct a barrier search to a distance of 75 miles around the ships. One aircraft developed engine trouble and had to make an emergency landing. At 1650 four Avengers were launched to search around the ships to 80 miles.

A U-boat was found and in an attack, one Avenger was hit, its pilot bringing back a slightly injured radioman at 1725. At 2203 two further aircraft were sent out and at 2228 one of these returned with engine trouble and its radar set u/s.

Finally at around 0300 hours, the carrier had radio contact with Lieutenant (jg) W A Dixon but then it was lost and not re-established. His last position was given as 4110/4742 – south-east of Newfoundland. He had reported radar contact but had lost it, so proceeded to drop Sonobuoys. It is unclear what happened to them, either they had hit the sea or had run out of fuel at low level. Whether the crew may have been lost to gun action is unknown.

Lt W A Dixon   AOM3c G J Scimio   ARM2c C G Melton

On 28 September 1944, U-219 was attacked by an Avenger of VC-6, west-south-west of the Cape Verde Islands. Using 'Ultra' information a task force centred around the escort carriers USS *Tripoli* and USS *Mission Bay* was waiting at a proposed rendezvous between U-219 (Korvettenkapitän Walter Burghagen) and U-1062 (Obtn Karl Albrecht) (1130/3440 – Grid EH 75).

At 1940 hours a searching Avenger from the *Tripoli*, piloted by Lieutenant W R Gillespie, reported making contact with a U-boat. Shortly thereafter he signalled that he was making an attack against flak – then silence.

Another Avenger saw part of the action as he came to the area, witnessing gunfire and rocket flashes in the darkening sky. It is not known for certain if it was U-219 as no KTB from this boat survives, but this was the only submarine known to be in Grid EH75 area on this date.

Gillespie and his two companions were the last escort carrier casualties in the Atlantic, fighting the undersea menace of Gemany's U-boats.

CHAPTER FIVE

BATTLES OVER THE BAY

Colliding with a U-boat

U-459, commanded by Korvettenkapitän Georg von Wilamowitz-Möllendorff and another Milch Cow U-tanker, a type IXV. She had begun her sixth patrol on 22 July, meeting up with U-117 at the mouth of the Gironde, having left Bordeaux the day previously. Due to the importance of getting these U-tankers safely out into the Atlantic, they were given a destroyer escort as far as 10° longitude. The escort departed on the morning of the 24th and that afternoon U-459 encountered Wellington 'Q' of 172 Squadron.

The U-tankers carried considerable defensive AA armament which U-459 had already used to good effect on 30 May 1943 by shooting down an attacking Whitley of 10 OTU. On this occasion the Wellington pilot managed to achieve some surprise and was down to 100 feet and heading in fast before the gunners reacted. They put up a heavy flak barrage and although it will never be known for certain, they either hit something vital or perhaps even the two pilots, for the Wellington smashed into the boat and broke up. Of the six-man crew, only the rear gunner, Sergeant A A Turner, survived, his turret breaking off on impact. He later ended up in the water and was lucky enough to find an inflated dinghy.

Meantime the submarine was in trouble; most of her guns had been carried away in the crash and their crews killed. Her situation was not helped by some sailors finding two depth charges lodged on the decking. Naturally they wanted to get rid of them, so quickly rolled them over the side. This, however, had the effect of setting them off once they fell beneath the waves, and the explosions beneath the stern badly damaged the steering gear and caused leaks in the rear hull area and a fire was started.

While in this hapless state, a second aircraft appeared, another Wellington, this time from 547 Squadron (F/O J Whyte). It dropped seven D/Cs around the stricken boat which caused further damage. By this time the German skipper realised there was no hope of saving his vessel, so ordered the boat scuttled – going down with his command.

The Polish destroyer *Orken* later arrived on the scene and picked up 37 U-boat men and Sergeant Turner. 'Ack-Ack' Turner, a keen football player, survived the war and played as an amateur for Charlton Athletic in the 1946 FA Cup Final. He had previously been in crews which had attacked and damaged U-525 and U-415 in March and May 1943.

F/O W H T Jennings	Pilot	F/O J Johnson	WOP/AG
F/O J G McCormack	2nd pilot	F/S L Harrop	WOP/AG
F/S J W Buxton	Nav	Sgt A A Turner	WOP/AG

The USAAF and RAF Sink U-404

In the Bay on the 28th were four outward-bound and one inward-bound U-boats. At 1107 hours, one of the outward boats, U-404, sailing on her 7th war cruise, under the command of Oberleutnant zur See Adolf Schönberg, was spotted by Major S D McElroy of the 4th US Squadron, 479th Group. U-404 had sailed from St Nazaire four days earlier, it being Schönberg's first patrol as her captain.

Major Stephen McElroy's crew had picked up a radar contact and he had brought Liberator 'Y' into visual contact and the boat was quickly seen and identified. The first attack failed due to non-release of the D/Cs and the German commander, seeing his chance, dived.

The Liberator remained in the area and finally their patience was rewarded at 1517 that afternoon as the boat returned to the surface. Whether the captain had not seen the aircraft or whether she was forced back to the surface to re-charge batteries is not known but her gunners were quickly at their posts and as McElroy came in again, the boat began firing, a 20 mm shell exploding inside the cockpit.

Miraculously no one was hurt, the shell passing through the co-pilot's fuse box before exploding behind the armoured plating to damage the radio. The American gunners replied, seeing three men fall from the bridge, but the boat was diving again. As it did so a turn to starboard was observed, the right waist and rear gunners spraying the decks as they went over.

McElroy had approached from directly ahead and let go eight D/Cs, the resulting explosions enveloping the swirl. As the Liberator circled so oil began to rise to the surface of the sea, but McElroy's attention was now focused on the oil pressure to his No.3 engine which was falling. Suspecting flak damage, and because of the damage to the fuse box, which caused the instruments to No's 2 and 3 engines to become useless, and the damaged radio, he left the scene and headed home.

U-404 may well have been damaged, but she resurfaced at 1745 and was found by another 4th Squadron B24 ('H') flown by First Lieutenant Arthur J Hammer, who had picked up McElroy's report. He made two attacks despite severe flak fire, and return fire knocked two men into the sea. However, amidst the D/C drop, the Lib had its port outer engine hit and it had to be feathered, with other hits on the tail and fuselage. As Hammer headed for home, a third Liberator came up.

This was a 224 Squadron RAF machine (BZ781 'W'), flown by an American, Flying Officer R V Sweeny. Bobby Sweeny was an anglophile having lived in England for some time and he had also gone to Oxford. He was a keen golfer, being the British amateur golf champion in 1937, and his brother Charles had helped form the American Eagle Squadron, the volunteer Americans who had flown Hurricanes and Spitfires in the two years prior to America's entry into the war. Bobby himself had been one of the adjutants.

The searching RAF crew had seen the exploding D/C plumes and headed for the action. As he came to a range of 1,000 yards his gunners began firing. Flight Sergeant Eddie Cheek recalled.

> 'During the run-up we were under heavy and sustained fire from the U-boat; the starboard outer engine was hit and seized. We were just able to see that our attack had been successful, but our immediate concern was our own predicament. At this time we were flying at about 15 to 20 feet, apparently unable to gain height and Bob ordered me to commence the radio distress procedure. I was able to make immediate W/T contact with HQ 19 Group at Plymouth, giving them details of our position. I now had a nasty suspicion that my 21st birthday party (July 29th) instead of being a riotous affair with the 'boys' would, at best, comprise a few Horlicks tablets in a heaving rubber dinghy.'

Looking back, some of the Lib crew saw the boat disappear then resurface. When the disturbed water settled down there was a good deal of floating debris around and about ten bodies in life belts. Bob Sweeny and his crew had finished off U-404, but her gunners had scored hits on three Liberators, knocking out an engine from each. In all 27 depth charges had finally sealed the boat's fate. None of her 50-man crew survived. This boat had sunk 14 ships and one destroyer during her six previous war cruises.

Bobby Sweeny got his Lib home but not before having to jettison guns and all loose equipment, including his engineer's prized tool box. Because of the three-engined landing coming up, Sweeny was diverted to St Mawgen as it had a longer runway. The SOS had been received, and when much later the crew finally got back to St Eval, and home, Eddie Cheek for one found most of his personal possessions had been 'liberated' by his pals. They were glad he had 'made it' of course, but sad that they had to give it all back, much of which he had picked up earlier in the war during a visit to America.

F/O R V Sweeny	Pilot	F/S E S Cheek	WOP/AG
P/O E Allen RCAF	2nd pilot	F/S I A Graham	WOP/AG
F/O R W King	Nav	Sgt A H Graham	AG
F/S C Owen	Eng	Sgt D Doncaster	AG

Likely due to his inexperience, Oberleutnant Schönberg had made several tactical errors resulting in three successive attacks on his boat. In each of these encounters accurate flak fire had knocked out an engine on his attackers' aircraft but had not prevented the completion of their attack runs.

U-461 and U/461

The action between a number of aircraft and three submarines on 30 July 1943, which resulted in all three boats being lost – two to aircraft, another by scuttling and the arrival of ships of Walker's 2nd Escort Group – is so well known that the details here will be brief.

The three boats had set out in company, U-461 and U-462 being U-tankers, U-504 a type IXC/40. They were sighted by a Liberator from 53 Squadron RAF (BZ730 'O') and it circled out of range while reporting the 'find'. This in turn brought further aircraft to the area, while Walker's sloops were also on their way.

The Liberator was joined by several aircraft, including a Sunderland from 228 Squadron (JM679), a Catalina of 210 Squadron, a Sunderland of 461 Squadron RAAF (W6077 'U'), two Halifaxes from 502 Squadron, and an American B24 from the 19th Squadron. In the battle which followed, one of the Halifax aircraft was hit and holed and the 53 Squadron Liberator was also badly shot up, and its D/Cs undershot. The latter was so badly damaged that the pilot had to limp to the nearest land – Spain – where the crew headed south, landing in Portugal to be interned.

However, with U-461 being sunk by Sunderland U/461 (F/L D Marrows RAAF) and U-462 credited to the other 502 Squadron Halifax, Coastal Command had scored well. When Walker's ships arrived and began to fire at the third boat she was forced under, and later suffered heavily from ships' D/Cs attacks which sent U-504 to the bottom.

The interned 53 Squadron (BZ370 'O') crew were:

F/O W J Irving	Pilot	Sgt A J Pudifin	WOP/AG
F/O R E Dobson	2nd pilot	Sgt J G Humphreys	WOP/AG
F/O J Haste	Nav	Sgt J Wildon	WOP/AG
P/O R G Sharpe	WOP/AG		

Bob Dobson recalls:

> 'We took off in the early hours of 30 July from Thorney Island and after some hours flying three U-boats were sighted. At that time, if more than one U-boat was sighted other aircraft had to be called.
>
> 'We began shadowing but if ever we got a bit nearer to them, the air seemed to be black with exploding shells. After some time, four or five other aircraft arrived and numerous efforts were made to establish radio contact but without success.
>
> 'Having failed to organise a concerted attack by radio, it was

decided to attack one of the outside U-boats. On our approach all boats fired at us but I do not think we were hit until going over the top of our target. The outer-starboard engine was put out of action and one of the port engines was also hit. The aircraft's controls became very difficult to handle and the main problem was to remain flying.

'We had dropped a stick of depth charges which were slightly under shot but it was thought that the last one may have caused some damage. However, a Sunderland flying boat had followed us in to the attack and our rear gunner shouted that he had blown the U-boat out of the water. This was U of 461 Squadron destroying U-boat U-461.

'As we were leaving the scene and struggling to climb, we flew over the Walker Escort Group. We eventually got up to 600 feet and set course for the nearest land which was Cape Finisterre. Having reached there, we decided to fly down the coast of Portugal and try to reach Gibraltar. When petrol was low we looked for somewhere to land but it wasn't until we reached Lisbon that it was possible and we landed (Portela) there after 13 hours in the air.

'We were treated well when we got out of the aircraft and I remember asking for a drink and being given some iced tea. I don't think I have ever enjoyed anything so much as that.'

The crew, after questioning, were housed in a hotel, the pilot or co-pilot having to report to the British Embassy each day. It so happened that Bob Dobson's father worked for a ship-building company on the Tyne, where most of the Portuguese Navy had been built. Once it was known the crew were safe, Dobson senior asked the Director if he could do anything to help. It was not long before the Portuguese authorities arranged for the crew to be flown back to England.[1]

This action was a complete disaster for the Germans. The loss of U-tankers virtually paralysed distant operations which at the time were the focus of BdU's efforts. The tactics of sailing U-boats in groups through the Bay of Biscay was abandoned as clearly any mutual support they could provide was more than out-weighed by Coastal Command's tactics of calling up other aircraft – and ships – to attack in force. In fact all outward sailings were temporarily suspended, pending the outfitting of boats with new equipment.

One for One
Two actions which heralded the end of the recent intense action over the Bay, and which also convinced Dönitz to change his 'fight back' policy, both came on 1 August 1943. In the first, a Sunderland of 10 Squadron

---

[1] (For full details of this action see *Conflict over the Bay*, (N Franks; Wm Kimber 1986;) *Search, Find & Kill* (N Franks; Grub Street, 1995) and *Dark Skies, Deep Water* (N Franks; Grub Street, 1997).

RAAF (W4020 'B') located U-454, commanded by Kapitänleutnant Burkhard Häcklander, in position 4536/1023. She was outbound and the time was 1440.

The Sunderland pilot went immediately into the attack, the U-boat captain electing to stay up, mainly because his batteries were low after a long period of being under water. The flak barrage was intense and accurate and the flying boat was hit repeatedly. Until I contacted one of the Australian crew a year or so ago, I went along with the oft-repeated story that both pilots must have been hit, but Don Conacher told me that this was not so.

As they made the run in, Don heard his pilot, Ken Fry, say that he was going to get the sub if it was the last thing he did. Unhappily, it was. The Sunderland had a single nose gun and the gunner, Tubby Fryer was blazing away but the flak fire was deadly. Don was in the rear gun turret and as they flew over and the D/Cs exploded, he saw the U-boat break in two. However, he could then tell that their engines were not sounding too well and they were not climbing, then he was told to vacate the turret and come forward.

When he reached the flight deck he could see there was a large hole in one of the tanks and fuel was gushing all over the place, a crew member was trying to plug it with a Mae West. He could see the second pilot was wounded but Fry seemed in control but the damage was forcing them to ditch. The Sunderland nosed in and suddenly there was a maelstrom of water as the flying boat began to sink.

Don and a few of the others clung to a section of broken wing until the sloop HMS *Wren* from the 2nd Escort Group came along and rescued them, but by then only six of the 12-man crew were alive. Another sloop, HMS *Kite* picked up 14 of the U-boat survivors (out of 45), including its captain.

F/L K G Fry	Pilot *	Sgt F O Pettersson	Fitter
F/O H R Budd	1st pilot *	F/S B E Cook	WOP/AG
F/O J M Curtis	2nd pilot *	F/S R G Welfare	WOP/AG
F/O J H Portus	Nav	Sgt J E Fryer	Fitter *
P/O A M Welch	Nav u/t *	Sgt J Haslam	Armourer
Sgt H B Lydeamore	Eng *	Sgt D I Conacher	AG
* Did not survive.			

That evening another Sunderland, this time from 228 Squadron (JM678 'V') found U-383, commanded by Kapitänleutnant Horst Kremser, in position 4724/1210, at 2002 hours. The pilot commenced a run, strafing the boat, but return fire scored hits, shooting away the starboard float and aileron as well as holing the hull and fuselage. This combined with the violent evasive action by the target boat, meant that the first attack was foiled.

Despite its heavy damage the Sunderland circled and came in for another run from the boat's starboard quarter, releasing a stick of seven D/Cs which seemed to make a good straddle. As the cascading water from the plumes subsided the boat could be seen listing heavily to port and men were jumping overboard. Due to the damage the Sunderland departed at once.

The boat was able to get off a signal to BdU but sank during the night. Those who had jumped into the water may well have been pulled back aboard, but the boat was effectively beyond help; all 52 crewmen were lost. U-boat men knew that if their boat went down their chances of survival and rescue were truly minimal. It had to be a sobering thought but one which must have concentrated the mind of the flak gunners in those final terrifying moments exchanging gunfire with a huge aeroplane as it headed for them. Sometimes it worked in their favour, sometimes not.

F/L S White	Pilot	Sgt B Hodgeman
F/O A Neville-Stack	2nd pilot	F/S T Robney
F/O K A Mooring	Nav	Sgt W Champion
P/O F Jackson		Sgt R Glazier
F/S E Kampton		Sgt W Carteen
Sgt F Baker RAAF		

* * *

It took two attacks on U-489 to stop her war. Oberleutnant Adalbert Schmandt was well out into the North Atlantic, south-east of Iceland on 3 August when he was attacked by a Catalina from 190 Squadron. Six days out of Kiel, which she left on 22 July, the boat had rescued three survivors from a Bv138 seaplane which had been shot down by Beaufighters, and they had to continue on with the U-boat.

Flight Sergeant E L J 'Peter' Brame flying a 269 Squadron Hudson III from Iceland had come on the scene of the action between the Catalina and U-489. 'U' of 190 (FP280) had flown from Sullom Voe at 2241 on 2 August on a Moorings Five patrol and at 0750 on the morning of the 3rd had sighted the U-boat from 1,150 feet five miles off and also another aircraft flying in and out of cloud, identified as a B17. The Fortress went in and U/190 strafed the boat to divert attention. The U-boat replied with 20-mm cannon fire, using self-destructive shells which was extremely accurate. The Catalina saw strikes on the boat but was also hit twice itself. The Fortress flew off and did not drop any D/Cs. At 0811 the boat was still on the surface as the Catalina crew, anxious about the damage their flying boat had sustained decided to head for base. As they did so they saw the Hudson arrive. The Catalina had had its IFF apparatus and DR compass destroyed by the gunfire and later the rudder cables were found to be almost severed. The D/Cs were jettisoned safe, and when base asked how many U-boats, they answered – one.

F/L B Crosland	Pilot	F/S H J Stammers

F/O H Marsden	Sgt A Eldridge
F/O W W D Lamb	Sgt R Q Marris
F/O T R Bishop	Sgt E Coulston-Smith
F/S W J O'Donnell	

Meantime, Peter Brame had attacked, his bombs badly damaging the U-boat. He noted in his log-book: 'Attacked surfaced U-boat for 50 mins with A/S bombs and gunfire. Met fierce anti-aircraft fire up to 2,000 ft. Submerged after front gun attack.'

| F/S E L J Brame | Pilot | Sgt Y T Borland | WOP/AG |
| F/S W Styring | Nav | Sgt E Beaudry | WOP/AG |

Soon after 9 o'clock the next morning, the 4th, the damaged boat was again found, this time by a Sunderland from 423 Squadron RCAF, in position 6111/1438. Sunderland DD859 'G' was captained by Flying Officer A A Bishop and he headed straight for the boat which began evasive action and firing; apart from the damage from Brame's Hudson, the boat's batteries were drained. Not far from the release point the flying boat was badly hit but Bishop managed to complete his run and drop the D/Cs before having to crash into the sea.

The story is told in some detail through the eyes of four living survivors from the crew including Al Bishop, in my book *Dark Sky, Deep Water*. Suffice it to say here that only six of the 11 crewmen survived, Bishop himself helping to support one of his wounded WOP/AGs who had a broken arm and other injuries. The U-boat was mortally hit and sank slowly, all the crew getting clear except for the chief engineer who was killed in an explosion just before the final plunge.

The British destroyers *Castletown* and *Orwell* arrived on the scene soon afterwards, for luckily an alert lookout on the former had seen the Sunderland go down. They picked up survivors from the aircraft and submarine. Bishop later received the DFC for this action, but Brame was not mentioned, although it had been his attack on the 3rd which had led to U-489's loss.

F/O A A Bishop RCAF	Pilot	F/S J S Kelly RAF	AG
F/O D M Wettlaufer RCAF	2nd pilot	Sgt F Handcroft RAF *	WOP
P/O H Parliament RCAF*	Nav	Sgt H E Finn RCAF	WOP/AG
Sgt P McDonnell RAF *	Eng	F/S J B Horsburgh	WOP
Sgt H Gossip *	Eng	RAF*	
F/O A E Mountford RCAF	1st WOP/AG	F/S J A V Richardson RAF	WOP

* Did not survive.

VC Action

On 11 August 1943 there was an action played out which would lead to a Liberator pilot being awarded the Victoria Cross. What was almost unique was that the report which led to this decoration being awarded came from the survivors of a German U-boat.

U-468 commanded by Oberleutnant zur See Klemens Schamong was off the West African coast, and the Liberator, of 200 Squadron (BZ832 'D') piloted by Flying Officer L A Trigg, was on patrol to the south-west of Dakar. No.200 Squadron was based at Yundum airfield, around four miles from the Gambia River estuary near Bathurst, 100 miles or so south of Dakar.

At 0945 am a surfaced U-boat was spotted and Trigg went straight into the attack but its approach had been seen by the boat's gunners who opened up on the oncoming bomber. Several hits were scored on the aeroplane and then it was seen to be trailing smoke and flame but on it came, though in obvious difficulty. It tracked over the submarine's port quarter and six D/Cs tumbled down. The aircraft's crew never knew the result of their attack for immediately after releasing its weaponry the Lib crashed into the sea and exploded. There were no survivors.

Aboard U-468 there was no celebrating. Two of the six D/Cs had exploded within six feet of the boat's hull and the effect was disastrous. Engines, motors and pumps were torn from their mountings, fuel tanks ruptured and sea water flooded the battery compartment, forming clouds of deadly chlorine gas. The boat sank rapidly in position 1220/2007. Less than half the boat's compliment managed to get out. Many of the men who managed to make the water were injured or gassed and sharks attracted to the blood also claimed victims. In the end only seven men, including Schamong, were rescued by HMS *Clarkia* on 13 August. Ironically they owed their survival to a rubber raft that had floated free from the wreckage of the Liberator. Based entirely on the testimony of the U-boat survivors, Leonard Trigg was posthumously awarded Britain's highest award for bravery.

Oddly enough, U-468 was being forced to return from patrol early because the plan to refuel her from U-462 (Milch Cow) had been foiled with the sinking of the latter boat on 30 July, referred to earlier.

F/O L A Trigg RNZAF	Pilot	F/S T J Soper RNZAF	WOP/AG
P/O G N Goodwin RCAF	2nd pilot	F/S A R Bonnick	WOP/AG
F/O I Marinovich RNZAF	Nav	F/S A G Bennett RNZAF	WOP/AG
F/O J J S Townshend	2nd Nav	F/S L J Frost RNZAF	WOP/AG

CHAPTER SIX

THE ANTI-U-BOAT WAR HOTS UP

September 1943
Although Admiral Dönitz had been forced to re-think and then rescind his stay-up-and-fight order following the disastrous summer, many U-boat commanders felt it was justified if circumstances were forced upon them. Therefore the number of gun actions with Allied aeroplanes increased.

On 7 September two Wellingtons from 172 Squadron at RAF Chivenor located U-402, commanded by Korvettenkapitän Siegfried Freiherr von Forstner. Aircraft 'D' and 'Q' were in the area of position 4635/090 (German Grid BF4597), 'Q' picking up an S/E contact at 2203 hours, distance six miles.

Flying Officer T Armstrong homed in MP791. There was no cloud and bright moonlight as he dropped to 200 feet. The Leigh Light was switched on at one mile, illuminating a U-boat on the surface, and moments later six D/Cs went down from 50 feet. The front gunner had opened up immediately and the boat had replied five seconds later with cannon and machine-gun fire. The rear gunner took up the firing as the Wellington went over but two of his guns jammed. Ten minutes later Armstrong went in again, this time only able to make a strafing attack.

As they circled, they saw, at 2213, another Leigh Light come on low down, a short distance from the submarine. They saw too the exchange of gun fire, the flashes lighting up the night sky. They also saw the aircraft catch fire near the boat and then dive into the sea where the wreckage burned for 20 minutes. They could do nothing but report to location, and later, had to return to base.

On landing they discovered their port tyre had been damaged and it burst on impact but Armstrong got it down safely. On inspection they found the Wellington had been hit twice in the port undercarriage, so unknown to the crew, U-402 had scored a hit on them too. The other Wellington's crew captained by Flying Officer C J Payne (in MP509) were all lost.

F/O T Armstrong	Pilot	Sgt N S Birch	WOP/AG
Lt P R Reumont USAAC	2nd Pilot	Sgt F A Wilkinson	WOP/AG
F/O T J Magee	Nav	Sgt W V Jones	WOP/AG

F/O C J Payne	Pilot	F/S R E J Cooper	WOP/AG
W/O A L Brigden	2nd pilot	Sgt L Vaughan-Harrison	WOP/AG
P/O R J Gerrett	Nav	Sgt C J E Moody	WOP/AG

U-402 was outbound, but she was not out of the woods yet. The next day she was under threat again, found by Wellington 'M' of 612 Squadron (HF126). The crew were heading for a *Percussion* J2 patrol as the radar operator picked up a blip at four miles and homed in his pilot, Flying Officer J M Bezer.

Shortly afterwards, at 0515, they tracked over the blip at 600 feet, the rear gunner spotting the wake of a U-boat. Bezer flew on for three miles before making a turn and dropping to 100 feet. At $3/4$ of a mile the Leigh Light went on, and the U-boat opened up with cannon and machine-gun fire, from what appeared to be from three positions. The front gunner attempted to reply but his armament jammed. Bezer released six D/Cs from 50 feet, but just before he did so he felt hits on his aircraft. Shells smashed into the nose, the perspex shattered cutting the pilot's cheek, others hitting the port engine and nacelle, starboard petrol tank and wing, tailplane and fuselage; the radar was also knocked out.

The boat's fire ceased as the D/Cs tumbled down, helped no doubt by the rear gunner's fire as the Wellington zoomed over them. Bezer didn't wait to discover more, and headed back to base, nursing his crippled machine to a British airfield, but it was a near thing. At 0602 base received an SOS call from the Wellington that its starboard engine had stopped and they were jettisoning as much loose equipment as they could. After a flight of $1^1/2$ hours, Bezer made a satisfactory crash landing at Portreath without injury to his crew. Thus had U-402 scored hits on all three attackers, and shot down one Wellington and damaged the other two.

F/O J M Bezer	Pilot	Sgt K H Scott	WOP/AG
F/O G Wallace	2nd pilot	Sgt H A Camp	WOP/AG
F/O E E G Pitt	Nav	Sgt R Higham	WOP/AG

Of interest is the radio traffic between U-402 and BdU concerning these attacks. On 11 September, the U-boat, then in Grid BE59 reported to BdU:

> "Air attack in BF48. One aircraft shot down." BdU responded with a signal of its own to U-402: "Your message of the attack in BF48 is too brief. Hour and date are not mentioned. The following are [our] intercepts of signals from enemy aircraft. 7 Sept – 1231 hours – BF4881 – U-boat observed; 1305 to 2335 – BF4597 – U-boat on course 280°; 8 Sept: – 0618 hours – BF4851 – U-boat, course 310°. By our calculations only U-402 was in these areas. If that is not correct, will you later report, when it is necessary to send a signal for other reasons."

U-402 responded on the 20th with,

> "... concerning FT 11.55 from 9 September, all is correct except the sighting by aircraft at 1231 hours."

U-402 was eventually sunk on 13 October 1943, by aircraft from the escort carrier *Card*, this time her gunners not being on target. She was credited to Lieutenant-Commander H M Avery of *Card*'s VC9 whom we met in Chapter Four. She had sunk 14 ships and one armed yacht. There were no survivors from the 50-man crew. However, during 7/8 September she had fought off three air attacks and shot down one hostile aircraft, damaging two others while crossing the Bay. All this was confirmed by signals between the boat and BdU.It was a fine example of effective fight-back tactics, warding off any damage to the boat.

* * *

Wellingtons were again to the fore on 11/12 September against U-617 – Kapitänleutnant Albrecht Brandi. She had been located and attacked initially by Wellington 'P' of 179 Squadron at 0050 am, off the northern Moroccan shore, heavy flak being met as soon as the Leigh Light went on. Squadron Leader D B Hodgkinson RCAF straddled the boat with his D/Cs and the boat began to leave a trail of oil. Keeping the boat under observation, they homed in Wellington 'J' of the same Squadron.

It appeared as if the submarine was trying to make neutral waters, the boat clearly seen by 'J''s crew on a calm sea under a cloudless sky. The radar picked her up then the oil trail could be clearly seen in the moonpath. 'J' attacked up the moonbeam in position 3517/0320, the boat opening up with heavy flak almost as soon as the Leigh Light came on, and the aircraft was hit in several places, the rear gunner being fatally wounded.

The front gunner had tried to keep the gunners' heads down, hits being seen to splatter around the conning tower, then the D/Cs were going down from 80 feet. Knowing his aircraft had been hit around the port side, the pilot kept on going and started a climb to 500 feet, but upon inspection the damage was not too severe so he turned back to see results.

About a minute later flames could be viewed coming from the conning tower for almost a minute and then the boat could be seen down by the stern. The aircraft continued to shadow the boat for 45 minutes until it finally beached herself on the Moroccan coast in position 3513/0329. Next morning U-617 was lying on her port side with her conning tower awash; her crew were ashore, drying their clothes. She was finished off by attacks from Hudsons, Swordfish and finally gunfire from HM ships. The German crew suffered no casualties and all 49 men survived. Interned by the Spanish, they were later repatriated to Germany. In seven patrols U-617 had sunk 11 ships including the minelayer HMS *Welshman*, gallant veteran of many Malta fast supply runs.

The Wellington's wounded rear gunner made no mention of being hit, but as the captain finally turned for home, there was no reply from an R/T check, so someone went to investigate. He had remained at his post and bled to death.

P/O W H Brunini	Pilot	Sgt F M Crowdis	WOP/AG
Sgt A Jones	2nd pilot	F/S H W Barnfield	WOP/AG
F/O V H Johnson	Nav	F/S W Jones RAAF	WOP/AG *

* Died of Wounds.

* * *

Peter Brame Again

We met Peter Brame in Chapter Five, making a damaging attack on U-489 which led to her loss on 4 August 1943. Still with 269 Squadron at Reykjavik on 21 September, he and his crew had another action on this date, this time with U-539, commanded by Oberleutnant zur See Hans-Jürgen Lauterbach-Emden.

Once again he was patrolling the Moorings area south-east of Iceland in a Hudson (V9161 'G') below 3/10ths cloud at 1,500 feet, sea calm with visibility 15 miles. Just as dawn was breaking they sighted a surfaced U-boat six miles away, in position 6222/1434. As Brame approached so the boat began to fire and the aircraft was hit a mighty blow in the port wing with cannon.

Brame began to circle at 2,000 feet and then climbed to 3,000 to make a high level bomb run, dropping one 100 lb A/S bomb, which undershot by 50 yards. A second run put another bomb 40 yards away, both attacks coming in from astern. Brame was trying to force the U-boat commander to dive so he could come in low without flak, but his ruse did not succeed.

Finally the U-boat increased speed so at 0750, Brame decided to make a D/C attack anyway, up wind in order to keep the spray in the faces of the U-boat men. Coming in he released his D/Cs from 30 feet, but the boat made a sudden last-minute turn to starboard causing the D/Cs to overshoot by 30 feet. During the run Brame opened fire with his front guns and saw hits on the conning tower, and return fire from the boat slackened off to almost nil over the final 100 yards.

After the attack the U-boat slowed down and gave off grey diesel smoke. Brame then lost it in the low morning sunlight, during which time the boat must have crash-dived for it was not seen again. Brame got his damaged Hudson back to base where later a photo was taken of the large hole in the starboard wing, with the crew looking through it smiling. Luckily they were able to smile; unfortunately the photo has been lost. When over the boat, the radio operator heard a strong R/T voice on 600 Kc in German. It was thought they were trying to contact another boat that may have been nearby. Peter Brame noted in his log-book:

'Attacked surfaced U-boat for 1 hr 17 mins. Dropped 2 A/S bombs from 3,000 ft, near miss. A/c hit by cannon fire on port aileron and starboard mainplane near engine nacelle. First about 1 ft in diameter with shrapnel, second 7 inches with much shrapnel.'

(U-539's story continues later in this chapter.)

Sgt E J L Brame	Pilot	F/S N W Elliston	
F/S G G McLean		F/L E Whitmore	
Sgt A H Hurle			

Heinrich Schröteler's Hard Fought Battles

Kapitänleutnant Schröteler had taken U-667 down to the Gibraltar area in September 1943 and ran into a RAF maelstrom. Shortly before dawn on the 24th he had suffered a Leigh Light attack from Flight Sergeant A W Ellis in Wellington 'P' of 179 Squadron off Portugal, fought back with flak but neither side suffered any damage.

That evening U-667 was attacked again by 179 Squadron, this time by Flying Officer A Chiltern in Wellington 'D', but on this occasion the boat was slightly damaged, in position 3652/0908. At 1035 on the 25th, Flight Sergeant D J McMahon in R/179 attacked, but despite six D/Cs falling near the boat, she survived. However, U-667 was forced to remain on the surface in order to recharge her batteries which were critically low.

At 0309 hours, Q/179 found her, having received the two previous sighting reports, and gunfire was exchanged but no D/Cs dropped as Flight Sergeant R W Dix's machine had been hit by flak. The D/Cs hung up and other hits were scored on the port engine and starboard wing, forcing the pilot to break off the action and return to base.

F/S R W Dix	Pilot	Sgt G Dade	WOP/AG
F/O J F Waters	2nd pilot	Sgt G W Green	WOP/AG
F/O R H Allen	Nav	Sgt H Chew	WOP/AG

The boat obviously kept below during the day but surfaced that night only to be located again by 179 Squadron. At 2218 hours the boat recorded an attack in Grid CG8584, with a Leigh Light heralding a D/C attack. The boat's gunners fired back and claimed hitting the attacker. U-667's KTB noted with surprise that in this case the Leigh Light had remained on after the attack and that there had been no strafing. Then at 0045 on the 26th, the boat intercepted an SOS distress signal from a British aircraft over the sea and assumed that this was the aircraft lost as a result of the boat's flak.

Wellington XIV 'F' of 179 Squadron did not return from patrol and as there is no matching attack by an RAF aircraft on a U-boat it must be assumed that F/179 was responsible. It seems too that the aircraft was not lost immediately following the encounter but in view of the circumstances and U-667's claim it is certainly reasonable that the boat scored this kill. Gibraltar also picked up the SOS, the aircraft giving its position as 3625/0930 at 2228 (ie: ten minutes after U-667's attack time), then silence. They had started their sortie at 1913 hours flying a north-west patrol. Riddell had been posted in from 172 Squadron as a flight commander on 6 September.

S/L G H M Riddell	Pilot	F/O H F Beale RCAF	WOP/AG
P/O H J Dowd RCAF	2nd pilot	F/S R Smith	WOP/AG
P/O S G Hoad	Nav	F/S D Abercrombie	WOP/AG

At 1040 that morning Flying Officer S H Nicholson in X/179 found and attacked the boat while engaged on an ASR search for Riddell and crew, along with a Hudson of 233 Squadron. Again the antagonists exchanged fire and the D/Cs this time exploded astern. Two other aircraft now appeared, identified by the boat lookouts as Beaufighters, but were in fact Hudsons. The first was the 233 Squadron aircraft, probably confusing the boat crew due to its use of rockets.

Flying Officer A G Frandson in T/233 rocketed the boat and strafed her but AE505 was hit in the tail. The pilot remained in the vicinity. He was lucky, for later it was found that several strands of his elevator controls had been severed. Frandson now homed in Flying Officer E L Ashbury flying N/48 (EW924) who also attacked with rockets and gun fire, the aircraft being hit also, withdrawing rapidly.

F/O A G Frandson	Pilot	Sgt J Graham RCAF
F/O A M Lipman		Sgt R Dexter
F/O E L Ashbury	Pilot	F/O L Honderich
F/O T Davison		F/S H P Roode

The accumulated damage of no less than eight air attacks and the virtual exhaustion of the batteries and crew caused U-667's captain to abandon the attempt to enter the Mediterranean. Despite this set-back she had been lucky to survive at all. Certainly the boat and crew had aquitted themselves well, having fought off a whole series of determined air assaults during which she had shot down one aircraft and damaged three others.

U-667 was lost on her fifth patrol which began on 22 July 1944, heading for the Cornish coast. She hit an RAF-laid mine on her return to port and sank off La Pallice on 25 August. None of her 45 crew survived, but on this occasion, Schröteler was not in command.

The Station Commander's Day(s) Out
On 27 September 1943 the Station Commander of RAF Holmesley South, Group Captain Roger Mead, decided to accompany one of the squadron's

aircraft on patrol, choosing to fly with Flying Officer Eric Hartley and his 58 Squadron crew, in a Halifax – HR982 'B'. It was a decision he might very well have regretted.

They were on a *Percussion* patrol to the south-west of Ireland. Having dropped down to 50 feet to investigate a possible periscope feather, the Halifax was just turning away when a surfaced U-boat was sighted dead ahead, six miles distant. Hartley decided to continue the approach at low level and upon reaching 1,000 yards from the target, the aircraft gunners opened fire. Almost simultaneously the U-boat began firing too.

The flak, strong at first, began to fall away but just as the bomber tracked over the boat a burst hit the No.2 fuel tank and set the starboard wing afire. It was too late to affect the attack and the eight D/Cs plummeted down and achieved a good straddle. The sub's bows were seen to rise and then the hull slid backwards and disappeared. No further observations were possible as the Halifax had likewise suffered mortal damage.

Hartley ditched the machine some three miles from the attack site and not until 11 days later were the six survivors picked up, totally by chance, by the destroyer HMS *Muhratta*, making her way home from Gibraltar. The ship's crew were not searching for anyone, her zigs just zagged in their direction at the right time! Eric Hartley received the DFC and Flight Sergeant Ken Ladds the DFM.

U-221 was the luckless submarine, on her fifth patrol, having left St Nazaire on 20 September. Her score of ships sunk amounted to 12 in all, including eight from convoy SC104 during the night of 12/13 October 1942, although only five were actually lost. None of the 50 crew survived, including her skipper, Kapitänleutnant Hans Troger. She had been sunk at 1713 hours in position 4700/1800.

F/O E L Hartley	Pilot	F/S K E Ladds	MU gunner
G/C R C Mead	2nd pilot	Sgt R K Triggol	Rear gunner*
F/O R C Bach RCAF	Nav	Sgt A S Fox	WOP
Sgt G R Robertson	Eng	Sgt M Griffiths	Front gunner*
* Lost.			

Another high ranking airmen was less fortunate than Roger Mead on 4 October. Wing Commander R M Longmore, the squadron commander, was piloting a Liberator V of 120 Squadron ('V-Victor') on this date from Rekyavik, having taken off at 0935.

Their task was to provide escort for convoy ONS19 (Britain to Halifax, Nova Scotia – slow). Some time around 1130 base received a message, which read: 'TOO 11.30 A – 465 – TZT – 2500 – 472 – 1 – FLR', which was corrupt but which meant: 'Am over U-boat on surface', but giving a corrupt position. 'FLR' may possibly have been corrupt for FLAK, but in any event the aircraft did not return. The actual position was believed to have been 6375/2850.

After exchanging gunfire with a surfaced U-boat which Longmore found, he decided to make an attack run but his Liberator was hit during the approach. Both starboard engines were set on fire but he completed his attack. The stick of D/Cs overshot and caused the boat – U-539 (Oberleutnant Hans-Jürgen Lauterbach-Emden), only slight damage, and one crewman was slightly wounded. U-539 reported the action at 1138 in position AD5769. This submarine, of course, was the one which had so nearly shot down Peter Brame and his Hudson crew back on 21 September. This time the flak gunners had done better.

W/C R M Longmore OBE	Pilot	F/S A E Parsons	Engineer
F/O R W Tait	2nd pilot	F/L A L Furr	AG/Sig
F/O R M Webber	3rd pilot	W/O E A Minchem	2/WOP/AG
F/L N Bruce	Nav	W/O W Stott	3/WOP/AG

October 1943
U-256, Oberleutnant Wilhelm Brauel's command, claimed an aircraft shot down in Grid BF4516 (Biscay) in the early hours of 8 October, identified only as a four-engined aircraft with a Leigh Light. They fought it off and saw hits on it, although they did not actually see it crash. Her KTB noted:

"0334 hours. Grid BF4516. Leigh Light distance 800 metres. Height 50 metres. Light flare. Flak. Four-engined aircraft turns off, puts off his searchlight. Hits on aircraft. 0340 hours, crash-dive."

So successful had the Leigh Light become that aircraft other than Wellingtons were using them. In this case, however, the four-motored bomber was in fact a twin-engined Wellington, aircraft 'J' of 612 Squadron (HF190). Thus are historians confused unless careful checks are made.

The Wellington was airborne at 0048 hours on the morning of the 8th, flying an Air Sea Rescue mission. However, at 0337 they found a U-boat in position 4728/0936, their six D/Cs exploding either side of the conning tower. A good straddle was no guarantee of success, ask any anti-U-boat airman, and this was again a case in point. U-256 sailed through undamaged, but its fire had put holes through the Wellington's starboard elevator and rear turret. The RAF crew were well aware of the boat's flak, red and white tracer reaching up for them, some of it exploding close to the bomber as well as the bullet hits. The aircraft replied, but when it came round for a second run, there was nothing on the surface but the flame floats dropped with the D/Cs, so no wonder U-256 was not around to observe the aircraft 'crash'. To complete the story, the Wellington later sighted sea markers and the dinghy it was seeking; they landed back at base at 0839 more than satisfied with the night's work.

P/O M H Paynter RAAF	Pilot	Sgt G Secklington	WOP/AG
Sgt G R Borlace	2nd pilot	Sgt D L Smith	WOP/AG
P/O J W MacKay RAAF	Nav	F/S W L Parsons	WOP/AG

Max Paynter and crew would sink U-545 on 10 February 1944, this time a perfect straddle being made. He received the DFC, Gazetted in May 1944.

Convoy ONS20

This convoy had U-844 sniffing around it on 15 October but during the night the destroyer HMS *Duncan* had kept her down over night until the latter returned to the convoy. Oberleutnant Günther Möller had surfaced on the 16th to increase his speed but was found by an escorting Liberator of 86 Squadron (FL952 'L'), 15 miles south of the ships, which were around position 5838/2643. The pilot, Flight Lieutenant E A Bland, attacked immediately but on the run-in both port engines were hit by flak and the D/Cs failed to release.

However, a second Liberator flying escort had picked up the sighting report and was now heading in – aircraft 'S' (FL984) of 59 Squadron. Pilot Officer W J Thomas attacked the still fully surfaced U-boat, which fired back and hit the starboard inner engine, straddled her and then saw her go down. Another run placed four more D/Cs on the swirl, position 5800/2720. (On his flight back to base at Meek's Field, Iceland, he found another surfaced U-boat but could only make a strafing attack on it as they were out of D/Cs. Just their luck!)

The U-boat was badly damaged and began to take on water. Bland, despite his aircraft's damaged state, tried to make another run, but the damaged release system again thwarted their attempt at releasing D/Cs on the area where the boat had disappeared. He was now in serious trouble and knew he would not be able to coax the Lib back to base. He put the damaged aircraft down near the corvette HMS *Pink*. One report says that two of the crew were lost, although the Squadron Diary says only one. All the others were injured in the ditching (Bland and Burridge being the more seriously hurt) but were all hauled aboard the corvette. There was no such rescue for the men of U-844 which went down with all hands; it was their first patrol, having sailed from Bergen ten days earlier. They had hit both attacking aircraft, one of which had been lost.

F/L E A Bland	Pilot	W/O R Lenton	WOP/AG
F/O R H Cox *	2nd pilot	Sgt S C Clements	WOP/AG
F/O B B Burridge	Nav	Sgt H J Payne	WOP/AG
W/O B Spencer	FC		

* Lost.

P/O W J Thomas	Pilot	Sgt G W Gerring	
Sgt J F E Seaver		Sgt J J Primeau	

W/O R N Pike   Sgt W C Wallace
Sgt E Ormerod

Eric Bland was awarded the DSO, while Walter James Thomas was also decorated, receiving the DFC.

A Tragic Loss

The next day over the same convoy, another aircraft was shot down, this time a Sunderland from 422 Squadron RCAF. Flight Lieutenant P T Sargent in 'S' (JM712) was covering convoy ONS20 and carrying this day not only the Squadron Gunnery Officer, but the Group Gunnery Officer too. Obtaining a radar contact he had homed in on two surfaced U-boats at 1350 hours in position 5950/3000. Coming out of a rain squall Sargent saw the two boats dead ahead and headed down into the attack.

He went for U-448, commanded by Oberleutnant zur See Helmut Dauter (the other was U-281, Oberleutnant Heinrich von Davidson), but his D/Cs fell short. Coming round again he once more went for U-448 after trading fire with both boats. During the second approach the Sunderland was badly hit by gunfire from both subs but the run was completed although only two of the three D/Cs released.

This time the attack was accurate and U-448 was heavily damaged and also suffered one crewman killed and two wounded. However, the flying boat was in even worse shape and had several casualties on board. At a height of just 100 feet the aircraft caught a full fusilade. Flight Lieutenant Woodwork and Flight Sergeant Needham appeared to have cleared the decks with their gunfire on the first pass, but the latter was killed at his post in the front turret on the second. The auto-pilot was smashed, radio destroyed, radar set damaged, control quadrant hit, throttle and pitch propexocters destroyed, wing dinghy blown out of its storage compartment, mid-upper turret damaged and the hull generally riddled. Steeves the navigator was mortally wounded but was able to give Sargent a course for the convoy before he died. Someone then found Woodwork was dead at his gun.

Sargent managed to bring his aircraft down near the convoy, ditching in heavy weather. Seven of his 11-man crew managed to scramble clear, to be picked up by the frigate HMS *Drury* but Sargent himself became entangled in the wreckage and went down, despite attempts to free him. Arthur Bellis and William Beals both received the DFC.

The two U-boats reported the action in Grid AK2488 at 1248 (German time) and the aircraft probably shot down, as the last they saw, it was staggering off towards the convoy although it was not observed to crash. As a result of the damage, U-488 had to abort her cruise and return to port.

F/L P T Sargent RCAF	Pilot	W/O J D Stafford	WOP/AG
F/O A R B Bellis RCAF	2nd pilot	F/S J Y Rutherford RAF	WOM **

F/S B Campbell RAF	3rd pilot	W/O J H Shand RCAF	WOP/AG
F/S L T Needham RAF	Eng *	F/S D Mesney RAF	FME **
F/O C B Steeves RCAF	Nav *	F/L P A S Woodwork	passenger */+
W/O W F Beals passenger ++		RAF	

* Lost. ** Injured. + Group Gunnery Officer. ++ Squadron Gunnery Officer.

The last recorded loss to a U-boat for the month came on the 30th. Wellington 'C' (HF205) of 612 Squadron RAF had begun a patrol half an hour before midnight on the 29th and at 0542 the next morning had found U-415 north of Cape Ortegal, in the Bay. The pilot carried out a strafing run, then released four D/Cs which did a fair bit of damage to the boat. However, she fought back and hits were seen on the aircraft which almost immediately plunged into the sea just 50 metres from the boat, which the crew later reported was in Grid BF8155.

The boat's KTB acknowledged that the Leigh Light was the first indication the crew had of danger and the aircraft swept in at 50 metres, heading for the conning tower and opening fire with its guns. The boat's crew reacted quickly and got their twin 20 mm into action. The target was raked on its approach and one of its engines was observed to catch fire. The aircraft overflew the boat, releasing a stick of four D/Cs but crashed burning into the sea some 50 metres away.

The D/Cs fell close astern and gave the boat a severe shaking and caused heavy damage. U-415 submerged at 0547 and a check of the boat's condition revealed she had to return to base for urgent repairs. U-415 was to suffer several such reverses trying to exit the Bay area, which must have been a nightmare for her captain and crew. There were, of course, no survivors from C/612.

F/O R S Yeadon	Pilot	F/O W Wilson
Sgt S R Jones		Sgt W F Ellis
F/O A M Davey		Sgt B Hall

USN Liberator Lost over the Bay

There was an attack on U-508, commanded by Kapitänleutnant Georg Staats, on the night of 11/12 November 1943. A Liberator from the US Navy's Squadron VB-103 ('C'), piloted by Lieutenant (jg) Ralph B Brownall USNR, was on anti-submarine patrol over the Bay and almost certainly encountered the outbound U-508.

At 0116 in the morning a flash message was received to the effect that the Navy crew were attacking a U-boat in position 4600/0730, 95 miles north of Cape Penas. Nothing more was heard from either antagonists. A search later that morning revealed two oil slicks, one larger than the other, about five miles apart. The assumption was made, probably correctly, that a fierce action had occurred between aircraft and U-boat from which not a man survived. Staats held the Knight's Cross and the boat had sunk 12 Allied ships; she was on her sixth war cruise having left St Nazaire on the 9th.

Lt R B Brownell	Pilot	ARM1c B R Holladay
Ens D A Schneider	2nd pilot	ARM3c W N Meroney
CAP (AA) R K Poole	Nav	AOM2c C K McClung
AMM1c W English		AOM2c L Eitel
AMM2c G B Simpson Jr		SEA1c W C Rodgers Jr

* * *

Oberleutnant Walter Hungerhausen's career came to an end on 16 November, and his U-280 was sunk, but not before it had tried to fend off an 86 Squadron Liberator (FL931 'M'). He was attempting an attack on convoy HX265 that morning, but in the air was the escorting Lib, flown by Flying Officer J H Bookless RAAF.

They located the boat at 1025 hours and attacked without delay. Liberators usually carried someone they called the Fire Controller, and on this occasion, this was Warrant Officer R H Carroll RCAF and he was in the front gun position. As they headed in he began firing, seeing his bullets slash in and around the conning tower. Return fire from the submarine was intense and accurate, one shell hitting the leading edge of the port wing and knocking out the outer engine.

In the attack the D/Cs overshot, the release hindered no doubt by the flak, but the Lib was being turned for another run. Carroll was firing again, his bullets seeming to knock out the boat's forward gunner. This time the D/Cs were closer and then it began to go down. Nothing more was seen and despite being down to three engines, Bookless continued to patrol around the convoy for another hour. However, the boat did not survive, credit being given to John Bookless and his crew, but not at the time.

F/O J H Bookless RAAF	Pilot	W/O R H Carroll	FC
P/O H Lewis	2nd pilot	RCAF	
P/O C C Cooper	Nav	F/S J Hamilton	WOM/AG
Sgt R F Burchett	Eng	Sgt B I Wade	WOP/AG
		Sgt R G McDonald	WOP/AG

A Hopeful Claim?

The KTB of Oberleutnant Wilhelm Brauel's U-256 for 16 November included the following reference to an encounter with Coastal Command:

> "0208 hours, Grid BF4616 (Biscay). Flying boat. Passes 200 metres astern of the boat. Flak. Hits on aircraft. Aircraft visibly looses height as it passes out of sight. No bombs no strafing."

The aircraft in fact was a Halifax II, 'D' of 502 Squadron. The crew had begun their anti-submarine patrol at 1720 the previous afternoon and had located the U-boat at 0205 hours the next morning, in position 4717/0820. At one mile they had seen the conning tower awash but immediately experienced gunfire from the boat, which hit the aircraft's starboard wing-tip. The pilot had taken immediate evasive action, flying away and reducing height, not because of the damage, but in order to lose altitude for an attack run. However, when the Halifax swept back over the area, radar contact was lost, so presumably U-256 had dived.

F/O F T Culling-Mannix	Pilot	P/O D J Williamson
RNZAF		Sgt E J Williams
F/O J K Keohane		F/S I N Botsford RCAF
P/O L Woolcott RAAF	Nav	F/S R F Upton RNZAF
F/O P Readings		

This crew landed back at base after recording 13 hours and 20 minutes of flight time, which was a record for 502 Squadron at this time. Culling-Mannix would be lost to U-boat gunfire on 5 February 1944 while still with the Squadron. Woolcott, Williamson and Botsford would be with him.

* * *

It was a 422 Squadron RCAF Sunderland that found itself in trouble on 20 November, this time while on escort to convoys SL139/MKS30. They had taken off from Castle Archdale and planned to land at Gibraltar after their escort. A '465' report was received at 1745 hours from the Canadian crew indicating that they had found a submarine and were about to attack.

The target had been U-648 – Oberleutnant Peter-Arthur Stahl – but alerted by her new *Naxos* search receiver, the boat's crew had been prepared [1]. Good shooting by the flak gunners did the rest and the flying boat (W6031 'G') was badly hit before the attack run was completed. It was to be her second kill, having shot down J/10 OTU back on 17 May (see earlier).

At Gibraltar a distress call was received and later an SOS came at 1910, the position given as 4240/1930, saying that they were about to ditch, which was 150 miles from the Rock. Whether they made a good landing will never be known and all 11 men were reported missing. By this time U-648 too was missing, sunk by HM frigates on the 23rd, north-east of the Azores.

F/O J D B Ulrichson RCAF	Pilot	F/S B G Burton RAF	WOM/AG
F/O W S Johnson RCAF	2nd pilot	Sgt W McKay RAF	WOP/AG

---

[1] *Naxos* was an improvement on *Metox* so that the Allies' centimetric radar could now be detected. It had been delayed for some time but was now being put into U-boats.

P/O C G Gorrie RCAF	3rd pilot	F/S N Barrett RCAF	WOP/AG
F/O R H Strauss RCAF	Nav	Sgt N N Lewis RAF	AG
Sgt H P Cook RAF	Eng	Sgt R A Peck RAF	AG
Sgt R M Fisher RAF	FME/AG		

* * *

There was another Coastal loss this 20 November, the second one also involved in escorting convoys SL139/MKS30. Kapitänleutnant Kurt Baberg commanded U-618 and she was found by a Liberator of 53 Squadron (BZ816 'N'). This was a Leigh Light equipped Liberator, flown by Squadron Leader K A Aldrich. It had taken off at 1530 and headed out for SL139 from St Eval.

Nothing further was heard from the crew on their night air cover patrol, except that we now know that they found U-618 and made an immediate attack. Met by fierce anti-aircraft fire the four-engined bomber crashed into the sea with total loss of life. U-618 reported her triumph to BdU by radio signal.

The boat's KTB noted:

> "Grid BE5885 [WNW Cape Finisterre] 1925 hrs. Attacked by 4-engined aircraft with searchlight. Aircraft engaged by quadruple and both twin mounts. Despite accurate fire, the aircraft comes on stubbornly, strafing-fire falling near the conning tower. Aircraft flies over but there are no bombs. The machine takes a wide circle and can now be seen to be on fire inside. Approaching again, this time from astern, once again engaged by accurate fire from the quad mount. The bomber falls into the sea 1,000 metres astern of the boat. Burns on the surface for about five minutes."

Historians have usually tried to indicate that Lib N/53 was shot down by U-648, and Sunderland G/422 by U-618. An examination of the facts indicate a reversal of this, U-648 shooting down the Sunderland, while U-618 got the Liberator. Clearly the description of a Leigh Light Lib by U-618, rather than a Sunderland, claimed (correctly) by U-648 is more plausible. U-648 also played a part in the loss of another aircraft the next day.

However, her days were numbered. Three days later, U-648 was caught by the Navy escorts of convoy KMS30/OG5, depth charges by HM frigate *Blackwood* of the 4th Escort Group in position 4240/2037. None of her 50 crew survived.

S/L K A Aldridge	Pilot	F/S A H Partington	
F/O A J Trennery		F/S T L Anderson	
F/L A G Warren		F/S W Smith	

F/L J Hoskin   W/O N R Bowman
W/O D H R Hill

Another Liberator was lost following an action around convoy SL139 on
the night of 20/21 November. 53 Squadron's aircraft 'A' (BZ819) flown by
the CO, Wing Commander H R A Edwards took off at 2312 and did not
return.

This crew too found a U-boat, and attacked in the face of gunfire and
D/Cs were dropped which fell astern as the boat started diving. It is unclear
if the Liberator suffered any damage, or even if the crew were aware of any
hits, but their Leigh Light did fail. At 0800 the captain turned for home but
some while later, flying at 200 feet, three of the aircraft's engines suddenly
failed and the bomber ditched. Edwards was the sole survivor, rescued later
by HM trawler *Lincolnshire* five miles from Longships at 0745 on the
22nd.

W/C H R A Edwards   Pilot   F/S W M Owen
   AFC   F/S G E Shield
F/O A Davis   Sgt L E Terry
F/L F Halliday   Sgt S C Johnson
F/O B Hamilton

Later, Wing Commander Hugh Edwards (who received the DFC
subsequently) made his report on the events. He recorded that they had
picked up a strong radar blip on ASV at 14 miles and had homed in. At one
mile, flying at 300 feet, the Leigh Light was switched on, illuminating a
surfaced U-boat in position 4510/2000. The boat opened fire and the mid-
upper and nose gunners replied. However, Edwards was dazzled by tracer
from these guns and lost sight of the sub. The D/Cs were dropped and then
the aircraft returned to the convoy, making a sweep astern.

Another contact was made at 15 miles but the Leigh Light did not work.
Then the second pilot reported that they had just passed over a U-boat and
reported the sighting to the escort ships. That was all they saw, and, as
mentioned earlier, they left the convoy at 8 am.

A note was made on the Attack Assessment Form to the effect that the
use of the mid-upper turret in night attacks should be discontinued. One
might have thought it would have been better to use the guns but delete
tracer ammunition from the belt make up, or even try anti-flash muzzle
attachments.

From U-648's last signals we can see the following: "BE8187, 0412 hrs,
aircraft attack." A signal the next day to BdU, noted: "To the signal of the
21st, 0412, direct approach. Searchlight and bombs and strafing. The
aircraft took several hits but managed to pull itself into the clouds." From
this it seems to indicate that the boat had a hand in the eventual loss of the
aircraft.

The second U-boat Edwards found was probably U-967, Oberleutnant Herbert Loeder's command. He reported driving off a Halifax-type with flak at 0612 in Grid BE81. Otherwise it could have been U-575 (Oberleutnant Wolfgang Boehmer) which reported a Leigh-Light assisted attack by a Liberator at 0740 in Grid BE5793. U-575 opened up with flak and the aircraft banked away without any bombs being dropped; ten minutes later the boat crash-dived.

*   *   *

It was proving a bad period for Coastal aircraft. Wellington 'O' (HF153) of 172 Squadron, was operating from Lagens, on the Azores on 27 November (the opening up of this island base further reduced the U-boats' area of freedom of movement).

It was flying escort to convoys SL140/MKS31 and at 2013 hours reported contact with a U-boat (U-764, Oberleutnant Hanskurt von Bremen). Two minutes later an SOS was picked up by shore stations, but that was all. Obviously the Wellington had come off second best during the attack and gone into the water. There were two survivors, including the/a pilot, who were rescued by another U-boat, Kapitänleutnant Horst Hepp's U-238.

U-764 had claimed having scored hits on an attacking aircraft, its KTB recording a strafing attack in position Grid CF6511, at 2122 hours, followed by a second attack during which the flak gunners scored hits on the machine, claiming a probable. U-262 did not claim shooting down an aircraft but whilst sailing nearby witnessed the 172 Squadron aircraft going down. U-764 was later sunk by VC-19 aircraft from the escort carrier *Bogue*. Unfortunately 172 Squadron's War Diary does not list the Wilkin crew but it can be made up from other records.

It is unclear what happened to one of the survivors, if indeed there were two. Of the usual six-man crew noted below, five were indeed lost this date, only Sergeant T B Semple being listed as a prisoner of war. It may be, of course, that there was another pilot aboard the Wellington, named as being Flight Sergeant N J Martin, not to be confused with S A Martin, who was killed. N J Martin and T B Semple both ended up in the same PoW Camp at Kopernikus.

P/O T B Wilkin	Pilot	Sgt J Stobo
F/S C R Farman		Sgt T B Semple
F/S S A Martin		Sgt K D Pitman
F/S N J Martin??		

Swamp
An attack on U-593, commanded by Kapitänleutnant Gerd Kelbling on 13 December, nearly ended in disaster for the 36 Squadron Wellington crew.

The aircraft – 'B' (MP816) – was part of a Swamp Operation [1], hunting the submarine responsible for the sinking of the escort ships HMS *Tynedale* and *Holcombe*. They took off at 2034 on the evening of the 12th.

At 0030 hours on the morning of the 13th, the aircraft made a radar contact in position 3730/0600, north-east of Bone, Western Mediterranean (Grid CH96). On approaching, the Leigh Light jammed as it was let down, and the bomber was met by very accurate flak fire which scored hits on the port wing and tailplane. The aircraft became unmanageable and fell off to port. The rear gunner opened fire in the moonlight on the sub, hammering 600 rounds towards the flak which then ceased.

The crew sent off both a sighting report and an SOS, and were preparing to ditch but the pilot finally managed to bring the machine under control and at 0140 landed it at Bone. The sighting report played an important role in the hunt which resulted in the destruction of U-593 later that same day by surface vessels.

F/O C F Parker	Pilot	F/S W Ashworth	WOP/AG
P/O P Thrower	2nd pilot	F/S T R Button	WOP/AG
F/O R J Shannon	Nav	F/S A T Emson	WOP/AG

* * *

Three days before Christmas, Beaufighter TFXs of 144 and 404 Squadrons were out on a Rover Patrol to the Norwegian coast. Four of the Beaus carried torpedoes, the others acting as escort and flak-suppression.

South of Egersund, they spotted a minesweeper [M-403], then a U-boat just on 1130 am, position 5759/0652. The Beaus attacked, raking the submarine heavily with cannon fire but all the torpedoes missed. Accurate return fire by both U-boat and the minesweeper escort hit two of the anti-flak aircraft – both from the Canadian 404 Squadron. The first one – 'H' (LZ452) – caught fire and nosed down towards the sea. Then 'F' (NE323) rolled over, its navigator still firing as it plunged into the waves. All four men were killed.

U-1062, commanded by Oberleutnant Karl Albrecht, sailing from Kiel to Bergen, suffered only superficial damage, although one crewman was killed and two badly wounded. She reached Bergen without further incident on the 23rd. She was finally sunk on 30 September 1944, by US destroyers south-west of Cape Verde Islands, returning from the Far East with strategic war materials.

F/O I Gillespie	Pilot	P/O J E Glendinning	Nav
RCAF		RCAF	
F/L R Munro RCAF	Pilot	F/O W B Conn RCAF	Nav

---

(1) Swamp will be explained at the beginning of Chapter Seven.

CHAPTER SEVEN

1944

Commander Left Top-Side

Two 224 Squadron Liberators were in action on the second day of the new year with an attack on U-625, commanded by Kapitänleutnant Hans Benker. Liberator 'G' (P/O J E Edwards), from St Eval, on a *Percussion* Sugar-2 patrol, beginning at 1854, picked up a radar contact at 2125, distance 20 miles, when at 1,000 feet. Homing in the Leigh Light went on at 2134 and this illuminated a U-boat which immediately opened fire from 300 yards range. This scored a hit on the port side of the aircraft and wounded one of the WOPs with a shell splinter to the head.

The pilot circled until 2205, homing in another aircraft, then because of the seriousness of the crew member's injury, he returned to base, landing 20 minutes after midnight. Liberator C/224 now arrived, flown by the redoubtable Flying Officer Ethan Allen, and the crew found the marker dropped by Edwards. They located a U-boat and attacked with eight D/Cs.

However, it was another U-boat, not U-625 which at that time was under water although the crew actually heard the D/Cs exploding nearby. Allen had most probably found the inbound U-421 (Oberleutnant Hans Kolbus) which reported an air attack with four bombs in Grid BF47, flak and strafing, at 0016.

During Edwards' attack the order was given to dive and the bridge party suffered in consequence. The attack was noted at 2138 hours by a four-engined Leigh Light aircraft in Grid BF4491. At 2140 the boat crash-dived, during which Hans Benker, and another man were left topside. The boat surfaced six minutes later and although one seaman was later found at 2201 hours, Benker was not recovered. The IWO, Oberleutnant sur See Kurt Sureth, brought U-625 into Brest on the 6th. A Sunderland sank her on the next – ninth – patrol, on 10 March 1944.

P/O J E Edwards	Pilot	F/S S K Price
F/S E C Browning		F/S S H White RCAF
F/S D J Villis		F/S A M Ball
F/S J McMahon *		P/O H Lord
* Wounded.		

Flying Fortress Down

A 206 Squadron B17 Flying Fortress (FA705 'U') was the next victim to
U-boat flak gunners aboard U-270 on 6 January, which was commanded by
Oberleutnant Paul-Friedrich Otto. The aircraft was on patrol north-north-
east of the Azores and radioed in a sighting report at 1812 hours in position
4353/2332. Nothing more was heard from it (FA705 'U') as it disappeared
with all eight members of her crew.

The loss of the aircraft was no mystery to the crew of U-270, for they
had shot it down. The boat reported the encounter at 1910 in Grid BE7349.

> "After two runs in which the boat was strafed but no bombs dropped,
> the Fortress began a third approach at 1918. Flak from U-270 fatally
> damaged the aircraft as she neared. The starboard inside motor was
> seen to be on fire and the aircraft lost height, releasing four D/Cs as
> she fell. They exploded 30-40 metres from the boat and the Fortress
> plunged a flaming wreck into the sea 300 metres further on."

The boat survived the action, although damaged, but was forced to break
off patrol and return to St Nazaire, which she entered on 17 January. This
boat's crew was to claim another victory on 13 June (see Chapter 9).

F/L A J Pinhorn	Pilot	W/O D L Heard RCAF	
F/O J H Duncan	2nd pilot	W/O O A Keddy RCAF	
F/S T Eckersley	Nav	Sgt R Fabian	WOP/AG
F/O F D Roberts		F/L R Brown	passenger+
+ Squadron Navigation Officer.			

Anthony James Pinhorn's DFC was Gazetted in February 1945, with effect
from 5 January 1944 noting his rank as Acting Squadron Leader.

* * *

On the night of 6/7 January, a 53 Squadron Halifax ran into trouble on a
Percussion M3 patrol. Canadian Flight Lieutenant E B A LeMaistre and his
almost totally Australian crew, had taken off at 2138 hours and at ten
minutes to midnight his radar operator picked up a contact at 37 miles. One
minute into the new day, and while still 18 miles off, they spotted a U-boat
in the moonlight in position 4708/0642.

LeMaistre attacked with six D/Cs and released markers. As he circled,
his radioman sent a contact report and then they were heading in again. On
the run-in a second S/E contact was made, two miles to starboard and then
another U-boat was sighted almost immediately. White tracer fire came
from this one, different from the red tracer from the first boat.

The second drop was made from 250 feet, four D/Cs, but this time hits
were scored on the Halifax in the rear of the bomb-bay and other hits
damaged the aircraft's control surfaces. Badly damaged, the Halifax limped

away, LeMaistre compelled to break off the action and head for home. Edward Benjamin Aycrigge LeMaistre was awarded the DFC in 1945.

This crew had encountered U-107 (Kapitänleutnant Volker Simmermacher), while the second boat appears to have been U-621 (Oberleutnant Max Kruschka). U-107 was probably the target in both attacks and she also had encounters with Halifax F/502 Squadron (Flying Officer J H Spurgeon) and probably Wellington J/407 Squadron RCAF (F/O Jordan) this same night.

The U-boat captain reported Liberator attacks in Grid BF54 at 0008 hours, 0040, 0104 and 0120 hours. Each attack was countered with flak fire and though bombs were reported on each occasion there was no damage. U-621, also in the area, reported opening fire on an aircraft at 0010 but was not herself attacked with bombs.

F/L E B A LeMaistre	Pilot	F/S J D Hunter RAAF
RCAF		F/S J A Kelly RAAF
F/O M B Hurley RAAF		F/S T C McGrath RAAF
F/S J H Hawkins RAAF		F/S H D Kohler RAAF
F/S A R Basted RAAF		

Swamp Operation

In my book *Dark Sky, Deep Water* I wrote a whole chapter on an episode concerning a Swamp Operation covering the events of 7 and 8 January 1944. Swamp, as the name suggests, was a plan to swamp an area with aircraft and surface vessels once a U-boat had been located. These operations took place in the relatively confined areas east of Gibraltar and/or north of the Moroccan or Algerian coasts, based on the assumption that with the boats operating near the coast in order to sink shipping, their area of movement had been halved. If then this area could be 'swamped' with ships and aircraft, the boat would eventually be forced to surface to recharge batteries etc, and thus be at a disadvantage.

Oberleutnant Wolfgang Rahn's U-343 was one boat that had the misfortune to be on the receiving end of a Swamp Operation at this time. She had been ordered into the Mediterranean just after Christmas, getting through the Straits of Gibraltar on 5 January.

Several aircraft were hunting for her and found her, but it was Flying Officer W F Mc Davidson that suffered most. First contact however, was by Wellingtons of 36 Squadron on the 7th. Having been located by the Polish destroyer *Slazak* too, U-343 knew she was in trouble. That evening, the crew of 'Y' of 36 Squadron (HF245) located her in position 3654/1056, captained by New Zealander, Flying Officer R D Bamford. However, at the moment of sighting, he was not at the controls, the second pilot making the attack.

F/O R D Bamford RNZAF	Pilot	F/O D G Cull RNZAF	WOP/AG

F/O T J Masters RCAF	2nd pilot	F/O W L Medcalf	WOP/AG
F/O L A Colquohoun	Nav	RNZAF	
RNZAF		F/S S W Layzell RAF	WOP/AG

They had been flying a CLA (creeping line ahead) search for two hours, on a clear night with a bright moon, so no Leigh Light needed to be used when contact came. Flak came up as the Wellington levelled off at 50 feet and just prior to release, hits were felt on the machine by its crew. After the pass-over, Masters noticed the port wing was on fire. Despite his efforts it continued to burn – time to ditch, and quickly.

It appears the machine started to break up on landing. Cull, Medcalf and Masters found themselves in the water, then, hearing Layzell calling that he couldn't swim, Masters got to him, found he was injured, and helped to keep him afloat until they were able to get themselves in the dinghy.

Layzell had got off an SOS immediately the wing began to burn, and the survivors were rescued the next morning by the *Slazak*. Bamford and Colquohoun did not survive the flak or the crash, although the latter was last seen getting rid of the astrodome prior to ditching.

Next to arrive that night was Wellington 'M' of 36 Squadron (HF221). It had received the sighting report from 'Y' and on arriving, picked up a radar contact and saw what the crew later realised was burning oil from the ditched 'Y'. Oddly, the second pilot of 'M' was in situ in this Wellington too, and he took the bomber into the attack.

Flak seemed to hose up to them, then the port engine was hit, but moments later the D/Cs were going down – then the rear gunner began hammering away. The aircraft became difficult to handle and before he could do much about it, the pilot found himself crossing the nearby Spanish coast. He was unable to close the bomb doors until the remaining D/Cs had been jettisoned and he must not do this while over land. Very gently the pilot eased the machine round, recrossed the coast and let go the D/Cs. With the bombs gone and the doors now closed, some height was managed. Meantime the submarine seemed to be stopped in the water. Diverted to Bone, the damaged Wellington was put down in a good landing.

F/O J T Hutton	Pilot	F/S C T Layson	WOP/AG
F/S R N Holton	2nd pilot	F/S P Kiln	WOP/AG
F/S F S Foxon	Nav	W/O I G Ricketts	WOP/AG

More aircraft arrived and attacked; 'B' of 36 Squadron, followed by the CO of 179 Squadron, Wing Commander J H Greswell DFC. They were followed by R/179, Flying Officer W F Mc Davidson.

Davidson, when he came along, found the boat south-west of Cartagena, Spain, in position 3654/0145 at 2240. With a full moon still shining he too

did not find it necessary to use his Leigh Light – perhaps if he had it may
have helped blind the gun crews – for the boat was not caught unawares and
during the bomber's approach it was hit several times.

Davidson made a fairly accurate attack with his D/Cs which caused
damage but with his port wing blazing furiously it became unmanageable
and crashed into the sea. Only Davidson was thrown clear and survived,
lucky enough too to find an inflated dinghy from the aircraft. He clambered
in, still groggy from the crash and with blood on his face. Then the U-boat
appeared out of the gloom and actually bumped into the dinghy. Davidson
pretended to be dead or unconscious, hoping the blood would convince
them not to pick him up. They didn't. William Fulton McGregor
Davidson's DFC was Gazetted on 8 February.

F/O W F Mc Davidson	Pilot	Sgt A G Fuller	WOP/AG
F/O L J Frost	2nd pilot	Sgt R S Eminsang	WOP/AG
Sgt C Parker	Nav	Sgt J V Dadson	WOP/AG

Another attack on the boat came a few minutes later, by a Catalina of 202
Squadron – Flight Lieutenant J Finch – attracted by the action between the
last Wellington and the U-boat. Finch made an approach and again the boat
put up a stiff defence, which wounded the Cat's flight engineer and
punctured the port wing, fuselage and both fuel tanks. Finch headed away
for home.

F/L J Finch	Pilot	Sgt E Wass	FM/AG
F/O R K Bell	2nd pilot	F/S A D S Sugden	WOP/AG
F/O B J Goodhew	Nav	F/S L Radcliffe	WOP/AG
F/S V Sheridan	Eng	F/S A P Newman	Rigger
P/O A F H Barber	WOP/WOM		

U-343 miraculously survived, limping into Toulon. She had acquitted
herself well but was sunk by the armed trawler HMS *Mull* on 10 March,
north-west of Bizerta. Davidson was rescued by HMS *Active* on the
morning of 9 January and later received the DFC. Tom Masters of 36
Squadron also received the DFC for his part in the action.

*   *   *

6th Escort Group Co-Op
Captain Walker's famous 2nd Escort Group was not the only Navy group
operating in the Atlantic, the 6th was another, and in early January 1944
was operating near the Azores. Whenever possible aircraft would co-
operate with the ships, and if a target was found would generally call up the
surface vessels and only attack if the U-boat looked as if it would dive
before they arrived.

On 13 January a 172 Squadron Wellington (HF168 'L'), operating from an airfield on the Azores was co-operating with the 6th and was flying a CLA (creeping line ahead) search pattern. Directed by a sighting report by aircraft from the American escort carrier *Block Island*, at 2255 hours the Wellington crew found a fully surfaced U-boat in position 4415/2038 and was greeted by heavy flak. It was U-231, commanded by Kapitänleutnant Wolfgang Wenzel. There seemed every indication that the boat would soon go down, so the pilot, a Canadian, Pilot Officer W N Armstrong, went in.

In the first run three D/Cs went down but as the aircraft went over the boat, flak fire smashed into it, seriously wounded the rear gunner, Flying Officer B W Heard, in both legs and arm, and knocked out his turret. Armstrong made other attacks but finally had to break off and head for home because of his wounded crewman.

However, he had done enough and the boat's captain ordered his men to abandon ship and they were later picked up by the *Block Island*. The crew had suffered seven casualties. William Norman Armstrong and Bernard William Heard both received DFCs for their actions.

P/O W N Armstrong	Pilot	F/O B W Heard	WOP/AG
RCAF		W/O Corbett	
F/O R D Haryett RCAF	2nd pilot	F/S R R Kersey RNZAF	
P/O N Ellis RCAF	Nav		

Wakes for the Wellingtons
Wellingtons appear to have taken a hammering this January. Following the events recorded above in the Western Mediterranean, other Wimpys were in trouble further north.

On the night of 30/31 January, aircraft 'K' of 172 Squadron (MP813) departed RAF Chivenor at 2011 hours on the 30th for a night *Percussion* patrol over the Bay. That was the last that was heard from the aircraft, assumed to have made a fatal rendezvous with U-364, commanded by Oberleutnant Paul-Heinrich Sass, returning to her French port.

The crew of aircraft B/304 Polish Squadron (F/S S Czekaski), witnessed an action that was possibly the end of K/172. They had a radar contact at 0027 and homing in saw a Leigh Light go on and exploding D/Cs. The contact disappeared and in fact the D/Cs may have been Leighton Richards' K/172 hitting the water. U-608's KTB (OL Wolfgang Reisener) noted:

"0128 hours, Grid BF8336 – search light – distance 300 metres, height 50 metres. Flak. Several hits seen. Aircraft banks away. Crash-dive."

It is also possible that U-608 fired upon another at this time and place, as R/304 also encountered flak. In any event it is probable that U-364 was not involved, as recent research indicates that the U-boat was very likely sunk on 29 January by Halifax U/502 Squadron.

F/S L D Richards	Pilot	W/O J Pritchard	WOP/AG
Sgt P Horsfield	2nd pilot	Sgt R C Fisher	WOP/AG
Sgt C J Lowther	Nav	Sgt A B Porter	WOP/AG

* * *

The next night a Wellington XIV from 172 Squadron – HF279 'Q' – failed to return from an anti-submarine patrol from Lagens, on the Azores. There were no calls and no signals.

17 Squadron South African Air Force

Encounters with enemy submarines were not in the exclusive domain of either Coastal Command or FAA aircraft operating in the Atlantic or the Med. On 4 February 1944 came an attack on U-453, commanded by Oberleutnant zur See Dierk Lührs, by Ventura 'Y' (565) from 17 Squadron SAAF. The Ventura, piloted by Lieutenant A de Jong, set out on an evening patrol from St Jean, Palestine, heading for Cyprus. At least two U-boats had been reported off the Levant coast. A Caique had been reported sunk off Lakatia and aircraft had reported attacking U-boats in position 3600/3510 and at 3414/3315 on the afternoon of the 3rd. De Jong's Ventura vanished together with her four-man crew.

No distress messages were received and a W/T contact at 1945 hours should have placed the Ventura in position 3433/3230, and a later fading RDF plot from Cyprus, in position 3429/3312 at 2014. Air Sea Rescue aircraft later found a large oil patch south of Cape Gata next morning. Another 17 Squadron aircraft sighted a U-boat on the 4th in position 3300/3431, which crash-dived.

According to the official SAAF history it was presumed to have been shot down by a U-boat and this is almost certainly correct. On this date the KTB of U-453 indicates she was attacked in Grid CP5244 (off the southern coast of Cyprus) at 1944 hours. The aircraft was twin-engined – identified curiously as a Mosquito – and made two approaches both aided by Leigh Light. No bombs fell on the first approach but on the second, as it flew 20 metres high across the boat, it released a stick of five bombs that fell to the port side. The KTB also noted that the searchlight proved an excellent target for the flak gunners.

Seen to be hit and the port motor catch fire, the Ventura burst into flames and crashed into the sea, 1,000 metres away. There is not much doubt that this KTB extract describes the final moments of the missing South African Ventura.

| Lt A de Jong | Pilot | 2/Lt M Pines |
| Lt G Josephson | | F/S T Smallwood |

U-763's Double Kills

Kapitänleutnant Ernst Cordes, commander of U-763, was bringing his boat

back to La Pallice at the beginning of February 1944, following a patrol to
the North Atlantic. Liberator 'F' of 53 Squadron (BZ795) had taken off on
a *Percussion* R3 patrol at 2230 hours on the night of the 3rd and found the
boat.

At 0811 the next morning a message to base advised: 'Am over enemy
submarine in position 4530/0700.' And that was all. In a fierce action to the
north-north-east of Cape Finisterre, the Liberator did not pull out of its
attack run and crashed into the sea, clawed down by the accurate gunfire
from the U-boat. The pilot had managed to drop his D/Cs but no damage
was done.

Sgt T A Patey	Pilot	F/S E J Fowler RAAF
F/S J O Lewis RAAF		Sgt R D Howard
F/O N J Williams RAAF		Sgt C Lidgett
F/S S G Hill RAAF		

Edging nearer to her base, U-763's crew thankful for the deliverance, she
survived the next day but the following night she was found by another 53
Squadron Liberator (BZ815 'D' – P/O L L Esler RCAF) in position
4527/0654 at 0135 hours. It was picked up by the boat's *Naxos* equipment
and although on an ASR sortie looking for the Bell crew, it homed in on the
sub and released its D/Cs. Flak fire put a few holes in the Liberator's
tailplane.

The crew of the Lib also picked up two more U-boats and reported this
to base, but in reality they were picking up *Aphrodite* decoys sent off by
U-763 which would give the radar operator multiple radar images. Boats
using these tried to hide amongst the aircraft's radar contacts, hoping the
searching aircraft would line up on one of the decoys and not them.

P/O L L Esler	Pilot	Sgt D M Holden
P/O J L Knight		Sgt T W Ellison
W/O W R Kinsman RAAF		W/O R C Lauer RCAF
F/S R J Crompton		F/S F Clegg RMZAF
F/S A W G Brown		

Not long after this event, the boat was located by Wellington 'M' of 172
Squadron (HF282), in position 4539/0640. An attack was met by more
gunfire, hits being scored in both wings and fuselage by cannon shells.
After the attack, the D/Cs exploding astern, the Wellington climbed away,
the pilot having difficulty due to some damage to the tail, so he broke off
the action and headed for home.

F/O C S Rowland	Pilot	W/O J F Wilmer RCAF	WOP/AG
F/O A Mason	2nd pilot	Sgt G B Schwinge	WOP/AG
F/S D R Pledger	Nav	Sgt E Oliver	WOP/AG

That evening, U-763 had reached an area west of Bordeaux, but at 2205 she was found yet again, this time by a Halifax ('R') of 502 Squadron. By now the flak gunners must have felt like seasoned veterans. The boat's guns slashed into the approaching bomber which was hit repeatedly and crashed. Again there were no survivors. Seaman Rudi Wieser had been the main antagonist with his 2 cm twin flak gun.

F/O F T Culling-Mannix RNZAF	Pilot	F/O D J Williamson
		W/O S Beaton
F/O L Woolcott RAAF		F/S I N Botsford RCAF
F/O D E Celdart RCAF		Sgt C Ostler
W/O M J Fahey	WOP/AG	

U-763 sailed into port on the 7th. She had been in five actions with aircraft, shot down two of them and damaged two others. (A full account of these encounters can be found in *Dark Sky, Deep Water*.)

Rudi Wieser, U-763's successful gunner, has written the following narrative about his duties aboard the U-boat, and about the training he and his fellow gunners had. It makes interesting reading:

'On the U-boat we were well acquainted with all of the systems. My personal focus in training was as Bridge look-out and gunner with the 8.8 cm and anti-aircraft guns. Furthermore, I operated the depth rudder aft and was a helmsman on the regular watches. In the torpedo section I was to set the parameters on the torpedo for multiple torpedo shots against convoys.

'Our AA training was carried out at a training camp at Swinemunde. There we underwent weapons instruction and firing at a passing aircraft – a Junkers W34 – with a target [drogue] in tow. Training took place during daytime and in twilight. Most important was precision firing and quick reaction. Cold blood and don't back off! Keep firing!

'Also during shipyard or base time we had AA instruction on our daily duty roster. There was also an AA training camp at Mimizan, France, [on the Biscay coast south of the Gironde] with similar conditions. My good training proved itself in quite a few battles with allied aeroplanes.

'In combat our own superiority had to be shown and proven because it was always one's own life and that of our fellow sailors at stake. It was either them or us!

'Our thoughts, I believe, were probably the same on both sides. There were no other feelings that I can remember. We also had absolutely no hatred against the enemy despite the propaganda efforts at home about the allied "terrorfliegers" bombing our towns. We really did not hate the RAF crews we encountered.

'We fought for our crew and the life we hoped to live. We never
fought a mean combat because when an action was over we always
tried to help and assist a downed opponent; you can read that in
U-763's KTB.'

A Mystery Claim and a Mystery Loss

U-608 (Oberleutnant Wolfgang Reisener) was attacked by an aircraft at
0506 hours on 10 February (Grid BE2561), using Leigh Light, and was met
by flak. The aircraft strafed the boat and dropped two bombs which fell 20
metres astern. The bridge crew reported seeing smoke coming from the
inner-starboard engine and the aeroplane losing height, but then the boat
dived. This may possibly have been an attack by Squadron Leader Tony
Spooner DFC, flying 'G' of 53 Squadron.

He was covering convoy HX277 this night and picked up an S/E contact
at 0500 and then attacked a U-boat in position 4953/1720 at 0508 hours
dropping six D/Cs on the first run, two on the second. Later some yellowish
planks were seen floating on the sea. However, the aircraft had not been hit.

On the night of 10/11 February, Oberleutnant Günter Ney's U-283 had
an encounter with an aircraft, but as she was lost just a few hours later to
another aircraft attack (by 407 Squadron RCAF), details are necessarily
sparse. All that is known is that she radioed base that an attack had been
made on her at 2110 hours, in Grid AE8899, and although her gunners fired
at the attacker, made no claim for it being shot down.

There was an aircraft lost, however, but it is not certain this was due to
hostile action by the U-boat. 612 Squadron were operating from RAF
Limavady that night on Moorings patrols, Wellington 'N' taking off at 1616
hours. At 2109 a signal was intercepted by aircraft 'B' of 612 Squadron,
flying in a nearby area, that 'N' was having engine trouble, but that was all.
There was no indication that the engine trouble might have been caused by
gunfire, but then such an emergency call would hardly be likely to enlarge
on the facts when the priority was to prepare someone for a potential rescue
mission. A possible position of the striken aircraft was 6032/1402, which
puts them in roughly the area of the action – the Iceland-Faeroes Gap – and
the time frame is about right too. The crew of 'N' consisted of:

F/O R E Durnford	Pilot	Sgt S J A Boon	WOP/AG
F/O J Bowmer	2nd pilot	Sgt R F Spanner	WOP/AG
F/O E H Hutcheson RCAF	Nav	Sgt R T B Howe	WOP/AG

Three Hours on One Engine

On the night of 1/2 March, a Wellington XIV of 179 Squadron, piloted by
one of the flight commanders, encountered Oberleutnant Hans Kolbus's
U-421 off the Portuguese coast. Squadron Leader R Knott set off for a
patrol to the north-west of Gibraltar half an hour after midnight and by

0214 was off Cape St Vincent. He was flying at 500 feet, under a cloudless sky, a calm sea below.

His radar operator picked up two S/E contacts at 11 and 12 miles and Knott closed in. The closer of the two turned out to be a lighted fishing boat, but the other was unlit so Knott headed towards it. At 400 feet and at $3/4$ of a mile the Leigh Light went on, illuminating a surfaced U-boat in position 3845/0943. The Wellington's front gunner began to fire but his gun jammed after about 40 rounds and by then the U-boat was firing too.

The bomber's starboard engine was hit but Knott pressed on and released six D/Cs from 100 feet. No sooner had the drop been made than a shell exploded in the centre of the bomb bay, knocked out the radar and caused other internal damage. The rear gunner saw a bright flash on the boat, which temporarily blinded him, but it seemed that streams of tracer came from it. It was later presumed that some ammunition had been hit on the bridge area.

Knott immediately set course for home on one engine. The useless ASV was jettisoned along with other loose equipment, and the engineer found one of the oil lines had also been severed. An SOS call was sent and the IFF switched to distress, but Knott got them home at 0610 after a stressful three hours of flying the badly damaged Wimpey.

U-421's KTB recorded:

> "Grid CG5586, 0309 hours. Searchlight 2,000 metres distant, height 100 metres. Probably a Sunderland. Flak, hits observed. Three bombs are released which fall far behind the boat, strafing. Aircraft crosses over at 30 metres height and disappears into the night."

Unfortunately there is no mention of what caused the bright flash. Nor had German aircraft identification improved!

Putting into Toulon on 1 April, U-421 was badly damaged in an American air-raid on 29 April and saw no further action in the war.

S/L R G Knott	Pilot	F/O W J Higgins
F/O M A Clifton		Sgt W D Moon
F/O C S Downes		F/S E E Hughes

Crash Landing – Written Off

Liberator V 'B' (BZ764) of 120 Squadron, flown by Flight Lieutenant H F Kerrigan, had a hard struggle to get home on 6 March 1944 following an encounter with U-737 (Oberleutnant Paul Brasack). Harold Kerrigan RCAF was an experienced pilot, and in October the previous year had helped sink U-470.

On this March day he and his crew, operating out of Meek's Field, Iceland, investigated a radar contact and found U-737 on the surface. During the approach flak from the boat hit and set fire to the No.4 engine.

In spite of the damage the attack was carried out and a stick of six D/Cs released, which the boat recorded fell within ten metres, then she dived. The KTB also noted that the right outside motor of the four-engined aircraft was seen to be on fire and trailing smoke.

Kerrigan circled as his crew took stock of the damage. While doing so they saw a second U-boat surfacing but this in fact was U-737 surfacing again. Kerrigan went into the attack but once more the boat put up a curtain of flak and the Lib was hit again in several places including the nose cupola. Both navigators were wounded and the bomb sight and D/C release gear put out of action, so that the D/Cs failed to drop. Kerrigan was given no choice but to head immediately for home, helped by his wounded navigator, Paul Rackham, despite wounds to his head, legs and body. The crew also managed to jettison the remaining D/Cs, and the engine fire was put out.

Because of the damage and with wounded aboard, he was diverted to Skitten, Scotland, where he successfully belly landed on two engines. The aircraft was so severely damaged that it was written off, being beyond repair. Kerrigan later received the DSO for his efforts, and the senior navigator, Paul Rackham, the DFC.

The aircrew recorded the action at 1748 hours in position 6857/0316 – west of the Lofoten Islands, Norway. The boat crew noted the time as 1745 in Grid AB8814, also west of the Lofotens but slightly to the north-east of the aircrew's position. U-737, on her fifth war cruise, having left Hammerfest on 28 February, was forced to abort and return to port, which she did on the 12th. She was eventually sunk on her 10th patrol, under another captain, on 19 December, colliding with a German minesweeper west of Tromso.

F/L H F Kerrigan RCAF	Pilot	W/O J T Foy	WOP/AG
F/O A M McLennan	2nd pilot	F/S T Levinsky	WOP/AG
F/O P R Rackham RCAF	1st Nav	F/S J J Grassam	WOP/AG
F/O W J Hartrick	2nd Nav	F/S T W Chapman	WOM
Sgt P Cole	Engineer		

* * *

The next recorded loss came just five days later, on 11 March, this time a Wellington on patrol to the west of Ireland. 407 Squadron RCAF were operating from Limavady, Northern Ireland, and aircraft 'H' (HF311) headed out at 1630 and was never heard of again.

The loss of this aircraft was probably witnessed by U-256, whose crew reported observing an aircraft crash into the sea near her, at 2148 hours on the night of the 11th, in Grid AL8434. The submarine did not open fire with her guns, and it was assumed that the crash occurred while the pilot was preparing to attack, turning in low for an approach run. None of the crew survived.

P/O E M O'Donnell	Pilot	W/O R C Gaudet	WOP/AG

F/S R C Sorley	2nd pilot	W/O I F Smithson	WOP/AG
P/O C Grant	Nav	W/O F L Travers	WOP/AG

The loss of this aircraft is sometimes attributed to U-741, but her claim was over a FAA aircraft (see Chapter 8).

More Bay Actions

On the 12th, U-311 (Kapitänleutnant Joachim Zander) was attacked by an aircraft identified as a Fortress which was shot down. As the boat did not return from her patrol the only evidence of this claim is a signal to BdU of the attack at 0120 hours in position Grid BF4585. The attack was made with bombs and strafing.

This ties in with the loss of a Halifax of 58 Squadron, HX225 'L' which had taken off at 1755 hours on the 11th on a *Percussion* S/1 sortie. At 0117 the next morning, control received a message from the aircraft giving a "465" call which meant: 'Am over an enemy submarine ....' was then abruptly broken off. There was no position stated but the time corresponds with U-311's attack time. The aircraft failed to return.

F/O L A Hayward	Pilot	F/O J Wilson	Sig
F/O W J Rice	2nd pilot	F/S F L Webster RAAF	WOP/AG
W/O R J McCormick RCAF	Nav	W/O R J Bonar	WOM/AG
		Sgt T Parkes	WOP/AG
Sgt R A Potter	Eng		

Position BF4585 is in the Bay of Biscay, roughly 4635/0925. There is another reported action by Wellington 'C' of 612 Squadron. The time was recorded as 0605 on the 12th, in position 4657/0905, and while this is close, and the aircraft was damaged in the tail and rear turret by flak fire, the time is way out. The pilot of the Wellington was Flight Sergeant D Bretherton, but that attack is recorded as a damaging attack on U-629, commanded by Oberleutnant Hans-Helmuth Bugs. There were no crew casualties, but only moments before the attack, the rear gunner, Sergeant J M Daly had vacated his turret in order to implement the usual change round position with the other WOP/AGs. After the attack, a flak hole was found in the bottom of the turret, the shell having passed upwards through and out of the top of the turret, shattering the perspex, so it was fortunate that Martyn Daly had not been sitting there.

F/S D Bretherton	Pilot	Sgt R A Campbell	WOP/AG
Sgt I W Green	2nd pilot	Sgt L J Cole	WOP/AG
F/S D E Sulis RAAF	Nav	Sgt J M Daly	WOP/AG

Liberator Down

The KTB of Oberleutnant Wilhelm Brauel's U-256 recorded an attack in

Grid BE4526 at 2312 hours on the evening of 19 March 1944.

> "Aircraft attacking with Leigh Light, distance 1,500 metres, height
> 50 metres. Strafing from aircraft. Flak opens up, hits scored by the
> 3.7 cm on the fuselage. Aircraft passes over at 50 metres behind the
> boat releasing six bombs. As it passes over flames observed in the
> bomb bay and starboard motor. Plunged into the sea 500 m away.
> Heavy explosion, pillar of fire, and nothing remains but burning oil."

The lost aircraft would seem to be a Liberator – 'F' of 224 Squadron –
which had taken off from St Eval on a *Percussion* Tere 4 sortie at 2105 and
failed to return. Three messages had been sent out but the aircraft did not
respond.

F/L R Dunn	Pilot	F/S H Penhale RCAF	WOP/AG
F/O A V Cormack	2nd pilot	F/S H Thornton RCAF	WOP/AG
F/S W F Stockwell	Nav	F/S A Souter RNZAF	WOP/AG
F/S W J Leahy RAAF	2nd Nav	Sgt G Jones	WOP/AG
Sgt J McCartney	Eng	W/O R H Cook	WOM/AG

Tsetse Mosquitoes

The hitting power of some RAF aircraft was enhanced by the introduction
of the 57 mm Molins Gun, used especially on Mosquito XVIII aircraft of
618 Squadron. Formed originally to use a bouncing bomb to attack ships
such as the battleship *Tirpitz*, when that idea was scrapped, the unit began
to develop the Molins Gun in their Mosquito aircraft, which became known
as the Tsetse gun.

With aircraft attached to 248 Squadron, equipped with Beaufighters, and
later Mosquito VIs, this unit provided escort, when the Tsetse Mosquitoes
were sent out to the northern Bay area in search of shipping, but especially
U-boats returning to or departing from French bases. The unit had had
some success since the winter of 1943, and on 27 March 1944, two crews
located U-960, commanded by Oberleutnant zur See Günther Heinrich.

Escorted by 248, the two 618 Squadron crews, led by Flying Officer D J
Turner, found two submarines off the French coast, escorted by four
minesweepers, and two converted merchant vessels (*Sperrbrechers*). The
RAF aircraft attacked, the Tsetse's big shells hammering into the boats. As
the second Mossie (HX903 'I') went over U-960, the pilot, Aubrey Hilliard
saw distinctly the boat's 3.7 gun firing up at him, the gunners having pulled
it virtually upright. He felt a thud as a shell hit the aircraft, and the machine-
gun doors in front of the cockpit blew open. At first the crew thought the
nose of their machine had been split apart.

Hilly got back safely, despite the damage, but U-960 had taken hits on
the conning tower which wounded 14 of her crew, four seriously, including
the captain with a wound above the left knee. U-960 was later sunk in the

Mediterranean on 27 April, Heini Heinrich surviving. He and Hilly Hilliard would later meet and become friends. Two days earlier, the 25th, the same Tsetse crews had attacked and sunk U-976.

F/O A H Hilliard   Pilot   W/O J B Hoyle   Nav

No. 53 Squadron's April Woes

On the night of 6/7 April, Liberator 'N' (BZ769) of 53 Squadron picked up a radar contact at 2324 hours, position 4413/0341, and the pilot manoeuvred into the moonpath, reporting the contact to base. At 2337 the Leigh Light picked out two surfaced U-boats broadside on in line astern, some 50 yards apart, the aircraft already tracking over the nearest (rearmost) boat. The navigator, only seeing the leading boat, directed the pilot to turn 20° to port, and the pilot, turning violently to comply, tracked between the two subs.

Intense flak opened up on the aircraft, which hit and damaged it, also wounding the beam gunner in the leg and buttock. The bomb doors had been closed after the initial run and now failed to re-open due to flak damage, and the radar set also became unserviceable. The Lib's port wing had also been hit with probable spar damage. The starboard wing centre-section had been holed, the flap damaged, port side fuselage and bomb bay holed. Flying Officer C Allison decided to haul off and when it was found the bomb doors would not budge, turned for home.

U-618, commanded by Kapitänleutnant Kurt Baberg, had been the main culprit for this damage despite mis-identifying the aircraft, as noted in the boat's KTB:

> "2333 hours, aircraft with Leigh Light. Distance 1.5 miles, two-engined, passes behind boat dropping two flares. No bombs, no strafing. Flak. 2337 hours – release *Afrodite*. 2340 hours, crash-dive."

Again in the confused action U-618 identified the attacker as a twin-engined aircraft but there is no doubt that U-618 was one of the boats involved. No claim to have scored hits but her gunner's shooting was obviously better than realised. There is no indication of a second U-boat and it may possibly have been a surface escort vessel or a trawler.

U-618 had earlier left for the Mediterranean, on 23 February, but failing to get through had been returning to France, where she eventually reached St Nazaire on 8 April.

F/O C Allison RCAF   Pilot   W/O H E Ritchie RCAF
Sgt D McGillivray RCAF   2nd pilot   Sgt G Langridge
F/O A W Goldstone   Nav   F/S D R Smith
  RCAF

W/O A P McKinnon RNZAF   Sgt J S Knapp
Sgt W C Tatum

On the night of 9/10 April, a Liberator V of 53 Squadron ('A' BZ781) was flying a *Percussion* D3 patrol over the Bay. At 0305 hours, in position 4620/0946, Flying Officer W J Irving's crew picked up a S/E contact at 17 miles and held it until illuminated by the Leigh Light. A second contact a short distance away was not watched, the radar operator concentrating on the first target.

However, as the Light came on, the stern and wake of a U-boat was seen disappearing to starboard. Flak came up from a range of 400-500 yards and the front gunner blazed away too but the D/Cs failed to release. Irving circled to port and came in again, the front gunner holding his fire in order not to advertise their position, but the U-boat's gunners were not fooled and as the range closed they opened up once again, this time their fire slashing into the Lib's bomb bay. Again the D/Cs failed to go down, either due to a continuation of a fault or on the second attempt due to flak damage. The rear gun turret also failed to operate. A third approach fared no better.

Irving broke off the action and headed home. The nose wheel, the crew discovered, had also been hit and punctured and the hydraulics damaged but Irving made an excellent landing at first light without flaps or brakes. William John Irving later received the DFC. (It will be recalled that Irving had been forced to land in Portugal after his aircraft was damaged by U-boats on 30 July 1943.)

F/O W J Irving RCAF	Pilot	F/S J G Humphreys	WOP/AG
Sgt A Thompson	2nd pilot	F/S J Wildon	WOP/AG
F/O J M Haste	Nav	Sgt R Brodskopp	
F/O R G Sharpe	WOP/AG	W/O T Collier	
W/O J E Hamilton		F/L R D Westlake	2nd Nav

Their target had been the inbound U-821, commanded by Oberleutnant Ulrich Knackfuss. His KTB extract noted:

> "0304 hours. Grid BF4569. First attack, Sunderland, Leigh Light. Light flare, no bombs. Second attack: Leigh Light strafing, light flare, no bombs. Third attack: No bombs, strafing. By manoeuvring the boat [we] prevented a cross over by the aircraft. During second and third runs many hits were observed on the aircraft by flak. 0325 hours, crash-dive."

There is no doubt that this attack was on U-821, the KTB matching V/53's report. Once again the German crew gave the seemingly ubiquitous Sunderland credit for an attack, as well as congratulating themselves on avoiding a damage due to their manoeuvres.

No. 53 Squadron Lose Two

A week later, on the 17th, 53 Squadron had far more serious encounters with submarines. The first came at 0351 hours in Grid BE6935 (outer Bay, north-west of Cape Finisterre). The German crew saw the Light come on and strafing began, being met by flak from Oberleutnant Kurt Hilbig's U-993. Then at least two bombs came down, but as the aircraft went over, the conning tower crew could see that one of the port engines was on fire. Moments later the bomber dived into the sea. No sooner had the aircraft gone in than there was a big explosion and the plane sank in flames. The boat's KTB records:

"Attack took place at 0351 hours in Grid BE6935. This was a Leigh-Light assisted attack. The aircraft strafed but was met with flak. As the plane crossed over the U-boat the port motor was seen to be on fire. The aircraft released two bombs and a small bomb; they did not fall close so may have been jettisoned due to damage. The aircraft plunged into the sea 600 metres away. There must have been further D/Cs aboard because the aircraft exploded and sank in flames. There were no survivors."

An hour later, U-546, commanded by Kapitänleutnant Paul Just, came under attack in Grid BF4458. This attack was also assisted by Leigh Light and developed from the boat's starboard side. The unidentified aircraft roared over at a height of 20 metres, releasing six D/Cs, two of which fell to starboard and the others to port. Hit by flak the bomber nosed over and crashed into the sea 500 metres to the port side of the boat. U-546 quickly dived in case other aircraft were about. Their KTB noted:

"Attack took place at 0453 hours in Grid BF4458 and not far from where U-993 had just shot down an aircraft an hour earlier. The aircraft crossed the boat at 20 metres, releasing six bombs; two fell to starboard, four to port. Hit by flak and crashed into the sea 500 metres to the port side of U-546. The U-boat crash-dived immediately after this action."

The two aircraft were both Liberators from 53 Squadron, 'O' (BZ945) and 'H' (BZ800). Flight Lieutenant F M Burton had taken off at 2152 hours on the 16th and at 0127 called in a sighting report but this was cancelled at 0230. At 0304 control instructed the aircraft to hunt for a U-boat, and given a position, and this was acknowledged. At 0349 came a flash report but nothing else. 19 Group noted the latter contact report as being in position 4700/0930.

Flight Lieutenant C Roberts, in 'H', had taken off at 2215 hours. At 0032 control had instructed him to search for a U-boat in position 4626/1041. At 0126 aircraft informed control it had reached this location and at 0457 a flash report was received but again, nothing further. From the available information it seems certain that 'O' was shot down by U-993 while 'H' fell to U-546.

F/L L M Burton	Pilot	Sgt R T McDennon RCAF
P/O E J Hagen RCAF		Sgt O R Newell RCAF
F/O A E Buckley		F/O L H Abbott
F/O K K Edwards		Sgt R L Pierce
Sgt W A Hallett RCAF		Sgt L G Reilly
F/O S B Critchlow		

F/L C Roberts	Pilot	F/S R J Lawrie RCAF
F/O D J Moore		F/S J L Stubbs RCAF
F/S N Box RAAF		Sgt R J Humbles
F/S A J Alexander RAAF		P/O H G Reed
F/S F H Nopper		

No.53 Squadron Again – but All That Glitters ......
The Liberators of 53 Squadron were having a bad period. On 25/26 April Flight Lieutenant C McC Forbes flew a Rover Patrol, which skirted the Spanish and French Bay coasts at 500 feet. At 0150 hours on the morning of the 26th, in position 4600/0146 – off La Pallice – the radar picked up several blips which turned out to be a dozen fishing trawlers. Then they reported finding two U-boats on the surface.

Only one was thought to be present as the Leigh Light came on at one mile during the run-in but as soon as the boats opened fire, the RAF crew became only too aware that there were two vessels – one each side of them – although they failed to see either. The Liberator was hit and Forbes hauled round for another approach, closing in on one of the targets from dead ahead; this time he could see the other on the port beam. The Light remained off on the second approach but flak came up at a quarter of a mile and further damage was inflicted on the aircraft. The No.3 engine was hit and set on fire and the D/Cs failed to release. A third attack-run was made, this time down wind on three engines, but again the D/Cs failed to fall.

Forbes gave up and headed away. He was only too aware of the close proximity of the French coast so kept all guns manned, climbing to 2,000 feet. At 0220 hours three radar contacts were seen on the screen, this time being aircraft. Forbes quickly descended to 200 feet and took evasive action for night fighters for over an hour, but finally brought the damaged aircraft home. Cameron Forbes received the DFC for this action and other attacks on U-boats.

However, on this occasion there were no U-boats in the area! Almost certainly he and his crew had chanced upon two German surface ships and therefore had been lucky to survive their combined AA fire.

F/L C McC Forbes   Pilot   Sgt E R A Steer
F/S H C Reay RNZAF   2nd pilot   F/S C J Falconer RNZAF
F/L T C Hood   F/S S G Hunt RNZAF
P/O G Steele   F/S W H J Barnes RNZAF
F/O R J Bromly

* * *

A 58 Squadron Halifax II ('M' HX152) had a narrow escape on 27 April, during an attack on U-473, commanded by Kapitänleutnant Heinz Sternberg. Flight Lieutenant W D C Erskine-Crum had taken off from Brawby at 1850, and at 0315 the next morning a S/E contact was found, lost and then regained. Flares were released from 600 feet to reveal, 1½ miles away, a surfaced U-boat which immediately opened fire, flak passing over the aircraft's port wing.

The navigator replied with a long burst from the nose gun and tracer struck the hull and bounced off the conning tower; the flak stopped. At 0327 seven D/Cs were dropped from 100 feet. The aircraft was hit simultaneously and the port wing dipped violently and the Halifax became unmanageable. The skipper ordered ditching positions but before vacating the rear turret the gunner saw four D/C plumes either side of the boat, and he maintained machine-gun fire.

Within one minute the captain cancelled the ditching order as he regained control and headed for home. The last they saw of the boat was bluish flames and a red glow along the length of it. Erskine-Crum got them back, landing at St Eval. On inspection, the Halifax had collected four cannon shell holes six feet outward of the landing light and one large hole on the underside of the port mainplane.

F/L W D C Erskine-Crum   Pilot   F/O C W Ellis
F/O R E Robinson   2nd pilot   Sgt S J Elliott   WOM/AG
F/L G L Conner   Nav   F/S A R Keech
Sgt W D Dewar   Engineer   Sgt R J Peake

The next night Wellington 'W' (HF386) of 304 Polish Squadron found U-473 in position 4530/1100 and attacked despite flak. Neither side did any damage to each other. U-473 did not return, becoming another victim of the 2nd Escort Group, sunk by *Starling*, *Wild Goose* and *Wren* on the night of 4/5 May. 24 of her crew were lost including Sternberg, 30 others being rescued.

On the evening of 1 May, another 58 Squadron Halifax, this time 'H' (HR741), flew a patrol, commencing at 2044 hours, and failed to return. A Liberator crew from 53 Squadron ('S' BZ873 F/Lt E B LeMaistre) saw some of the action in which this aircraft presumably was shot down. In the early hours of the 2nd (0112 am), the Lib crew reported seeing three flares and tracers from sea level, followed by a dull red explosion.

On investigating the burning wreckage, clearly seen on the surface, the outline of the frame of an aircraft was visible, but no survivors were evident. The attack had been upon U-846, Oberleutnant Berthold Hashagen's boat, who reported attacks to BdU at 0115 on the 1st and at 0407 on the 2nd, the latter in position BF8111. It seems probable that the second attack had involved H/58, if for no other reason than that 58 Squadron's Halifax aircraft were using flares at night rather than Leigh Lights.

F/O D E Taylor	Pilot	Sgt Y J D Riddell	WOM/AG
F/O D C N Sullivan	2nd pilot	F/S B J Forsyth	WOP/AG
F/L S T Geary	Nav	F/S M C E Lewis	WOP/AG
F/S G I Stoddart	Eng	Sgt L V Ashton	WOP/AG

The Norwegians get a U-boat and Damage Another Despite Casualties
A Sunderland of No.330 Norwegian Squadron ('V' JM667) attacked a submarine in the late afternoon of 16 May 1944. The front gunner sighted an object eight miles off on the port bow, and closing in a U-boat was identified at 1720 in position 6305/0310 – west-north-west of Alesund, Norway.

In the initial attack heavy flak was met but fire was returned and some of the German gunners were seen to fall, but only one D/C was released. A second approach was made. The flak had lessened but the Sunderland took several hits that killed the front gunner and wounded two other crewmen. One shell exploded in the cockpit, the flash temporarily blinding the captain.

Despite the damage and smoke, and fires in the cockpit and front turret, the attack was pressed home from 50 feet. A stick of four D/Cs exploded off the boat's port side causing it to sink stern first at a sharp angle one minute later. As well as the casualties, both starboard engines of the Sunderland had been hit, one of which cut out shortly after the attack. By jettisoning fuel the flying boat managed to regain height and eventually returned safely to Sullom Voe.

S/Lt C T Johnsen	Pilot	QM K I Halvorsen	FME/AG **
S/Lt F Meyer	2nd pilot	QM A J Johansen	FMA/AG *
S/Lt F Buck	3rd pilot **	QM L Faberg	WOM
S/Lt E S Pedersen	Nav	QM D J Brannvoll	AG
QM N Borresen	Engineer	QM K Naevdahl	WOP/AG
QM J E Johnsen	WOP/AG		
* Killed; ** Wounded.			

It has always been assumed that this attack was upon U-240, commanded by Oberleutnant Günther Link. However, it is now believed to have been

Kapitänleutnant Wolfgang von Eickstedt's U-668. His KTB recorded:

"AF8115, 1715 hours, attack by Sunderland, distance 6,500 metres, height 100 metres. When at 3,500 metres, flak. Cross-over strafing. A second attack, bombs, 100-150 metres behind the boat. Hits on aircraft (starboard wing). Strafing, aircraft disappears."

U-668 was a boat from the Artic Flotilla on her way to Bergen, having yet to start her first war patrol. Her skipper reported the encounter in Grid AF81, being surprised and forced to fight on the surface, firing both its 3.7-cm and 20-mm guns. Taking violent evasive action the D/Cs did some minor damage and one crewman was wounded in the hand by a bullet.

U-240, it is now believed, was attacked and sunk by 333 Squadron's Catalina 'C' (FP121, S/Lt H E Hartmann pilot) on the 17th. This had been U-240's first real war cruise, making her way from Kristiansand to Narvik which she had begun three days earlier. None of her gallant crew survived.

On patrol in a similar area to the Sunderland's encounter, the Catalina crew located a suspicious looking water disturbance at 2221 hours, 125 miles west of Alesund. On closer inspection a U-boat was made out in the twilight-type night of northern latitudes during May.

The Catalina was met by flak and in return strafed the U-boat. From 50 feet a stick of D/Cs was released but the results not clearly observed. Meantime, the flying boat was struck by an explosive shell, detonating in the aft compartment. One air gunner manning the starboard blister gun was killed and a large hole blown in the bottom of the hull. The pilot managed to fly back to the River Tay where the Catalina was landed and beached. Damaged beyond repair, the Cat was considered a total loss and broken up.

S/Lt H E Hartmann	Pilot	Pty/O L Sjonnesen	WOP/AG
Pty/O J H Frogner	2nd pilot	Pty/O H N Stein	WOM/AG
Pty/O F C Christiansen	Eng	Pty/O K D Berg	FME/AG *
Pty/O E M Marcussen	Obs (Nav)	Pty/O H Lochting	FMA/AG
Pty/O O W Hofsrud	WOP/AG		
* Killed.			

* * *

On 24 May 1944, U-921, under the captaincy of Oberleutnant Wolfgang Leu, was attacked by Sunderland 'R' (DV990) of 422 Squadron RCAF, which had taken off from Sullom Voe at 0800 that morning. The flying boat did not return from the action. The U-boat had been sent to the area to look for survivors from U-476 which had been severely damaged that morning by a Catalina from 210 Squadron.

The sub was seen to go down but later resurfaced but it was clear she was not going to last long. Two other U-boats were sent to her aid and later picked up 21 of her 56 crew, one of the subs then finishing off U-476 with a torpedo.

Until fairly recently most sources have credited U-476 with downing the aircraft but this is incorrect. It is all but certain that R/422 was shot down by U-921. This boat's KTB shows that she was attacked by an aircraft at 1420 in Grid AF5748. The attacking plane, identified as a Catalina, strafed her and dropped three D/Cs but was seen to be hit on the run in. The boat was not damaged and claimed the aircraft shot down.

Another Sunderland, 'S' (DW111) of 423 Squadron RCAF (Flight Lieutenant R H Nesbitt and crew) was also in the area and at 1419 this aircraft intercepted a weak SOS message from position 6358/0357, which falls in Grid AF57. This was a 'QR' and a long dash, and moments later the crew sighted a puff or splash 10-15 miles to the north. On investigating, a surfaced U-boat was spotted. This was U-921 again. While closing in to attack some wreckage was seen on the water by the Canadian crew, but it was ignored until after the attack.

The boat was strafed and then five D/Cs were dropped. Smart manoeuvring by U-921 avoided the D/Cs but the gunfire wounded the IWO and one crewman. Worse yet, during the crash-dive, Oberleutnant Leu was left topside and lost. In fact he knew he did not have time to get down the hatch and bravely shut it from the outside in order to save his boat, thereby sacrificing his own life. The IWO, Leutnant Hans Neumann, took command and brought the boat into Trondheim on the 26th.

The Sunderland then went back to inspect the wreckage and there can be little doubt it was from R/422 and there are no other recorded attacks that match that of the action between this aircraft and U-921. The only dispute is in the aircraft type, and as we have already seen, aircraft identification was often wrong.

F/O G E Holley	Pilot	W/O J O Burke	WOP/AG
F/O G B Gingell	2nd pilot	Sgt D J Harvey RAF	WOP/AG
F/S I W Guggiard RAF	3rd pilot	Sgt P D Andrew RAF	FME/AG
F/O T E Friar	Nav	W/O C Senton	AG
F/S J H Hamilton	Eng	W/O J M G Fleming	AG
Sgt J C Seely	WOP/AG	F/L E W Baillie	passenger +
+Station Gunnery Leader.			

U-921 had joined the Arctic Flotilla on 21 May and was on her way from Kristiansand to Trondheim when she was attacked and damaged, not making her first patrol as a result until 2 July. She was sunk on her third on 30 September by FAA aircraft.

A second aircraft lost this 24th day of May was from 612 Squadron. Wellington 'L' had taken off from RAF Chivenor at 2019 that evening, her crew flying their first operation, having arrived on the Squadron on the 11th

from No.6 OTU. No signals at all were received from the crew from the
time they took off and they were reported missing.

However, U-736 (Oberleutnant Reinhard Relf), on weather reporting
duty, was making for a Bay port after an unsuccessful attack on a convoy
south-west of Ireland a week earlier. She was located and attacked by a
Wellington, which was claimed as shot down. It seems certain that L/612
was her victim. She reached Lorient two days later but was sunk by a RN
frigate on her next patrol in August.

F/O K M Davies	Pilot	F/O C E Scott
F/S K S Collins		W/O J A Rooney
F/S J Bailey		Sgt H C Trump

CHAPTER EIGHT

FLEET AIR ARM AND US NAVY ACTIONS

First Actions
As early as 14 September 1939 aircraft of the Fleet Air Arm were meeting German U-boats, not that they had very good equipment with which either to search out the boats or to fight them when found. They, like some of their RAF counterparts, had been way down the queue for more modern aeroplanes.

On this September day the action revealed only too well the serious deficiencies in aircraft, tactics and weapons. Three Blackburn Skuas of No.803 Squadron from the aircraft carrier HMS *Ark Royal* were in the vicinity of Rockall Bank, German Grid reference AM19, or 5643/1521 – the scene of the loss of the SS *Fanad Head*. They found U-30, commanded by Oberleutnant zur See Fritz-Julius Lemp.

The first two attacking aircraft dived, only to be enveloped in the explosions of their own bombs, and crashed. The pilots of both aircraft, Lieutenants G B K Griffiths (L2873) and R P Thurston (L2957) were later picked up by the U-boat to become prisoners of war, the second crewmen in both machines, Petty Officers J Simpson and G V McKay, being lost. The third Skua subsequently strafed U-30 which suffered three crewmen wounded in the whole attack. It was not a good beginning.

* * *

While there were other actions, the next event covered by the remit of this book skips forward in time two years, to 17 December 1941. A Martlet fighter (the name given to the American Grumman F4F Wildcat) of 802 Squadron FAA, from the escort carrier HMS *Audacity*, found and attacked U-131, commanded by Korvettenkapitän Arend Baumann. The time was 1330 hours, in Grid DH3349, west-south-west of Gibraltar.

Sub-Lieutenant G R P Fletcher was in the fighter and made a diving attack, but on his approach for a strafing run was shot down by the boat's flak gunners and killed. U-131 was herself sunk only minutes later by surface escorts of convoy HG-76, of which the escort carrier had been part.

The convoy had left Gibraltar on the 14th and that night, a Swordfish biplane from the carrier had found and attacked a U-boat just over six miles from the ships. The attack had frustrated attempts to torpedo the convoy.

On 23 July 1942 a Swordfish from 815 Squadron (V4365) failed to return from an anti-U-boat patrol between Alexandria and Mersa Matruh. While the reason for its loss is not known for certain, an attack upon a U-boat cannot be ruled out, but Sub-Lieutenant O Dixon and his two crewmen were never seen again.

Pilot	Observer	Telegraphist/AG
Sub-Lt O Dixon	Sub-Lt H G Newbold	LA W E Way

A similar thing happened on the night of 16/17 August, although there is more evidence to support a shoot down by a submarine. Again it was a Swordfish of 815 Squadron (V4373) last seen in position 3143/3338. Lieutenant Hedley Vernon Day RNVR, Sub-Lieutenant G F Fenton-Livingstone and Leading Seaman Frank Edward Brown, assigned to HMS *Grebe* failed to return.

The Biter is Bitten

HMS *Biter* was another of the gallant band of escort carriers which operated valiantly in the Atlantic with Allied ship convoys. On 12 May 1943 a Fairey Swordfish from her decks, 811 Squadron, flown by Sub-Lieutenant V W Witts, was helping to cover convoy HX237 and had been sent off to investigate a HF/DF bearing, and discovered U-230, commanded by Kapitänleutnant Paul Siegmann, on the surface.

The biplane's slow approach speed did nothing to help the FAA crew and gave the flak gunners time to find the range and the Swordfish was hit hard during the run in. Before the aircraft could complete its attack it was either knocked into the sea by the accurate AA fire or as the Germans thought, hit the sea. Depth-charges meant for the submarine exploded under the wreck of the machine and if any of the three-man crew had survived the crash, they would certainly have died in the explosions.

Sub-Lt V W Witts RNVR   Sub-Lt R J Lee RNVR   LA G H Marsden RNVR

U-230 escaped unscathed, of course, later reporting the action in Grid BD6831, at 0920 – north of the Azores. Her KTB recorded:

> "Aircraft from carrier strafing. No result. Flak. Aircraft banks off and attempts to attack from front side. The boat is helmed to foil this attack. These manoeuvres cause the pilot to undershoot his approach and crash into the sea 100 metres from the boat. The aircraft is destroyed by the explosion of its bombs."

* * *

It was not until March 1944 that the next recorded action of a FAA aircraft being shot down by a U-boat occurred, and that came on the 12th of that month. It involved the escort carrier HMS *Vindex*, on hunter-killer operations in the north Atlantic, actually in the area west of Ireland.

A Swordfish of 825 Squadron, piloted by Sub-Lieutenant P E Cumberland, was one of two aircraft on a night patrol and shortly after 0100 hours they picked up a radar contact. Investigating, a U-boat was sighted and the first Swordfish attacked in the moonlight and dropped two D/Cs which splashed into the sea close on the boat's starboard quarter.

Peter Cumberland's observer then picked up the ASV contact and guided Cumberland to the spot. This time the U-boat began firing, but Cumberland, wondering what all the pretty lights were, carried out his run on the target and just as the D/C release was completed, and he realised he was being shot at, the 'Stringbag' was hit in the cockpit area by a cannon shell. The observer, leaning over the port side of the aircraft, was hit in the back and crumpled to the floor, while the air gunner called that he too had been hit.

Because of this, Cumberland was understandably too involved with keeping his aircraft in the air to see his D/Cs explode, and immediately headed back to the carrier. On landing he discovered that his air gunner was dead, and his observer wounded. The observer, forgetting his injury for the moment, reported to the Commander and his staff, the men noting his tattered parachute harness. It was only then that he was sent off to sick bay where they found he had been nicked in the back by a piece of metal. The doctor extracted some aluminium slivers and dressed the wound.

There is no doubt that the U-boat encountered was U-741, commanded by Oberleutnant zur See Gerhard Palgren. He later reported hitting and shooting down a Swordfish at 0308 hours in Grid AL8524. Other than the fact that the aircraft was not actually shot down, the claim is a perfect match. A third Swordfish had also attacked the boat, but there is no evidence that any of the D/Cs actually exploded.

T/Sub-Lieutenant Frank R Jackson was the wounded observer, Leading Airman John Stone RN, a 19-year-old lad from Birmingham, who had already been mentioned in despatches, the fatal casualty. The Swordfish, LS428, was repaired and returned to duty, only to be lost in a take-off accident 11 days later.

Russian Convoy

On April 1st, the escort carrier HMS *Tracker*, part of the escort to convoy JW58, had her aircraft out searching north of the Kola Peninsula, Russia's northerly arctic area, and at 0952, Avenger FN877 'L' of 846 Squadron sighted a U-boat on the surface and attacked, but the pilot, Sub-Lieutenant A E Ballentyne RNVR, found he could not release the D/Cs. The boat dived and Brown marked the spot then returned to the carrier, managing, he thought, to jettison three of the four D/Cs before he had to land. The pilot misjudged his landing and hit the curve of the bow decking. The fuel tank burst into flames and it took some time for the danger from the burning aircraft to be sorted out. The remaining D/C needed to be chopped free, but it was then found that all four must have been jettisoned. Alan Ballentyne stumbled from the wreck on fire and although helping hands put out the flames, he died soon afterwards. His observer, Sub-Lieutenant K D Callaway was badly burned but the gunner, Leading Airman G E Hearn, was not hurt.

In the afternoon, another 846 Squadron Avenger attacked two U-boats its pilot found on the surface, while another was attacked a short while later. This latter one left a trail of oil and was later finished off by an escorting destroyer. In this action Lieutenant F J Brown had his aircraft hit in one wing by flak which caused the D/C's release gear to malfunction.

The next day, a Wildcat from 846 Squadron (JV420), piloted by Sub-Lieutenant T D Lucey, attacked another U-boat, but fire from the sub hit the fighter and Lucey notified the carrier of his problem then baled out into the icy waters. He managed to get into his dinghy and after nearly two hours he was rescued by HMS *Beagle*. Another Avenger dived through a snow squall and attacked a target, only to find he had attacked a destroyer, whose captain sent a message to the carrier – 'Call off unfriendly Avenger!'

During this three-day period (1-3 April), aircraft and ships had sunk three U-boats – U-355, U-360 and U-288 – while fighters had shot down a Blohm & Voss 138 and a Focke Wulf 200. All 153 submariners were lost. In addition to the three lost boats, U-716, U-361, U-313, U-990 and U-968 all reported attacks by aircraft, the latter boat twice, which were fought off by flak.

* * *

Operations in support of Russian convoy RA59 in May 1944 called for the FAA to provide air cover and anti-submarine patrols in the Arctic waters. No.842 Squadron was aboard HMS *Fencer* equipped with Swordfish and Wildcat Vs. During the period, 11 attacks were made on U-boats, three being sunk on 1 and 2 May.

On the 3rd, they found U-278 – Kapitänleutnant Joachim Franze – as his later KTB report noted:

> "0332 hours, Grid AF1525. Three aircraft emerging from a dark cloud in echelon formation. One single-winged plane is in the centre, flanked by bi-planes. Aircraft opened fire scoring 33 hits on conning tower and deck. Four or five badly placed bombs are released. The sudden attack was a surprise but renewed attempts to approach are held off with accurate flak. The aircraft dart in and out of the clouds. After the initial shock the crew respond well and all weapons functioned well with only minor problems which were quickly remedied. All three planes now try a simultaneous approach from different directions. This manoeuvre is defeated. First the monoplane approached from 130 degrees. Accurate bursts from the

quadruple hit the port wing. The plane banked sharply to port trailing smoke and jettisoned a bomb which fell some 2,000 metres distant. The aircraft banked again to starboard, almost a new approach and received a further blast from the quadruple mount. Fire is interrupted by a heavy swell; the aircraft is last observed trailing smoke and disappearing into the sea at 170 degrees to our course. Only one of the bi-planes made a further approach which was easily defeated by flak. Appearing to have lost their nerve due to the loss of the single-wing plane both bi-planes disappear."

Although the aircraft was seemingly lost, there do not appear to be any personnel casualties, so the pilot must either have got back, or if he did come down, to have been rescued. And a report by HMS *Fencer* makes no reference to any losses.

MAC Ship Actions
We can also make reference to an action on 25 May 1944 by aircraft from two MAC ships (Merchant Aircraft Carriers – merchant ships converted to carry aeroplanes), HMS *Ancylus* and HMS *Empire MacKendrick*.

They were part of the escort for convoy ON237 (GB to Halifax), and their aircraft located U-853, commanded by Kapitänleutnant Helmut Sommer, which was on weather reporting duties in the North Atlantic. One of their aircraft picked up the boat visually astern of the convoy and its report quickly brought three biplanes to the scene, two being Sub-Lieutenant B J Cooper in Swordfish 'G3' (HS622) of 836H Flight, and Swordfish 'M3' from 836M Flight – Lieutenant D Shaw. (The third was HS621 'M2' of 836G Flight, crew not known.)

Despite the odds of three aircraft to one boat, Sommer remained on the surface and fought it out, his gunners scoring hits on all three biplanes. No rocket hits were claimed thanks no doubt to the fierce gunfire. All three machines landed back on their respective MAC ship, but each had been badly damaged, 'M3' in fact being deemed beyond repair and jettisoned off the *Empire MacKendrick*.

Lt D Shaw	Sub-Lt H W M Hodges	LA J M King
Sub-Lt B J Cooper	Sub-Lt Owen	LA F L Turner

U-853's KTB recorded the action:

"At 1701 hours, Grid AK8520, three double-winged aircraft, type Vought SU4. Too late to dive. At 2,500 metres opened up with flak on two aircraft approaching from starboard. After seven rounds the 3.7 cm gun jammed. The third aircraft was held off by the 2 cm gun. Boat turned 90°. The third aircraft attacked and released seven bombs that look like rockets. They passed ahead of the bows. Flak!

Top left: U-415's 2 twin 20-mm AA guns.

*Top right:*Gunner behind a 20-mm flak gun training on the aircraft as it flies by.

Middle: U-960 at La Pallice in February 1944, being welcomed by Flottillenchef Zapf. This boat was damaged by a Mosquito of 618 Squadron on 27 March 1944 but her gunners damaged their attacker.   *(G Heinrich)*

Left: Catalina of 265 Squadron patrolling over the Indian Ocean. Note ASV aerials.

(L Eccles)

Top left: Swordfish 'C' of 811 Squadron taking off from HMS *Biter*. *(via R Sturtivant)*

Top right: A Swordfish of 811 Squadron (NF190 'F') on HMS *Biter*, suffering an undercarriage collapse.

(J W G Wellham, via R Sturtivant)

Middle: An 846 Squadron Wildcat – JV579

'F', 1944, with D-Day invasion stripes.

(R Sturtivant)

Bottom left: Fleet Air Arm Avenger taxies with wings folded, similar to the F4F set-up.

(B Tillman)

Bottom right: Avengers of 846 Squadron FAA. *(via R Sturtivant)*

Top left: Firefly 'Q' of 1771 Squadron. Fireflies of this unit were in action on 27 October 1944 off the Norwegian coast.

(via R Sturtivant)

Top right: A US Navy PBY Catalina.

Middle: U-848 under attack by VB-107 on 5 November 1943, showing 105-mm deck gun, and eight 20-mm guns (2 twin and 1 quad mounts). Note crouching sailors, one with a German 'coal-skuttle' helmet. The boat was sunk but not before her gunners had damaged one USN Liberator.

Left: Joe Spurgeon DFC, 502 Squadron. On the night of 6/7 June 1944 he had his port-inner engine hit attacking a U-boat.

Top: A VLR Liberator of 224 Squadron, on St. Eval airfield, summer 1944. Note Leigh Light under the wing and the heavier front turret guns.

Middle: S/L Les Baveystock DFC DFM and crew of 201 Squadron sank U-955 on 7 June 1944. Three nights later, his crew, flying with S/L Ruth, failed to return, possibly shot down by U-333. Picture shows the crew with their previous skipper, F/L Longford. All except Anderson died on 10 June. Front: F/O P Hunt, F/O C Griffith, F/L Longford, P/O M Anderson, F/O A V Philp; Rear: (not thought to be in order) - Flight Sergeants Hobson, Currie, Humphrey, Sharland, Watson, Foster and South.

(John Evans Collection)

Right: Peter Cremer, commander of U-333, whose gunners shot down a 228 Squadron Sunderland on 12 June 1944.

Top: David Hornell won the VC during the attack and sinking of U-1225, but did not survive his ordeal in a dinghy. L to r: Sgt F St Laurent, F/O F W Lawrence, Sgt D S Scott, F/O S E Matheson, F/O G Campbell, F/L D E Hornell, F/S I J Bodnoff, S/L W F Poag. (Poag and Lawrence were not involved in the VC action.)

Bottom: F/L Geoff Parker with some of his 86 Squadron crew. They sank U-317 on 26 June 1944 but not before they had their Liberator damaged by flak. L to r: F/S A H Hogan, F/S D Carter, F/L G W T Parker, F/S M Garrett, F/S D Jones.   *(S Norris)*

Top left: U-boat under attack, 17 July 1944. Initially it was believed that John Cruickshank and crew attacked U-347, but it is thought now that it was U-361.

Top right: F/L R E MacBride of 162 Squadron RCAF. His Catalina was damaged by U-478 on 30 June 1944 causing the release mechanism of the D/Cs to fail.

Middle: John Cruickshank and crew (standing l to r): Sgt Stockton, F/O J Coulson, F/O J A Cruickshank (VC), F/O J C Dickson, Sgt F J Appleton; (front) Sgt S B Harbison, Sgt Westby, Sgt Wallis, F/S J Smith, Sgt C J Webber. Only Dickson, Appleton and Harbison were with him during the VC action, but this was his crew on 7 July 1943 during a damaging attack on U-267.   *(F J Appleton)*

Right: Wing Commander C StG W Chapman, OC 161 Squadron RCAF, brought down by U-715 on 12 June 1944. Survivors from his crew were rescued later that day.

Top left: F/O John Mills, 210 Squadron navigator. On 18 July 1944 the Catalina he was in was hit by gunfire from U-742, but the submarine was destroyed. *(J Mills)*

Top and middle right: U-968 under attack.

Middle left: Oberleutnant Otto Westphalen, commander of U-968. His gunners despatched an 86 Squadron Liberator on 18 July 1944.

Bottom left: John Scott, 58 Squadron, was flying in a Halifax which was hit by U-boats on 13 August 1944. *(J J Scott)*

Bottom right: A commanding view of a 201 Squadron Sunderland, with Leigh Light beneath the starboard wing. It was far more usual to have Wellingtons and Liberators using the Leigh Light but as the picture shows, some Sunderlands had them too.

Above: U-534 sunk 5 May 1945 and raised in August 1993. Her gunners had shot down a 172 Squadron Wellington on 27 August 1944. Photos taken at Birkenhead prior to restoration work. *(M Fahey)*

Right: Aprés la Guerre. Former enemies now friends. Günther Heinrich (left), CO of U-960 wounded by fire from Aubrey 'Hilly' Hilliard's tetze gun fire on 27 March 1944, while his gunners damaged the attacking Mosquito. *(A Hilliard)*

A flame came out of the engine, then was extinguished. Different objects, including a dinghy, were jettisoned by the aircraft in an attempt to gain height. Aircraft descends to ten metres and touches the water before regaining height and slowly disappears from sight. The first of the other two aircraft also hit by flak. It turns away, loses height until 10 metres above the water. It too jettisons articles, including a small rocket, then flies away, barely above the sea. Previously this aircraft had fired seven rockets, all of which passed over the boat as did its strafing. It seems certain both aircraft will not reach their carrier. The third aircraft fired only three rockets and was not so offensive as the other two. Remained at 1,000 metres and when the 3.7 cm gun opened fire, she released her weapons at a great distance. Crash-dived at 1732."

Other aircraft to be on the receiving end of U-boat flak were Fairey Fireflies of 1771 Squadron FAA, and Barracudas of 828 and 841 Squadrons on 27 October 1944. These aircraft were operating from HMS *Implacable* along the Norwegian coast during the period 26-28 October. U-1060, escorted by minesweeper M-433, was on a torpedo transport mission to Trondheim, and they came under two separate attacks. In addition to her own complement, U-1060 had on board 28 survivors from U-957 which had been damaged in a collision on 19 October and paid off.

The initial sighting was made by a patrol of four Fireflies at 0820 hours, and in a fierce action, M-433 was set on fire although one aircraft was shot down by the U-boat. One of the FAA crew was later found drifting in a dinghy and taken aboard the submarine, which also took the burning minesweeper in tow near Tong Fjord.

At 1100 hours a second strike consisting of Barracudas, Fireflies and Seafires, found the vessels. The strike was led by Lieutenant A V Donaghy RNR, having been launched half an hour earlier. The U-boat, under heavy attack, cut the line to M-433 and was abandoned, after blowing up in Vaaga Fjord. U-1060 put up an effective defense but was overwhelmed by numbers and firepower and she was finally beached near Fleina Island, south of Bronnoysund (6521/1150). Again one attacking Firefly was hit by AA fire and plunged into the sea, and once more one of the crew was rescued by the Germans.

U-1060 was a wreck. Twelve of her crew, including Oberleutnant Herbert Brammer, had been killed and the boat was abandoned, the hulk being totally destroyed by Coastal Command Liberator aircraft two days later.

The Fireflies lost were those of Sub-Lieutenant G C Weir (Z1978), who was rescued, but Sub-Lieutenant Sam A W Waters RNVR, the pilot, was killed. The second Firefly had Sub-Lieutenant G M Maitland rescued, although there is some doubt whether or not a second aircraft was indeed lost in this action.

US Navy Land-Based Squadrons

Once America was in the war and German U-boats began operating off the eastern coasts of North and South America, US Army and Navy squadrons began operating over the western Atlantic seaboard. They had their successes and also shared the dangers and losses.

On 24 June 1943, Kapitänleutnant Curt Barleban was taking his U-271 south-south-east of Cape Farewell, travelling through Grid AK7253. At 0850 hours German time they were attacked by an unidentified aircraft, but thought to have been an American flying boat, Martin type. The boat remained on the surface and fought back as the aircraft came into a range of 800 metres.

Hits were seen to be scored on the aircraft which came in strafing, and then released four D/Cs. They were way off target and may have been jettisoned as the aircraft was now seen to be on fire and trailing smoke. It crashed about 1,500 metres off the starboard side of the boat leaving a high column of smoke.

The boat nosed to the area but found nothing other than oil and two green-painted sections of wreckage. We have yet to identify this aircraft. Although a long way from Iceland – and there were no RAF losses this day – and not much closer to Greenland or Newfoundland, all we know for sure is that U-271 brought down its attacker.

* * *

Down in the Southern Atlantic, we know for certain that VP-74 lost an aircraft on 3 July 1943. U-199, commanded by Kapitänleutnant Hans-Werner Kraus, was attacked by a Martin Mariner of this unit whilst she was searching for targets off the south-east coast of Brazil, near Rio de Janeiro.

The boat's presence had already been picked up and on this day she was spotted by Brazilian aircraft and forced to submerge. Attempting to re-charge her batteries that evening, U-199 was located by a searing Mariner piloted by Lieutenant (jg) H C Carey. He dived to attack but alert gunners on U-199 were prepared and the aircraft was shot down before it could drop its D/Cs.

U-199 reported this victory by radio in Grid GB1815, and there were no survivors from the Mariner's crew. On the last day of this month, U-199 encountered aircraft again and came off second best, this time being damaged by a Mariner of VP-74 (Lt N F Smith). Unable to submerge she was later attacked and sunk by a Brazilian Catalina while also being strafed by a Brazilian Hudson. Only 12 men, including the captain, were rescued. (Sometimes U-199 is noted as having shot down an aircraft on 27 June, but this is incorrect. She sank an unescorted Liberty ship on that date.)

Lt H C Carey	Pilot	ACRT W F Magic
Lt J A Helms		AMM2c R R Hundt
Ens R G Smith		AVM2c N A Miller

Ens R R Roberts   AOM2c G W Persinger
ACMM J L Mason   S1c J E Burke
AMM2c Kofka

Action South of the Canary Islands

Three days later, on the 6th, a PBY Catalina of Squadron VP-92, was patrolling on the other side of the ocean, and came into contact with U-193, commanded by Korvettenkapitän Hans Pauckstadt.

U-193 reported this attack at 1534 hours (German time) in position Grid DU2361, south of the Canary Islands. The flying boat was at 100 metres on the boat's starboard side and recognised as a Catalina. Pauckstadt stayed on the surface and began firing as the Cat reached 800-1,000 metres from the boat.

The PBY roared over the conning tower at low height and released six bombs which fell close, explosions lifting the quarter deck. There was also a strafing attack but the aircraft was hit.   A second approach was also met with gunfire with more hits which forced the American pilot to break away. Circling some 4-5,000 metres away it was held off by more flak fire. However, U-193 had been damaged and two of her crew had been wounded but eventually the boat went down and escaped.

Another Catalina from VP-92, piloted by Lieutenant (jg) G Morris, was en route to escort convoy SL132. He attacked the boat at 1431 hours (Allied time) after it had resurfaced south of the Canaries, position 2645/1435. Visibility was four to five miles because of haze but the wake of the boat as it surfaced was clearly seen. The PBY traded four D/Cs for heavy flak fire, the flying boat taking hits in the wings, rudder and fuselage. One crewman, Gibson, was killed and five others wounded but Morris managed to get his machine back to its base at Agadir, Morocco. Gibson was observed to be having trouble with the camera on the first run and was fatally wounded during the second approach.

The others wounded were Morris, a flesh wound to the right calf; co-pilot a wound to the left knee; Frnka, abrasion to the right forearm; Postle, abrasions to the left arm; Curlin, puncture wounds to forehead and left eyeball with a splinter to the eyeball itself. Gibson had been killed by a hit in the upper abdomen. A detailed report of the damage caused by the U-boat's fire listed the following:

> "One shell hit the starboard wing, a ricochet on the trailing edge causing some slight cuts on the under-surface. Another shell went through the radar antenna on the port wing, one splinter went into the left aileron and lodged there. Yet another shell went into the lower side of the port wing about 18 inches from the wing splice, the explosion blowing a few holes through the bulkhead of the after wing spar as well as causing several holes to appear in the top wing

fabric. A fourth shell entered the bow compartment to the right of the bomber's window and continued on to hit the right rudder pedal of the first pilot and then ricocheted under his seat. Fragments from this shell evidently hit both pilots in the legs. One shell in the bow compartment entered low on the starboard side, passed through No.1 bulkhead into the nose-wheel compartment and into the cockpit under the first pilot's seat, hitting the supporting angle frame for the seat and partly severing the SBAE rudder cable, then shot through No.2 bulkhead and exited the aircraft on the port side under the navigator's table. The shell in the radio compartment went through the propeller anti-vibration plate on the starboard side, severing the starboard elevator control cable. Fragments from the shell entered the main fuse panel completely demolishing one ameter. Some fragments also hit the first radioman in the face. A shell also went into the bunk compartment, passed through the keel and lodged in a parachute pack located on No.6 bulkhead.

"A second shell went into the bunk compartment just aft of the starboard window and continued through No.6 bulkhead, through the fore-and-aft stringer of the turtleback of the waist compartment and finally lodged in the revolving windshield. Fragments of this shell evidently injured the port waist gunner. A nut 'popped' off the window as the shell entered and the nut went through the port wheel-well and hit the port tyre but did not damage it.

"A shell also smashed into the waist compartment through the lower stationary part of the starboard blister, passing through the opened revolving windshield and continued through the starboard fore-and-aft stringer of the turtleback, severing the down-throw elevator control cable and cut all but two strands of the rudder control cable and exited the 'plane through the skin of the turtleback between the two blisters. Another shell which hit the waist compartment aft and below the starboard blister, went through the door of No.7 bulkhead which was open, and left the machine on the port side above and aft of the port blister. This shell evidently passed through the photographer."

Lt G K Morris	Pilot *	ARM3c M J Curlin	Radioman *
Lt R W Hall	Co-pilot *	ARM3c E J Gibson	Cameraman/
AP1c C O Butcher	Bow Gunner		AG +
AMM2c F R Frnka	Port	AOM2c W R Postle	Std Waist
	Waist AG *		AG *

* Wounded; + Killed.

Morris and crew reported that the U-boat had the number '88' in a dark colour on the starboard forward side of the conning tower and a swastika next to it. This led the intelligence people into believing the attack had been on U-88. However, U-88 had been sunk on 12 September 1942 during operations against convoy PQ18 in the Arctic.

* * *

On 9 July, U-590, commanded by Oberleutnant zur See Werner Krüer was off the north-east Brazilian coast in position 0354/4852 at 1230 hours. Here she was spotted by a Catalina of Squadron VP-94, captained by Lieutenant (jg) F F Hare, engaged on an anti-submarine sweep around convoy TJ-1. He immediately launched an attack but the boat remained on the surface and accurate gunfire from her scored hits on the PBY's port wing and the cockpit, where instruments were shattered and a fire started.

Frank Hare was mortally wounded by shrapnel in the head and throat and the radioman was also hit but he managed to put out the fire. The co-pilot, Lieutenant (jg) J P Phelps, continued the attack and released D/Cs which exploded within 30 feet of the sub's starboard quarter. Despite the damage to the flying boat Phelps got it back to base at Belem, Brazil.

Less than two hours after this clash, U-590 had another run in with the Catalinas of VP-94. Lieutenant (jg) S E Auslander found the boat as it surfaced, and made a surprise attack which sank her with all hands.

USN Blimp Downed

On 18/19 July U-134 – Kapitänleutnant Hans-Günther Brosin – was attacked by a Navy Blimp No.K-74 – a rigid airship used for anti-submarine patrols. This unique action occurred in the Florida Straits, 30 miles off Key West, as the submarine was *en route* for her patrol station of Havana, Cuba. The Blimp, piloted by Lieutenant N G Grills, was providing air cover in the region and he had been informed that two valuable merchant ships would be crossing his area that night.

At about midnight, a U-boat was picked up on the Blimp's radar and Grills chose to bear in and attack. The slow speed and large size of his airship made it a less than ideal vehicle to attack a U-boat and so it proved this night.

K-74 was shredded by flak from alert gunners on U-134 during the Blimp's run-in but even so its momentum carried it over the target. At the critical moment the Blimp's bomb release mechanism failed and so K-74's crew did not even have the satisfaction of delivering its pay load. U-134 submerged and escaped, while the airship collapsed on the water. The destroyer USS *Dahlgren* arrived to pick up Lieutenant Grills and all but one of his ten-man crew.

In any event, U-134's days were numbered. Returning home in August she was attacked by aircraft of the 21st, but survived. Three nights later 179 Squadron sank her west of Vigo, Spain. There were no survivors.

* * *

On 24 July, U-466 (VIIC), commanded by Oberleutnant zur See Gerhard Thäter, was also in the wars, having been attacked twice the previous day off the Brazilian coast. The first had been by a US Navy Catalina of VP-94 which the gunners had damaged. Now a Liberator of the 35th USAAF Squadron, operating from Zandery, Surinam, Dutch Guyana found her at 1430 hours. The 35th was bomber outfit but had been used on anti-submarine duties since Pearl Harbor.

The boat had no time to dive so responded as she had previously done, with her guns. The Liberator took several hits during the run in but also gave the boat a heavy strafing with its own .50s. Four D/Cs also splashed down but exploded outside lethal range. Realising the aircraft had suffered damage, Thäter quickly took the opportunity to dive and safely cleared the area. Damage to U-466 was not serious but five of her crew, including the captain, the IWO and IIWO had been wounded.

The aircraft had also suffered heavily. The outer port engine was on fire and shrapnel had wounded at least two of the crew. Nevertheless the pilot dropped a further D/C on the swirl before heading back to base. U-466 reported the attack in Grid EP4327 and claimed hits on the aircraft which had departed with one engine on fire. There is no doubt that the U-boat's gunners had saved the boat twice in two days, while damaging two attacking aeroplanes.

Flak fire is thought to have hit and driven off another American aeroplane (an Army B18) five days later in the same area. U-653 – Kapitänleutnant Gerhard Feiler – reported an attack at 0307 hours on the 29th in Grid EO37, just to the north of Dutch Guyana. Certainly there was no attack by the aircraft, understood to be from the 18th USAAF Squadron, also operating out of Zandery. It reported an action with a U-boat 90 miles north of Paramaribo, which was against U-466.

Death in the Caribbean

U-359, commanded by Oberleutnant Heinz Förster, had left for the Caribbean on 29 June 1943, being refuelled at sea around 10 July. Off Puerto Rico on the 28th she was attacked by a USN Mariner from VP-32, flown by Lieutenant D C Pinholster.

On its first pass the boat opened up on the aircraft and turned sharply to port, four bombs straddling the vessel. On the second run both antagonists exchanged gunfire and the Mariner was hit. Two of its gun turrets were knocked out and two crewmen wounded.

Breaking off to return to base, the Mariner crew observed an explosion in the area they had just left. An aircraft flying to the spot the next day found a large oil slick but nothing else. U-359 went down in position 1557/6830, taking her 47-man crew with her. She had been on her third war cruise.[1]

U-406, commanded by Kapitänleutnant Horst Dieterichs, had been on

---

(1) Recent research may indicate the boat was U-159 (OL Heinz Beckmann).

several war patrols since early 1942 but had only one sinking to her credit with three other ships damaged. She left on her seventh cruise on 26 June 1943, destined initially for the central Atlantic, then after refuelling at sea, patrolled south-west of the Azores. Then by the end of July she was one of seven U-boats operating between Trinidad and the mouth of the Amazon.

She had no success on this cruise but there was some luck. She was found on the 30th by an aircraft from VP-204 (P-11) flown by Lieutenant L D Crockett in position 0758/5458. His first attack run was not low enough to make a successful drop so he pulled out and opened the range for a better approach.

On his second run, Lewis Crockett had the length of the U-boat as a target but unfortunately, one of the (estimated) 30 calibre rounds from the boat severed the lead to the navigator's micophone shorting out the intercom system. When Crockett gave the order for the co-pilot to drop the D/Cs he could not hear him, and although a drop was then instigated two seconds later, it was enough for a miss. The tail gunner saw a tremendous explosion, but it was just astern of the sub.

The same round which cut the intercom wire also resulted in tragedy aboard the Mariner. This bullet hit Lieutenant (jg) Robert Kistler Hershey USNR (the 3rd pilot) in the stomach. He had been standing by the navigator's table in the waist hatch and was fatally wounded, dying ten minutes after the aircraft made the beach at base. Lewis Crockett later helped to sink U-615 on 6 August 1943, whilst flying a machine of VP-205.

On 23 August, U-406 was damaged by aircraft attack and had one crewman killed and three others wounded, but survived again, returning to St Nazaire on 15 September. She was finally sunk by HM ships on 18 February 1944.

* * *

On the last day of July 1943, U-572, commanded by Oberleutnant Heinz Kummetat, was found by a Mariner aircraft from Squadron VP-205 (P-2), 180 miles east of Trinidad, at 2310 hours. The Mariner used flares to carry out a high level bomb run on the target. A second attack was made at low level with a stick of four D/Cs.

U-572 fought back with flak and may have scored several hits on the Mariner – captained by Lieutenant H B Lawrence – but it returned safely to its Trinidad base. The U-boat commander reported this air attack to BdU as happening in Grid E016. Three days later she would encounter aircraft from VP-205 again, from which there were no survivors from her crew nor from the aeroplane.

This occurred on 3 August, again east of Trinidad. The Mariner (P-6) was piloted by Lieutenant (jg) Clifford C Cox, who signalled at 25 minutes past midnight that he was attacking a surfaced U-boat in position 1135/5405. Only 20 minutes earlier U-572 had signalled BdU from approximately this location. Nothing further was heard from either antagonist and it must be assumed that they annihilated each other in a

fierce action from which not a single man survived. The Mariner carried a
crew of 12, four officers and eight enlisted men, the U-boat a crew of 47.

Lt C C Cox USN	Pilot	ARM3c R A Guthrie USNR
Lt O K La Craft USNR		ARM3c K G Anderson USN
Lt W A Schwant USNR		AOM2c C R Campbell USN
Lt E G Wood USNR		S2c W L Beckman USN
AMM2c W J Dier Jr USNR		AOM3c J B Martin USN
AMM3c R L Courtney USNR		S2c S C Boggs USN

U-615's Epic Struggle

The US Navy's Squadron VP-205 were back in action three days later. A
U-boat had been located and attacked by a USAAF aircraft on the 1st, so
aircraft were on the alert. They found her again on the 5th, Lieutenant (jg)
John M Erskine of VP-204 attacking her in position 12128/6510 but
without result. There followed a 'hold down' operation by a succession of
aircraft designed to keep the boat below the surface so as to exhaust her
batteries and air supply as well as reduce her speed.

On the 6th, Mariner P-4 of VP-205, piloted by Lieutenant Anthony R
Matuski, found the sub, U-615 (KL Ralf Kapitzky), on the surface that
afternoon at 1320 hours, north-west of Blanquilla Island (1254/6434). The
boat attempted to submerge but was too slow. The Mariner dropped a stick
of four D/Cs that seemed to bracket the boat and blow it back to the surface.

Matuski radioed base of his actions saying that the boat was damaged but
there was no damage to the aircraft, but then eight minutes later another
signal was received: 'Damage, damage, fire!' This was the last that was
heard from P-4 and her 11-man crew. In a second run on the now surfaced
U-615 the gunners on the boat had shot down the Mariner. However, the
boat was now in serious trouble from Matuski's initial attack and she was
given no chance to effect an escape, but she was still a force to be reckoned
with.

At 1537, Mariner P-11 of VP-205 piloted by Lieutenant Lewis D
Crockett (he and his crew were actually members of VP-204, the 205
machine having been loaned to 204 as all their aircraft were undergoing
repairs) was vectored to the last position reported by P-4 and while looking
for both the missing aircraft and the U-boat, found the latter. Crockett made
two runs, first at high altitude dropping two A/S bombs, then a lower one
with four D/Cs. In both attacks U-615 remained on the surface putting up
flak, and scored hits on the aircraft's wing which also started a fire. As far
as they could tell, a 30 calibre round, apparently an incendiary, ruptured the
fuel line between the hull and wing tank. The inside of the starboard wing
became a mass of flames and although Crockett fully realised there was the
likelihood of the machine exploding, he decided to continue with the
attack.

Warrant Machinist Anthony Spence Creider USN, taking a shirt that was convenient, crawled into the starboard wing root in an attempt to smother the flames. With two $2^1/_2$ pound CO^2 bottles, his efforts proved effective. In all the aircraft had taken six hits.

Crockett saw a tremendous explosion about 50 feet astern of the sub and the hull from the conning tower to the stern was wholly underwater. Water was breaking around the forward part of the conning tower with the bow sticking up at a sharp angle out of the water. Now out of D/Cs, Crockett called for assistance.

More damage had been suffered by U-615 and despite hits on his aircraft, Crockett remained on station for the next five hours directing and supporting follow-up attacks. Another attack was made by Lieutenant-Commander Robert S Null of VP-205 (P-2). Later interrogation of survivors from the boat confirmed they had shot down P-4 in flames, but no trace of her crew had been found.

Lt A R Matuski USNR	Pilot	AMM2c R M Gilchrist USNR
Lt J L Milmoe USNR		S2c E W Moore USNR
Lt C E Donahue USNR		ARM3c M G Rankin USNR
AMM2c J L Egnew USNR		AOM3c C R Steely USNR
AMM2c R B Fisher USNR		ARM2c G T Worrell USNR
ACM1c H E Frederickson USNR		

The next aircraft on the scene was a USN Ventura of VB-130, piloted by Lieutenant (jg) T M Holmes at 1630 hours. Five minutes after arriving he attacked, supported by a strafing run by Crockett, but the U-boat men knew that Crockett was a spent force and concentrated their fire on the Ventura, but failed to hit it. Four D/Cs straddled the boat as both aircraft hurtled over it, the force of the explosions temporarily pushing the boat underwater, and the captain and other crewmen were wounded by the strafing.

Now in desperate straits the U-boat was unable to dive, could no longer manoeuvre properly as its rudder was jammed, so it could only circle at a speed of less than two knots. Nevertheless the boat continued to fight back.

Now Mariner P-8 of VP-204 arrived, flown by Lieutenant (jg) John W Dresbach. He arrived at 1815 and attacked, again supported by a strafing run by Crockett, but the new arrival was hit by flak in the initial run. Dresbach was shot through the chest and shoulder by 30-calibre fire. Just before losing consciousness he released his D/Cs, then slumped in his seat. He looked at his co-pilot, Lieutenant (jg) Oren R Christian, motioning him to take over the controls, and at less than 200 feet Christian pulled the Mariner out of its dive and even made a second high-level bombing run before departing for base.

Flak from U-615 scored hits on the Mariner during this run too but Christian got the aircraft home with its dead captain and four other crewmen wounded. AMM1c Edsel H Baites USN, bow gunner, was shot in the leg, and Seaman 2c Howard E Kerr USNR, bombardier, was shot in the leg, hip and left side, resulting in three broken ribs. Lieutenant (jg) Thomas M Hurley was hit in the face with splinters from the instrument panel and bullet, while Radioman 3c Paul R Lanigan USNR received a wound to his wrist.

P-2 of VP-205 arrived at 1834, captained by Lieutenant-Commander Robert S Null. He made two runs – once again covered by a strafing run by Crockett and his crew – but inadvertently the pilot, whilst opening the bomb-bay doors, released the D/Cs which exploded 600 yards astern of the boat, but flak smashed into the Mariner and once more an aircraft was going home with wounded on board. However, U-615's time was running out.

The final air assault came from a B18 bomber of the 10th Bombing Squadron USAAF at around 2118. Crockett, still on the scene, dropped flares but the submarine could not be located. A Blimp – K-68 of squadron ZP-21 flown by Lieutenant (jg) W Wydean – had also arrived on the scene. Despite Crockett ordering the Blimp pilot to stay clear and keep watch for disabled aircraft, the pilot guided the bomber in but it met a hail of flak and was hit, its bombs again failing to inflict fatal damage. However, the Blimp remained too long over the scene and ran out of fuel, force-landing on Blanquilla Island where it was wrecked.

When the B18 staggered away U-615 was nothing better than a floating wreck but she remained defiant. Her end finally came as the USS *Walker* from Port of Spain, Trinidad reached the area at 0552 am on the 7th. Realising nothing further could be achieved, Kapitzky ordered his men over the side then scuttled his command, going down with her. As dawn broke over the Caribbean, the destroyer found a group of 43 survivors and one dead seaman, floating in the water.

U-566 Runs the Gauntlet

The next actions recorded in this chapter occurred a little further north, off the American east coast and involved Ventura aircraft of VB-128. The date was the same as the finalé to U-615, namely 7 August 1943.

Kapitänleutnant Hans Hornkhol, commander of U-566, was hunting off the US coast and became involved in a bizarre succession of events. On the night of 1 August a Flying Fortress from Mitchell Field was on routine patrol. At 2050 her radar picked up a blip near position 3909/7110, 120 miles off Montauk Point but in the darkness nothing could be seen so all that could be done was to inform base of a possible U-boat.

Less than three hours later coastal DF net picked up a submarine radio message from 3900/6800 and the following day searches were made but nothing found. However, a Navy PBM, flying escort to a Gib to Norfolk (Virginia) convoy the next night again picked up a blip and then dropped flares but these failed to ignite, but the 'sub' opened up with tracer fire, and it was assumed that this was the same U-boat. Further searches were made but nothing further developed until the afternoon of the 3rd – a disappearing radar contact from another Navy PBM.

Nothing more until the afternoon of the 5th. Although a New York to Key West convoy had moved into the danger area the submarine managed to move into an attacking position. The gunboat USS *Plymouth* on search escort had just picked up a contact as a torpedo hit her on the starboard side and sank soon afterwards. Further air and sea searches quickly followed but the sub had gone, moving out to sea eastwards. But her radio messages to base on the 6th were again picked up, putting her in position 3800/7115. Next day 11 aircraft and one Blimp were scouring the area.

One of the aircraft was a PV-1 from VB-128, operating out of Floyd Bennett Field, and flown by Lieutenant (jg) F C Cross USNR, and his co-pilot J T Aylward Jr, USNR, with three enlisted men in the back. Shortly after 0700 they picked up a radar contact at 14 miles from 3,500 feet and at six miles spotted a surfaced U-boat. As they approached the aircraft opened fire with the bow guns, quickly returned by the boat's gunners. One of the first shells from the boat hit the starboard engine which not only stopped it but mortally wounded the pilot too, and seriously injured the co-pilot.

Despite his injury the pilot shifted to one-engine operation, opened the windows to clear the cockpit of smoke, then continued his attack run. All four D/Cs were dropped in a stick across the bows of the sub, the attack timed at 0730, position 3755/7120. There was no chance of a circle back and the immediate question was whether the aircraft could be kept flying, for the pilot was unable to feather the damaged propeller. The increasing drag combined with resistance caused by a torn and bent cowling, was forcing the aircraft down. Finally the order was given to stand-by for ditching and it then carried out a perfect full-stall landing on the sea.

Both pilots and the radioman, the latter having broadcast the standard distress message before clamping down the key, climbed out through the escape hatch during the 12 minutes the damaged plane remained floating. The other two men in the rear cabin were not seen because of the smoke and quite possibly they were suffocated or temporarily blinded by smoke and fumes. They may also have attempted to bale out but were too low. Two closed parachutes were later seen in the water. In any event they did not survive.

The three men floated in their life jackets for about 20 minutes, then the wounded pilot succumbed to his wounds and before the others could reach him, he slipped out of his jacket and went under. One of the other search planes in the area later arrived and landed on the sea, picking up the two survivors, then flew them back to Norfolk Naval Air Station.

Eastern Sea Frontier HQ did not receive word of the attack for some time as the 'sub sighted' reports from the PV-1 had not been picked up. Even when a message was later received that survivors had been rescued it was not clear if the flying boat had been shot down or lost due to mechanical problems, therefore further action against the U-boat was delayed.

There was some confusion now trying to sort out who knew what, who was doing what, what had been the causes, and were people being rescued or needing to be rescued. Another aircraft sent to the area to search, Ventura 'P-8' of VB-128, was never heard from again and it was supposed that she too had found the sub and been shot down. The pilot was Lieutenant J M George, the Squadron's Executive Officer (2nd in Command). Later it transpired that this second aircraft had indeed come across the U-boat, made a run, but its D/Cs failed to explode. The Ventura was shot down and the crew lost.

The search continued. Another PV-1 from VB-126 out of Quonset located U-566 at 1223, position 3736/7035 and as it came in it too was fired at, but then the boat was crash-diving. Four D/Cs went down over the swirl, the explosions seeming to lift the boat back to the surface and smoke started to come from the conning tower as the boat lay still on the surface with just her bows breaking the surface. The Ventura crew were:

Lt J R Smith	Pilot	ARM2c A Ozvath
Ens A Q Mathews	Nav	AMM2c J S Rectenwold

At this moment another aircraft took a crack at U-566, a PBM from Elizabeth City. The crew picked up a contact at 18 miles, ran in and found the boat just as the PV-1 was making ready to run in. The PBM opened its bomb doors and headed in as the German crewmen were seen manning the guns. However, the D/Cs failed to release and the aircraft was hit and damaged. The pilot turned to come in again, but again the D/Cs remained stubbornly inside the machine. Seeing that nothing was falling from the aircraft, the U-boat began to dive and in desperation the Navy pilot pulled the emergency release toggle, dropping all eight bombs. The explosions were close enough to blow the boat back to the surface again.

For the next 30 minutes the two aircraft circled her, then the PV-1 made a strafing attack and started another. As the machine got to within 200 yards the boat's gunners opened fire and the plane pulled out of range to the left. The Ventura crew thought they heard a hit although none were found on landing. However, one of the jettisonable wing tanks had not released, but after the attack it was found to have done, so it may have been this stubborn tank that had taken a hit. Five minutes later the boat got under way, making tight circles to the left for the next quarter of an hour, her bows still riding high, the stern under water, but finally trim was restored; then she began to go down.

More ships and planes were now rushed to the area but both aircraft had now to clear the scene and could not home anyone to the exact spot. Finally, at around 2220 on the evening of the 7th, a PBM picked up a radar contact in 3735/6852, and dropped flares in preparation for an attack but they failed to go off. As the plane ran over the target the setting moon gave enough light to reveal to the pilot the shape of a submarine. Climbing round for another approach, flares again failed to ignite but now the moon had dropped further and its light had decreased. Radar contact was then lost.

As the search continued a destroyer was despatched from the convoy but another PBM which was in the area was not informed so that when a radar contact was effected and an approach made, flares suddenly illuminated the destroyer. (Fortunately the pilot did not drop his D/Cs!) The plane rapidly withdrew, but then picked up another contact three miles to the north-east, but the pilot was so worried about illuminating another destroyer that he went to another search area. It was thought the illuminated destroyer had been seen by the U-boat's lookouts and that the boat had dived. However, Hans Hornkohl confirmed to Norman Franks that he does not recall having seen the destroyer, nor does it appear in his KTB.

The cat-and-mouse game continued on the 8th but without any sightings. However, at 2100 that evening a Catalina picked up a contact in 3812/6639 and then the escort destroyer *Lawrence* established a contact an hour after midnight and made a D/C attack with Hedghogs but without results. The ship continued its search until the evening of the 10th, but by then it was obvious the U-boat had got away.

Hornkohl's KTB extract makes interesting reading when compared to the above actions:

"1322 hours, Grid CA6845 – Air attack. Mitchell [Ventura]. Flak. Starboard motor seen to be on fire. Aircraft releases 3-4 bombs, they do not explode. Following the attack the motor is no longer burning, probable that the pilot has cut the motor. No second attack. It's probable that this aircraft did not reach base.

"1815 hours, Grid CA6885 – Attack by Mitchell. Flak, 4 bombs, 4 explosions. Following the attack heavy flak at the aircraft. Motor is burning and the aircraft crashed into the sea 1,200 metres away. We head for the crash scene.

"1820 hours, Grid CA6885 – A second Mitchell appears. A Lerwick is also observed on the horizon. Flak on both aircraft. No attacks.

"1828 hours – Crash-dive.

"1829 hours – 3-5 bomb explosions heard, no damage. Boat plunges heavily at a 50° angle. Motors of the diving rudders fail, reason unknown. At 60 metres the LI [chief engineer] blows the tanks.

"1830 hours – Boat surfaces. Commander and flak crew to the bridge. The two aircraft are still there. Boat dips under the water. Technical failure. Commander holds himself fast on the periscope stand. The entire flak crew of eight men go over board, 300-400 metres behind the boat. Commander calls a new flak crew to the bridge. No new attack from the aircraft. After 20 minutes all eight men are recovered. The rescued men state they were strafed by the aircraft while in the water. Commander saw how the Mitchell was strafing the dinghy of his downed comrades, probably to prevent our men in the water from using it. The IWO believes that he had seen one of the downed aircrew near the dinghy.

"1908 hours – Attack by the Mitchell with open bomb bay. Heavy strafing. Flak. The flying boat does not attack, probably because he had received some hits from our flak.

"1925 hours – Crash-dive.

"1935 hours – Several bombs. No damage."

It is entirely clear that when compared to the Eastern Sea Frontier's War Diary, U-566 shot down two Venturas and badly damaged a Mariner during this prolonged action. Both Venturas, identified as Mitchells, were from Floyd Bennett Field. (Note – there was a six-hour time difference between German and American times.)

The first action is clearly the attack Hornkohl reported at 1322, in fact the match is perfect right down to the guess that the pilot had feathered the starboard engine and that the aircraft would be unable to return to its base. The bombs released in Cross's attack were either duds or unarmed, a fact that the aircrew were unable to take in due to the damage to their plane.

The second attack at 1815 hours in which the aircraft was observed to crash was obviously Ventura 'P-8' which vanished after acknowledging a routine message at 1206 [1806 German time] when she was estimated to have been in the immediate area of the U-boat. Clearly nine minutes later she ran into U-566 and as the war diarist supposed, was shot down with the loss of her entire crew.

The third and fourth aircraft on the scene were another Ventura of VB-126 (Smith) and a Mariner PBM 'P-10' (reported as a Lerwick by U-566) and USN patrol squadron VB-211 from Elizabeth City, piloted by Lieutenant (jg) E C Scully. This latter aircraft also suffered considerable flak damage in the course of runs over the submarine.

U-566 made Brest on 1 September but was lost on her next (15th) cruise. Damaged by 179 Squadron RAF, the boat was scuttled, her crew taken to Spain by a Spanish trawler. They were soon returned to Germany.

USN Libs in the South Atlantic

Back to the South Atlantic, VB-107 lost not only an aircraft on 11 August, but its Commanding Officer too. Lieutenant-Commander B J Prueher USN went out from Natal, Brazil at 0900 in search of two reported U-boats. One of these had earlier been attacked by Ventura aircraft from VB-129 (Lt-Cdr T D Davies) escorting convoy TJ2, and the destroyer *Moffat* on 3 August. These attacks had damaged U-604 (KL Horst Höltring) and caused crew casualties.

Prueher knew the reported location of these boats was at extreme range so his fuel load had been increased to 3,400 gallons, enough for a 15-hour trip. He flew 800 miles due east then 200 miles north-west. His last radio call came at about 1130, changing radio frequencies – then silence.

We now know that the Navy PB4Y Liberator came upon the two boats north-west of Ascension Island. The damaged U-604 had made rendezvous with U-185 and U-172 but then the Liberator arrived. U-172 crash-dived but the other two remained on the surface and opened fire. Two attack runs were made by Preuher and while banking to come in for a third it was hit by flak and dived into the sea. There were no survivors.

While this was a victory for the U-boats' AA gunners it did not change U-604's plight, for it was in such a bad state that she had to be scuttled, her crew split between the other two boats. The choice was arbitrary but luck as in most things determined the future, for U-185 failed to return from the patrol. [1]

In fact she was sunk by aircraft of VC-13 (USS *Core*) – see Chapter Four. As U-185 was sinking, Hans Höltring went into the forward torpedo room where two of his own U-604 crewmen were. They could not be moved and they pleaded with their skipper for him to shoot them. Seeing no alternative but a slow death by drowning, Höltring did so, then turned his gun on himself. The Lib crew:

Lt Cdr B J Preuher USN Pilot	ARM2c D W Gardner USNR
Lt (jg) G C Hannever USNR	AOM1c G G Merrick USNR
Ens R Tehan USNR	S2c J Milhalsky USN
Ens E L Coupe USNR	ACMM C A Smith
ACRM(A) H C Brandon USN	AMM1c J R Van Horn USNR

U-161's Loss

The United States Navy Squadron VP-74, from Aratu, Brazil, sank U-161 on 27 September 1943, despite flak damage. A type IXC, and commanded by Kapitänleutnant Albrecht Achilles, U-161 was detected by aircraft radar off the Brazilian Coast at 1050, the position given as 1230/3535, which was 250 miles north-east of Bahia.

The aircraft was Mariner 'P-2', piloted by Lieutenant (jg) H G Patterson USNR, and he closed in until the crew sighted first a wake and then the boat itself. U-161 began to open fire at extremely long range, 7-8 miles, so it was obvious she was not going to crash-dive. As the range decreased return fire began to splatter the boat, then Harry Patterson was ranging over his target, six D/Cs tumbling down as he went over from the port quarter.

Hauling round for a second approach the Mariner was hit several times. Airman Bealer on the radio, and Ensign Brett were both wounded. The inverter line was shot away which rendered all electrical instruments u/s. Coming over the boat the last two D/Cs went down, falling on the starboard quarter. All the time the boat's gun crews kept up return fire but now the boat seemed to be down by the stern and her speed was dropping off.

The boat finally went under the waves at 1122 and as no survivors were seen it must be assumed it was a dive which once below, proved fatal. The

---

(1) For a potted history of VB-107 see Chapter 8 of *Dark Sky, Deep Water*, N Franks, Grub Street, 1997.

boat was not heard from again and it took all 53 men aboard her to their deaths. Due to damage and because Ensign Brett's wounds were serious, Patterson did not stay around and headed back to base.

In her six war patrols U-161 had sunk a total of 14 merchant ships and damaged six others. Three of those sunk had occurred between 20-26 September, hence the knowledge of her presence and the search for her.

CHAPTER NINE

JUNE AND D-DAY

Operation Cork

The German submarine force knew just as well as the German army and airforce that the Allies would at some stage attempt a landing on the coast of Europe, but like everyone else, had no idea where. It could be attempted anywhere from Holland to Cherbourg. What they did recognise was the daunting prospect of being sent into the Channel to attack the invasion fleets. They knew that in the confined space of the English Channel, danger from air and sea attack would not be helped by the narrowness of the sea they would have to operate in, and the further east up the Channel, the worse it would be.

Once the first landings took place along the Normandy coast, there must have been some small relief that at least the actions would take place at the western end of the Channel, provided that another – and the more expected – landing did not take place somewhere by the Pas de Calais.

The Allied planners of D-Day, possessing the knowledge of where the landings would take place, had also planned to make it as difficult as possible for U-boats to operate against the vast array of ships that would be off Normandy and sailing to and from southern English ports. As the Channel would, in any event, cause a bottleneck for the submarines it was little wonder that the cover plane to exclude U-boats from getting into the Channel was known as 'Cork'.

As history now records, the Allied D-Day invasion of France began in the early hours of 6 June 1944. Once it became known that something big was happening off the Normandy coast, Admiral Karl Dönitz was told to attack shipping in the Channel, and however reluctant he was to give the order, had to instruct his U-boat commanders to do just that. During the 6th U-boats in the area of the Western Approaches, or in ports around Cherbourg and the Biscay coast, were ordered out to do battle.

For their part, Coastal Command saturated the sky with aircraft with orders to stop U-boats getting in amongst the invasion force at any cost. If they did not, the already tenuous and fragile landing plan, hampered very much by bad weather and the unknown German reaction to the invasion, would be made more critical.

The Night of D-Day
There is a great deal of confusion over the encounters between U-boats and aircraft this day. Four Coastal Command aircraft were lost on the night of 6/7 June, three of which were Liberators and the fourth a Wellington. Almost certainly all were brought down by U-boat flak. Confirming exactly what happened during this night is next to impossible. Of the missing aircraft only one passed a signal after becoming airborne and of the U-boats involved, several did not return or make any signals.

In one case, that of U-256 which was heavily engaged, her diary was damaged in the attack and it has not survived. One thing does appear certain; all four aircraft were downed in action against the boats which departed from Brest. Several of the boats stationed in the Biscay area were attacked but in most cases the aircraft involved can be identified or the engagement was not of the 'battle to the death' kind.

Of the Biscay boats only U-981 (Oberleutnant Walter Sitek) made a claim to have scored hits on an attacking aircraft which was identified as a Halifax (see later). Examining the relevant records of both sides reveals that without doubt the attacking aircraft was Halifax U/502, flown by Flight Lieutenant W G Powell, which was not in fact damaged. With U-981's claim dismissed, we can turn to the Brest boats.

Fifteen U-boats departed from Brest on D-Day, which was the offensive counter force to the Allied invasion of Normandy. Code named Group 'Holzbein', the task of these boats was to penetrate the Channel defences and get amongst the invasion shipping plying back and forth between England and the Beachhead.

It was decided by BdU that a high speed night surface run would provide the best chance of putting the boats into the operational target areas in the quickest possible way. Given the expected air defences that the RAF were bound to put up, this would be a near-suicide type of sortie. Nevertheless it was hoped that the majority of boats could battle their way through the aircraft during the night and continue submerged during the next day. Obviously those boats with a schnorkel had a better chance of accomplishing this mission but all the boats were at severe risk.

The boats began to sail on the evening of the 6th, most of the non-schnorkel boats departing about the same time. They began their run as a group, under escort. It has proved difficult to be sure precisely which boats had and which had not been fitted with the schnorkel apparatus. Those known not to have been converted were Oberleutnant Wilhelm Brauel's U-256, Oberleutnant Dietrich Sachse's U-413, Oberleutnant Herbert Werner's U-415, Oberleutnant Hans-Helmuth Bugs' U-629, Kapitänleutnant Günther Stark's U-740, Oberleutnant Ulrich Knackfuss' U-821, Oberleutnant Karl Boddenberg's U-963 and Kapitänleutnant Hardo Rodler von Roithberg's U-989. They were apparently led out by U-441, Kapitänleutnant Klaus Hartmann, which seems to have been fitted with a schnorkel.

Unfortunately, of these nine boats, only the KTBs of U-415, U-963 and U-989 are available to consult. The observations in Oberleutnant Hermann Stuckmann's KTB from U-621, a schnorkel boat which departed Brest just prior to the non-schnorkel group, is also of interest. Finally, reference to Herbert Werner's book *Iron Coffins* (Arthur Barker Ltd, London, 1970), is of value concerning his U-415, although his memory appears faulty on some details.

The Assault Begins

The air attacks on the Brest boats started shortly after 0130 hours on the 7th. By this point the surface escort had already turned back to port and the boats were on their own. According to the KTB of U-621, which was on the surface just to the east of the non-schnorkel group (Grid BF51), an aircraft passed 100 metres behind the boat at 0135. Her gun crew opened fire with 2 cm flak but the aircraft flew on in an easterly direction – ie: towards the non-schnorkel group's location.

Just two minutes later this same boat observed flak (in fact the KTB entry says there was flak everywhere, indicating at least two and possibly several U-boats had opened fire) and the crew observed an aircraft being shot down some six miles to the east. The logical assumption here is that this was the same aircraft which had passed by U-621 moments earlier. This aircraft has not been identified.

Four minutes later, at 0141 hours, another aircraft was observed to be hit and this too crashed. The KTB notes that Brauel's U-256 was likely responsible. The final entry of note is that U-621 dived at 0224 and two minutes later heard two series of bombs exploding in the immediate vicinity. These may have been attacks on U-415 – see later.

At these times, the KTB of U-989 reported:

> "0138 hours, Grid BF5211, three aircraft, distance 5,000 metres, two of these are shot down by other boats."

The KTB of U-963 noted:

> "0136 hours – the shooting down of an aircraft was observed .... at 0138 hours, a second aircraft is seen to be shot down."

Finally U-415's KTB recorded:

> "0145 hours, next astern attacked by aircraft. I open fire with her. Aircraft shot down by U-256."

In his book, Herbert Werner indicates that the aircraft was a Liberator, confirming the boat was U-256 but confuses the issue by naming the boat's captain as Boddenberg, the skipper of U-963!

It is logical to assume that all of these KTB entries refer to the same actions in which two Allied aircraft were seen to be shot down. One was definitely a Liberator which two of the four KTBs (U-415 and U-621's) indicate was shot down by U-256. The War Diary of BdU agrees in crediting U-256 with shooting down a Liberator although she herself was badly damaged by bombs and forced to return to port. As mentioned earlier, this boat's KTB was lost – a great pity.

The first aircraft shot down was presumably as a result of the fire from U-441, U-740, U-629 or U-413. Most likely some combination of the listed boats and even U-621 may have played a part as this was likely the aircraft she fired upon. U-821 was not attacked this night. This boat did not return but a survivor report indicates she sighted an aircraft at 0112 hours and crash-dived. This may have been Mosquito Q/404 Squadron whose crew sighted the conning tower of a U-boat in position 4814/0515 at 0121 hours.

Of several aircraft that would have been able to attack Group 'Holzbein' only the crew of one aircraft returned. This was Wellington 'G' of 179 Squadron which sighted a surfaced U-boat at 0212 hours in position 4827/0512. Just minutes beforehand, at 0207, the last signal from Liberator B/224 Squadron was received, in which the crew reported being over a U-boat in position 4833/0452. These two aircraft actually encountered three boats – U-989, U-415 and U-963, all westbound and in the described order from north to south.

First encountered was U-989 which when sighted by G/179 (Flight Lieutenant W J Hill) was initially too close to get in an attack run. The aircraft circled but as it flew back an attack was balked by a Liberator, which must have been B/224 Squadron. The Lib carried out a front-gun attack then broke away to starboard while the Wellington passed over but could not attack due to concerns about the Liberator. Flak was experienced and the fire was returned by both front and rear gunners. U-989 reported this attack thus:

> "0215 hours, Grid BF5211, type Mitchell, no bombs, flak, hits on aircraft. Aircraft flies away disappearing."

Then – and this is important because no time is referred to with these entries –

> "Second attack, Leigh Light, 5-6 bombs, strafing. Two aircraft, type Mosquito and a third with a rear armour-plated cupola. The 2 cm flak [gun] put out of action. Commander wounded, crash-dive."

It would seem that the first part of this entry refers to the passing over of the Wellington. The time and the position are correct, there were no bombs dropped, and although flak was encountered it was not hit. At no time did the Wellington use its Leigh Light so the second KTB entry must refer to the

Liberator which seems must have carried out an attack on U-989 immediately after her strafing run. Meanwhile, the Wellington on circling to port did not resight U-989 – which was presumed, incorrectly, to have dived – but instead, found U-963. When the pilot closed in on this boat a third U-boat was spotted, which was actually closer, and this was Werner's U-415.

The Wellington pilot switched targets at this point and carried out an attack on the closer boat. He attacked from 80 degrees to U-boat's course with a stick of six D/Cs, estimating a straddle amidships. The boat was completely obscured by explosion plumes, but no flak was encountered as the Liberator, still on the prowl, drew the flak fire and then the boat was heavily strafed by the Wellington. As it did so it came under heavy fire from the third U-boat, U-963, so the pilot took evasive action, carried out a circuit and then departed the scene, resuming patrol at 0225 hours.

Five minutes later a brilliant flash was seen on the surface of the sea, close to where the attack had been carried out. The probability is that this was B/224 Squadron carrying out yet another attack run during which she was shot down, crashing in flames. The 224 Squadron crew were:

F/O R H Buchan-Hepburn RAAF	Pilot	F/S B Hands RAAF
F/S G J Faire		F/S A Kennedy RAAF
F/S P Hogan RAAF		F/S H Earl RAAF
F/S J D Whitby RAAF		F/S L Barnes
F/S M Dickenson RAAF		Sgt A Collins

The KTB of U-963 records:

> "U-Werner (415) runs forward of us on the starboard side, distance 2,000 metres, also on a westerly course. 0213 hours, aircraft distance 8,000 metres. 0214 hours, a second aircraft, 1,000 metres behind the first. 0222 hours, aircraft attacks. 0223 hours, distance 5,000 metres, first aircraft attacks U-Werner with four bombs, turns above our own boat. Sunderland, height 15 metres, no bombs, strafing, no hits on our boat, which instead, was directed on the second aircraft also attacking U-Werner. Flak from U-415, hits on aircraft. The aircraft turns in a great curve round our boat. Flak from U-963 but the aircraft is already doomed by hits from U-415. 0228 hours it crashes into the sea 800 metres from us, shot down by U-415. Following the explosions no more is seen of U-415."

Werner's KTB noted:

> "0220 hours, Sunderland approaches from green 40. I open fire. Four bombs fall just ahead and detonate under the boat. A Liberator attacks simultaneously from the starboard beam, firing her guns and

scoring hits on the bridge. She drops no bombs. The Sunderland's bombs have brought my diesels to a standstill. The boat rises high in the water and settles by the stern, so that water enters the conning tower hatch. Order – 'clear lower deck; clear away the rubber dinghy.' Radio out of action .... Boat remains afloat, so all ammunition is brought on to the bridge. Rudder jammed to starboard. 1228 hours, Sunderland renews attack from starboard, firing her guns and dropping bombs from low altitude. Bombs straddle us amidships. Directly afterwards the Liberator flies in from the port bow. I open fire. My twin 2 cm [gun crew] shoot well and the aircraft crashes in flames. My Wanze and Fliege have been shot out of action. Some time later the LT reports all clear for diving on one electric motor, so I order all hands below and commence a return passage."

As one can read, it is difficult to follow some actions due to the misidentifying of aircraft types. Often the high-winged big-bellied Liberator was thought to be a Sunderland, and in some instances, submariners identified with Sunderlands, much like Luftwaffe bomber pilots in the Battle of Britain were 'always' shot down by Spitfires, as if Hurricanes did not exist. There were no Sunderlands operating in the area off Brest – nor were there any Mitchells.

Both the Liberator and the Wellington appear to have been variously reported as a Sunderland by both boats. There is also the mystery of how both U-415 and U-963 report a second attack by both aircraft at 0228 hours when G/179 carried out only one attack. Also, U-989 reported attacks by Mosquito aircraft – time unknown – in which she was damaged and her captain wounded. No matching Allied report seems to exist unless this attack was carried out by Beaufighters of 144 and 404 Squadrons. At different times these aircraft seem to have found and attacked what were reported as surface vessels off the Brest estuary. Perhaps at least one of these aircraft unknowingly attacked U-989.

At 0324 hours came the final Allied loss of the night. Once again the only description is from the KTB of U-963:

"0324 hours. Aircraft with search-light attacking; 0325 hours, FT [signal] – 'Air attack, BF5253, U-963.' The aircraft receives flak from a U-boat which was involved in the action and proceeds on its way."

Again we have no description of the aircraft and no identification of the U-boat. It could have been either U-441, U-629 or U-740. Naval Historical Branch of the MoD in a letter dated September 1990 hazarded a guess that the lost aircraft was Liberator M/53 flown by Squadron Leader G Crawford. This is most logical from the take-off time and it is known that this aircraft was assigned patrol area 'G' which included the area directly off Brest. Assuming it was indeed M/53, this would make the first aircraft lost Wellington C/407, Squadron Leader D W Farrell and crew, as the aircraft shot down by U-256 was identified by the Germans as a Liberator. This would make that aircraft M/224, flown by Flying Officer E E Allen, which agrees pretty much with this same MoD letter.

S/L D W Farrell RCAF	Pilot	F/O A D Callander RCAF
F/L W H Brown RCAF		F/O E C N Kent RCAF
F/O W P Johnston RCAF		W/O C J Hall RCAF

F/O E E Allen	Pilot	Sgt A R Croft
DFC RCAF		Sgt J Mitchell
P/O M E Maynard RCAF		Sgt J B G Gray
F/L W J Esler RAAF		Sgt A McLaughlin
P/O H E Pugaley		F/L L R Aust DFC DFM
W/O H McIllaney		
Sgt D E Froggatt		

Of the other attacks this night, it is certain that the first attack by Liberator L/53 Squadron – Flight Lieutenant J W Carmichael – was upon U-963. This boat reported the attack at 0435 hours in Grid BF2769, by a four-engined aircraft which dropped six 'bombs' and strafed them. After the attack the boat was able to dive but other damage caused her to return to base. The aircraft returned with serious damage.

Carmichael found the U-boat in position 4836/0521 and attacked with six D/Cs while his gunners raked the target. They met intense flak after passing over the conning tower and the D/Cs overshot. Coming round for a second run the aircraft met flak from three different vessels so stood off and sent a report to base.

At 0513 Carmichael went in against another of the boats, his D/Cs going down forward of the conning tower. After this the flak stopped except for a twin-gun which fired a few more rounds very wide before ceasing. The crew thought the firing was caused by the trigger gripped by a dead man! The aircraft, although damaged, suffered no crew casualties.

A second attack was made by this aircraft at 0513 hours, in position 4834/0523, on what until recently had been an unidentified submarine, which was very likely sunk, although the aircraft and crew has yet to receive official credit. The Navy assessment of the attack was: 'damaging, possibly lethal.' Axel Niestlé, an expert on U-boat warfare, now considers the attack probably sank U-629.

F/L J W Carmichael	Pilot	F/S R H Curner RAAF	
F/S E E Stevens	2nd pilot	F/S K J Campbell RAAF	
F/S J T McKeown	Nav	F/S L W Shaw	

F/O A C Peters RAAF   F/S I E Martin RAAF
F/O V R White   Sgt V H Lusher

This was the largest single pitched battle between U-boats and aircraft of the entire war with more than 20 U-boat sightings having been made. Sadly there were few survivors on either side so that piecing together the events of the night with any certainty is next to impossible. One summary might be:

C/407 likely shot down at 0137 hours by a combination of U-441, U-413, U-629, U-740 and possibly U-621.

M/224 likely shot down at 0141 hours by U-256.

B/224 definitely shot down at 0228 hours by U-415.

M/53 likely shot down at 0325 hours by U-441, U-629 or U-740.

L/53 damaged in an attack at 0513 hours, probably by U-441, U-629 or U-740.

D-Day +1

At 0437 hours on the morning of the 7th, Oberleutnant zur See Walter Sitek, commander of U-981, knew he had been located by an aircraft, in position 4655/0326. He had been spotted two minutes earlier by Halifax 'U' of 502 Squadron, flown by Flight Lieutenant W G Powell.

The Halifax went into the attack in the face of intense AA fire and released three 600 lb anti-submarine bombs which overshot. U-981's KTB recorded:

> "Grid BF5532, 0437 hours. Strong signal on radar-receiver. Starboard side, a Halifax passes astern the boat, then turns and comes in. Flak. Aircraft passes over the boat releasing 4-6 bombs. Strafing. No damage. Aircraft is hit and is burning. Disappears into heavy cloud. Probably crashed into the sea."

On the face of it there seem to be two conflicting reports, for the Halifax, whose attack and position matches the scenario, was not hit. Whether it was wishful thinking after perhaps seeing exhaust flame and smoke from one of the engines is unclear, but a claim for a probable victory appears over-optimistic. In any event, the boat immediately crash-dived.

On 8 June U-413, commanded by Oberleutnant zur See Dietrich Sachse, was found and attacked by O/58 Squadron (HR744) flying Patrol 'F' and F/502 Squadron. 'O' found the boat first, at 0133 hours, in position 4743/0526, in the moonpath. The crew met flak – they thought from at least one boat if not two. Their seven D/Cs dropped from 600 feet were close. Shortly afterwards the crew found another submarine. At 0200 hours they saw a four-engined aircraft attacking a vessel on the surface and shortly afterwards an unidentified aircraft also made an attack in the same spot.

S/L A T Brock	Pilot	Sgt R J Peake	WOP/AG
F/O A T C Wilmot-Dear	2nd pilot	Sgt J C Seadon	
F/O D Phillips	Nav	F/S D N Cocks	
Sgt D T Bax		F/S W Halbert	

F/502 from Brawdy had left its base at 2205 the previous evening and picked up a target at 0028 am at 5-6 miles. These proved to be three surface vessels which opened fire. Just over an hour later, at 0145, Flying Officer J Spurgeon, the Halifax pilot, saw a U-boat on the surface in the moonlight 3-4 miles away. He went in.

Flak began at once but the Halifax was not in a good attack position so Spurgeon turned for another approach. On this occasion the ordnance failed to release, so a third run was begun, this time four 600 lb bombs going down, seen to explode close to the submarine. This time the aircraft was hit, the port inner engine being damaged, while other shells smashed into the tailplane and elevators. Joe Spurgeon headed for home, landing at Predannack at 0412. (He received the DFC at the war's end.)

F/O J H Spurgeon	Pilot	W/O A Watt RCAF
F/S J Cowan RAAF		Sgt A Davies
F/S E Ward		Sgt V Efstathiou
Sgt H Collingridge		Sgt R Chittleborer

With the blood-letting of the night of D-Day over, both sides had a respite – until the 10/11th June 1944.

228 Versus 228

A Sunderland of 228 Squadron (ML762) took off at 2010 hours on the 10th on a Patrol 34 sortie and failed to return. It was captained by Flight Lieutenant Dudley Hewitt DFC. Weather was noted as very cloudy, some rain, but fair later. Information is scarce but it is likely it was shot down by U-228, commanded by Kapitänleutnant Erwin Christopherson. They were found at 0437 hours on the 11th in Grid BF5591, an area of the Bay over which Sunderland squadrons were operating.

The boat's KTB recorded:

> "Aircraft approaching, no detection, type Stirling, four-engined, 600 metres distance, 50 metres height. Finally detected (electronically) far too late for the aircraft has already been identified. At 200 metres, flak and boat turned to starboard. Six bombs fall 30-40 metres off. Two bursts from the twin 3 cm set the aircraft on fire. It banks giving us a full broadside, further hits. Starboard side of the 'plane from mid-wings on fire – aircraft gradually looses height heading towards land, possibly attempting a belly landing. Burning aircraft disappears over the water, then the fire seems to become waterborne.

No further movement. For a few seconds the fire is very visible, then a big black cloud appears over the water. Apparently the aircraft crashed."

F/L D Hewitt DFC	Pilot	F/S J Gilroy
F/L R T Forgen		F/S A Davison
F/L J J Emery		F/S N Wilson
W/O D Macfarlane RNZAF		Sgt C Abram
F/S C Ellis		Sgt W Pierce
Sgt H Filmer		

Home on Three Engines

Flight Lieutenant Johnnie Posnett, 24 Squadron, found a U-boat on the morning of the 11th, having taken off on patrol at 1907 hours the previous evening. As they headed out, they were spotted by some Spitfires, highly noticeable with their D-Day black-and-white invasion stripes. For a few minutes they buzzed the Liberator before leaving to head for home.

Posnett's crew then located an empty dinghy, complete with oars, which they attempted to destroy with machine-gun fire. One has to wonder at a possible story behind this empty rubber boat. Night came upon the Lib and her crew but the vigil continued with the radar set. At 0233 came the contact, at six miles. The radar operator homed in his pilot and they spotted a surfaced U-boat in the gloom, which was made suddenly daylight at one mile as the Leigh Light went on.

Immediately, the boat's gunners began to fire, 37 and 20-mm stuff coming up at them, the Lib's front gunner firing in return. However, the boat's gun crews scored hits on the aircraft, knocking out the No.4 engine, while other shells smashed into the bomb bay. As the bomber roared over the submarine, one man looking straight down through the bomb bay at the sub saw the guns pointing almost vertically at him, then the firing ceased as one of the deck crew must have either seen a depth charge heading for him, or yelled out in expectation of them.

As it happened, only one D/C released, for unknown to the RAF crew, the flak fire had also hit and shot away the bomb release gear. Apart from the damaged engine, there was a gaping hole in the rear of the bomb bay, flap and aileron trim tabs had been knocked out, the bomb doors would not close, and there was other sundry damage. Posnett began to circle to establish how bad the damage was, and was hoping that someone might be able to fix the bomb release gear, but it was totally useless.

Noting the U-boat's position – 4919/0415 – they headed back to England, feathering the crippled engine, and then set about jettisoning the D/Cs manually, which they did at intervals as they headed for home. Once again U-boat fire had saved the day for the German crew.

Welshman Keith Bettany, the Flight Engineer, later recorded:

'While I was sitting on the flight deck, two cannon shells exploded in the bomb bay. It shook me quite a bit and I thought of my mother and father, as one does at a time like that. I waited for the depth charges to fall, but they didn't, and I realised that something had been hit. The electric circuit had been broken by the cannon fire.

'I looked down at the sea through the open bomb doors; there was a little light from the sun [dawn] and our Leigh Light, still shining on the water. I could see the U-boat 200 feet below, and the flak coming up towards me. I tried to close the bomb doors, but two of them had jammed. One depth charge was hanging down, with its nose through the bomb door, so I pulled the lever and released it. Then I was able to close that door, but the other one was still open. The other depth charges would not fall so there was nothing to do but set course for home.'

For twenty minutes Bettany stood on the narrow, twelve inch, cat-walk, which was also covered in oil. With the sea below and a gale blowing up at him, he hung on to the bomb rack with one hand and one by one released the rest of the D/Cs with the other. As each one went out, the Liberator was able to gain a bit more height, Posnett having got her up to 700 feet by the time the last one went. Finally Bettany was able to close the other bomb door, so they were clear for landing.[1] John Posnett received the DFC later that summer.

F/L J W A Posnett	Pilot	W/O T Evans	
F/S B Chapple RAAF	2nd pilot	W/O H C Kuhn RCAF	WOP/AG
F/O R E Smith	Nav	Sgt D Wilkinson	
P/O J E Stanton		F/S L Dixon	WOM/AG
Sgt K B Bettany	Eng	W/O J Kilburn	WOP/AG

Posnett's encounter must have been with U-269, commanded by Oberleutnant Georg Uhl. There can be no final confirmation because U-269 was sunk on 25 June by the frigate HMS *Bickerton*. However, the Allied position falls in Grid BF25 and U-269 signalled BdU on 10 June that she had been attacked from the air in Grid BF25. There was no elaboration on this as to whether she had fought back with flak, but confirms the time as 2331, Grid BF2597. As Posnett's encounter is the only identified air engagement on the 10th in or near Grid BF25, this must be the attack to which the submarine's signal referred.

More Problems on the 12th
If there was difficulty with matching claims and losses on D-Day, 12 June

---

[1] As related to Hector Bolitho and recorded in the latter's book *A Penguin in the Eyrie*, Hutchinson, & Co, London, 1955.

proves equally problematical. All we can do is report the facts and our suggestions.

Kapitänleutnant Peter Erich Cremer commanded U-333. He was a Knight's Cross holder and the boat was on her 10th war cruise and had already been attacked and damaged by Y/10 RAAF Squadron the previous night. The sub's 37-mm gun was out of action as was the boat's radar; there were also some leaks in the hull. Cremer aborted his mission and began to return to La Pallice.

On the 12th the boat was attacked by a Sunderland which was shot down in a well known action and often this aircraft is reported as being U/228 (Flight Lieutenant M E Slaughter RCAF), which had left Pembroke Dock at 1810 hours on the 11th. However, there is another possibility, that it was Sunderland 'S' of 201 Squadron which had taken off at 2012 on the 11th. Whichever flying boat it was, U-333 reported that it went down with one engine on fire and its rear gunner blazing away with his four .303s to the last. The 201 Squadron crew had been:

S/L W D B Ruth DFC*	Pilot	F/O A V Philp	WOP
F/O C J Griffith	2nd pilot	F/S D J Currie DFM	WOP/
F/O F A C Hunt	Nav		Radar
F/S J C L Humphrey	Eng	F/S D E South DFM	WOP/
F/S J W Hobson	Eng		Radar
F/S D E Sharland	WOP/AG	F/S E Watson	FMA/AG
		Sgt J R French	AG
		F/S F Foster	AG

William Denys Butterworth Ruth had won his first DFC in 1940 flying with 50 Squadron, and a Bar in 1942 whilst with 207 Squadron. Both Duncan Currie and Dennis South had won their DFMs while flying with Les Baveystock DSO DFC* DFM, of 201 Squadron, sinking U-955 on 7 June 1944. In fact the above crew had been Baveystock's on that night. Baveystock had been on compassionate leave, attending his father's funeral in London, and Ruth had taken the crew on this fatal sortie.

* * *

The observations of a 172 Squadron Wellington crew at 0045 hours on the 12th, in position 4815/0545, that an aircraft was shot down by flak does not appear to fit very well with any loss either in time or location. If correct, the position is too far north for the Sunderland losses and the time is too early for it to have been Liberator S/224 Squadron or Wellington K/179 Squadron.

It is certain U-333 downed one of the Sunderlands and it is probable that the second was lost during an attack on U-993, captained by Oberleutnant Kurt Hilbig, in Grid BF5153 (approx 4750/0600) at nine minutes past midnight on the 12th. This boat's KTB noted:

"0005 hours, Sunderland, strafing, four bombs fall 50 metres to port
side, flak. One crewman killed, two seriously wounded. 0009 hours,
crash-dive. 0010 hours at 50 metres, three bombs."

It has not been possible to locate any Allied attack report to match this KTB
so it seems the aircraft did not return to its base. The KTB does not claim
to have hit the Sunderland but it is certainly possible, probable even as
there is no Allied report. The three 'bombs' at 0010 could have been the
Sunderland crashing and its remaining D/Cs exploding. The position is not
far from where Wellington J/172 observed an aircraft shot down and could
be a possible match apart from the time. The crew for Sunderland 'U' of
228 Squadron comprised:

F/L M E Slaughter RCAF	Pilot	F/S H Chester
F/L D H Griffiths		Sgt J Bleach
F/O R L Griffin		Sgt G Channing
F/O L C Dadds		Sgt W Patterson
W/O J Foubister		Sgt L Segaloff
Sgt W Carr		

Loss lists which indicate that S/201 Squadron fell victim to U-437 (KL
Hermann Lamby) are certainly incorrect. Her KTB states:

"2243 hours, Grid BF9276. Attack by two-engined aircraft, probably
a Hudson, 30 metres height, port side. Three shots from 3.7 cm flak.
Aircraft turns away to the west, keeps in touch for a few minutes at
a distance of 10,000 metres, then disappears."

No indication at all that the aircraft was hit or damaged and the time is
clearly too late for either of the lost Sunderlands or any of the other missing
aircraft. Other than the attacks on U-333 and U-993, this was the only air
attack for which there is a surviving KTB on the 12th.

Another loss this night was of a 224 Squadron Liberator. Aircraft 'S'
took off at 0105 hours on the morning of the 12th from St Eval to Patrol
area 'G' – West Channel area – and failed to return. A position report at
0305, noting 4837/0526 and U-boats, was the last anyone heard from the
Lib. It has long been presumed that S/224 went down to U-boat flak despite
no direct German evidence. U-441 has been mentioned, but the boat's KTB
was lost when she was sunk. It has been presumed that she was damaged
in an air attack on the 12th having left Brest six days earlier and was
thought to be limping back to this base but then was lost to unknown
causes. Perhaps a mine, or perhaps her damage proved too much and she
foundered. There has been suggestions that she went down on the 18th, but
it is now believed she was lost before this date. In fact it is thought likely
she went down to the attack by Liberator G/224 Squadron (K O Moore)
which was previously believed to have sunk U-629.

There is no evidence at all from the German side that Jenkison, the pilot of 'S', and crew were lost to a U-boat and no signal from U-441, which was not heard from again after departing from Brest. An attack on the 18th by Polish Wellington A/304 Squadron was not successful and may have even been on a non-submarine contact.

F/L J E Jenkison RNZAF	Pilot	W/O F J Reid	
F/S K Graves		F/S L Starr	
F/L A M McCleod RNZAF	Nav	F/S L Dixon	WOM/AG
F/S T F Jones RAAF		Sgt R T Green	
P/O C C Chitty		Sgt A Jenkins	

Canadian Cats – Triumph and Tragedy

Catalina flying boats of 162 Squadron RCAF were in serious actions on 13 June, and although they sank one U-boat they lost two aircraft, including that of the Squadron's commanding officer.

Wing Commander C StG W Chapman RCAF was on patrol in Canso 'T' (9816). At 1012 two periscope 'feathers' were seen from 2,000 feet, three miles away. Chapman closed in and attacked from 50 feet and the U-boat surfaced, or at least, seemed to half surface while turning to starboard, and seemed down at the stern and some men were spotted in the water.

As the aircraft flew over, taking pictures, a man was seen to run to the guns, and then a shot hit the Canso and the port engine began to leak oil and trail smoke. The engine was shut down but could not be feathered, and excess fuel could not be jettisoned in case of fire from the smoking engine. The machine lost height and finally hit the sea.

Water began to pour through holes in the hull and the Canso sank in 20 minutes. However, Warrant Officer Joe Bercevin remained at the wireless set sending distress signals until the last moment. The crew got into their dinghies, but then one exploded and two others were discovered to have holes in them. Taking it in turns to be in the remaining dinghy and in the water, the men hoped for rescue but gradually cold, and other problems, made the swop over of positions virtually impossible.

Some time later a Liberator from 86 Squadron found them, and then a Warwick aircraft from 281 Squadron arrived and dropped an airborne lifeboat which Flying Officer David Waterbury swam to, but it took him an hour of hard endeavour. Meanwhile, Flight Sergeant H C Leatherdale lost his grip on the dinghy and disappeared. The seven others clambered into the lifeboat, but it had been damaged and was leaking, soon being half under water.

Another Warwick arrived and dropped a Lindholme dinghy but when one of the weaker men was pulled into it, a hole was torn in it. The lifeboat's sail was raised and they tried to reach a second dinghy but it drifted away. Two other crewmen, Reed and Staples, were both in a bad way now, everyone was sitting up to their armpits in sea water, but these two had to have their heads supported above the water. Finally an ASR launch arrived (No.2723), its crew taking off all the survivors and taking them to Lerwick, but Reed and Staples both died.

Their antagonist, Kapitänleutnant Helmut Röttger's U-715 – a schnorkel boat as confirmed by the twin 'feather' wakes – was on her first cruise, having sailed from Stavanger on the 8th. The boat went down with all hands in position 6245/0259. Chapman received an Immediate DSO, while all the other survivors received DFCs and DFMs.

W/C C StG W Chapman RCAF	Pilot	Sgt R F Cromarty RCAF	2nd Eng
F/O J M McRae RCAF	2nd pilot	W/O J J C Bercevin RCAF	WOP/AG
F/O D J C Waterbury RCAF	Nav	F/S G F Staples RCAF	WOP/AG *
F/S H C Leatherdale RAF	Eng *	W/O F K Reed RCAF	WOP/AG *

* Lost.

Submarine U-480, commanded by Oberleutnant Hans-Joachim Förster, was attacked on this same 13 June by another Catalina (Canso) of No.162 Squadron ('B' 9842), piloted by Flight Lieutenant L Sherman. The flying boat departed from Wick at 2200 hours on the 12th to patrol in the north-west transit zone. In the early hours, base received a flash report of a U-boat sighting in position 6410/0011, west of Trondheim, Norway, but this was the final signal from 'B'.

U-480's KTB describes what happened:

> "0401 hours, Grid AF4995 (west of Trondheim). Attack by flying boat, type Catalina, flak, strafing, hits observed on aircraft. A single bomb falls 20 metres to starboard. 0405 hours, aircraft is burning, plunges into the sea."

In fact the pilots of the severely damaged Catalina were able to ditch and five of her crew managed to get out and into a dinghy. Sherman, who had been badly burned, was swept away by the waves before the others could pull him into the raft. Two other crewmen were also lost with the aircraft.

As a result of the Cat's last signal, search and rescue aircraft were despatched but no sign of the missing aircraft was found, probably because it actually went down south-west of its radioed position. The plight of the men in the dinghy was terrible. They had no food, water or survival gear. After a week the men began to die of exposure and all except Flight Sergeant J E Roberts succumbed to the temptation to drink sea water. Finally on 22 June, a Norwegian fishing vessel found the dinghy quite by chance. Roberts, seriously ill and suffering badly from exposure, was taken into Alesund. The Canadian survived the ordeal and spent the remainder of the war as a PoW.

Sherman and crew had sunk U-980 on 11 June for which Sherman was awarded an Immediate DFC. Sadly their next operation proved to be their last, encountering U-480.

F/L L Sherman	Pilot	Sgt J E Roberts RCAF	2nd Eng
DFC RCAF		F/S M A Gislason RCAF	WOP/AG
F/O G W Besley RCAF	2nd pilot	F/O R R Ward RCAF	WOP/AG
F/O J L Harrison RCAF	Nav	F/O F W Lawrence	WOP/AG
F/S F R Dreger RCAF	Eng	RCAF	

Carmichael Fails to Return

Flight Lieutenant John William Carmichael's DFC was Gazetted on 25 August 1944, but by this time, he had been dead for over two months. Carmichael's actions on the night of D-Day are recorded above, but he failed to survive the momentous month of June 1944.

As we have already seen, 13 June proved a hard one for the anti-submarine fraternity, and 53 Squadron lost this gallant pilot and his crew on this date. They had left St Eval for a night *Cork* patrol at 2130 and the last message received from them was at 2355 hours, the signal indicating they were attacking a U-boat to the south-west of Ushant. There is no doubt that the Liberator ('C') was shot down by U-270, commanded by Kapitänleutnant Paul-Friedrich Otto, another boat which had sallied forth on the 6th as part of the 'Landwirt' Group.

The boat was found and attacked first by Wellington 'Y' of 172 Squadron (MP789), flown by Pilot Officer L G Harris, at 2342 hours. Leslie Harris made a Leigh-Light assisted attack with six D/Cs in position 4759/0528, his front gunner firing as they came in, and afterwards they remained in radar contact. Eighteen minutes later his crew observed an explosion and then a fire on the water from the position of the submarine. This was the last moment of Carmichael's C/53 – BZ818.

The KTB of U-270 records the action thus:

"Grid BF5244, time 2340 hours. Air attack – Liberator, Leigh Light, distance 1,500 metres, height 50 metres. Strafing, flak. At 2341, three bombs, they fall 20 metres from the boat. At 2357 hours, attack, Liberator, no Leigh Light, flak, distance 800 metres. Starboard inside motor is on fire as the aircraft crosses over at 30 metres height. 2358 hours, three bombs nearby and four far away. When the aircraft is at a distance of 600 metres there is a bright flash. 2359 hours, aircraft plunges into the sea, heavy fire and smoke."

U-270 was damaged in the attack and returned to harbour, the credit going to Harris and crew of 172 Squadron; Harris received the DFC shortly afterwards. This submarine had shot down Fortress U/206 Squadron on 6 January 1944 (see Chapter 7). Under a new commander, U-270 was severely damaged by 461 Squadron RAAF on 12 August 1944 and had to be abandoned the next day.

F/L J W Carmichael DFC	Pilot	F/S R H Curner RAAF	
F/S E E Stevens	2nd pilot	F/S K J Campbell RAAF	
F/S J T McKeown	Nav	F/L H C Shaw	
F/O A C Peters RAAF		F/S I E Martin RAAF	
F/O V R White		Sgt V M Lusher	

Norwegian Mosquito Down

No.333 Norwegian Squadron had a variety of aircraft, Sunderlands, Catalinas and Mosquitos. On 16 June, one of their Mosquito IVs – HP860 'R' – was on patrol late in the day and at 2259 a corrupted message indicated the crew was in trouble, and they failed to return.

In fact they had found U-804 – Oberleutnant Herbert Meyer – and attacked. Return fire hit the Mossie's port engine and split open the wing and the pilot had no choice but to ditch. This he did successfully and both men then spent 30 hours in their dinghy until, amazingly, they were rescued by another U-boat on the 18th – Oberleutnant Willi Müller's U-1000 – and brought into Bergen, the first steps into a PoW camp for the rest of the war.

The boat's KTB recorded:

> "Grid AN2333, 2259 hours. Attack by two-engined aircraft. Flak, strafing, hits observed on the aircraft. It crosses over the boat emitting a heavy smoke stream. It disappears into the darkness rapidly losing height. No bombs. Five crewmen wounded on the boat."

Lt J M Jacobsen	Pilot	2/Lt P C Hansen	Nav

VC Action

It was another 162 Squadron Canso ('P' 9754) from Wick which was involved in an action on 24 June which resulted in the loss of both U-boat and aircraft, the pilot of which would receive a Posthumous Victoria Cross.

The pilot was Flight Lieutenant D E Hornell RCAF, and he sighted a U-boat at 1900 hours in position 6300/0050, north-east of the Faeroe Islands. The action has been described numerous times but briefly, Hornell made an immediate attack but was met by heavy and accurate AA fire. Coming in astern of the boat – U-1225, commanded by Oberleutnant Ernst Sauerberg – the flying boat was hit in the starboard wing and engine, setting the aircraft on fire.

With his aircraft ablaze, Hornell continued his run, releasing a stick of four D/Cs from low altitude. The boat had by now turned broadside to the attack but the charges straddled the target across the bow, and the explosions were seen to lift the boat out of the water. As the Canso crossed over the U-boat, its burning starboard engine fell right out of its frame. Despite this mortal damage, David Hornell managed to coax his machine into a semi-smooth landing on the sea. All eight men clambered into a four-man dinghy. At first they took it in turns to have four men in the dinghy, four hanging on while in the water, but later all eight crammed in.

The D/Cs meanwhile, had proved fatal to U-1225. A Norwegian Catalina (333 Squadron) that flew over the scene later sighted the wreckage, oil and bodies. A rescue launch was sent out but there were no survivors from the submarine. The aircrew were in the water for 21 hours before rescue arrived, and three men, including Hornell, did not live through the ordeal, Hornell dying 20 minutes after rescue. His Victoria Cross, the first to a Coastal Command Catalina pilot, was Gazetted on 28 July 1944, while a DSO went to Bernard Denomy, DFCs to Ed Matheson and Graham Campbell, with DFMs going to Joe Bodnoff and Syd Cole.

F/L D E Hornell RCAF	Pilot *	Sgt F St Laurent RCAF	Eng *
F/O B C Denomy RCAF	2nd pilot	F/S I J Bodnoff RCAF	WOP/AG
F/O S E Matheson RCAF	Nav	F/S S R Cole RCAF	WOP/AG
Sgt D S Scott RCAF	Eng *	F/O G Campbell RCAF	WOP/AG

* Did not survive.

Norwegian Coastal Area

With the war in the Atlantic more or less won, the main action continued in the areas off Norway or in the Faeroes-Iceland Gap. Two days after Hornell's heroic action, U-771, commanded by Oberleutnant Helmut Block, was found and attacked by a Liberator of 86 Squadron, piloted by a veteran Coastal pilot, Flying Officer E D Moffit.

He and his crew had taken off at 0256 hours (Lib 'M' FL931) to patrol off the Norwegian coast (a Blue Peter patrol) but failed to return. U-771 later gave the following description of the action.

> "Grid AF8447 (west of Alesund), time 0659 hours. Four-engined aircraft seen approaching at a distance of 7-8,000 metres. Attacking from astern. At 4,000 metres the U-boat opens fire with the 37-mm gun and with the 20-mm guns at 2,000 metres. The aircraft passes over the boat aft of the conning tower, strafing, but releasing no bombs. Many hits seen by the 20-mm gun but the 37-mm has jammed. Aircraft crashed into the sea 200 metres to starboard and disappears in a few minutes. The aircraft was certainly a Liberator."

Moffit and crew had damaged U-743 on 20 June 1944.

F/O E D Moffit RAAF	Pilot	Sgt J Moffat	Eng
P/O S W Whitby RAAF	2nd pilot	Sgt L H Mason RAAF	WOP/AG

F/O H Pearson	Nav	Sgt J G Williams RAAF	WOP/AG
Sgt K Richardson RAAF	2nd Nav	F/S D O'Beirne	FC/AG

* * *

This same 26 June, an 86 Squadron Liberator sank U-317, commanded by Oberleutnant sur See Peter Rahlff, but did not get off without damage. Geoff 'Farmer' Parker flew FL916 'N' out on a *Blue Peter* patrol at 2045 hours and at 2320 they found the submarine in position 6203/0145.

Des Carter, the second navigator and Syd Norris the second pilot spotted it, and their hours of practice paid off as they went into their set routine. Bomb doors open and D/Cs armed, the Lib hurtled down from cloud cover and it was soon obvious to the crew that the U-boat was going to fight it out.

Carter began firing with the front gun as the boat too opened fire. In the first attack the D/Cs undershot and Parker hauled round for a second run. Flak became more intense on this run, the boat trying to keep its stern towards the aeroplane. The No.3 engine was hit and had to be feathered, but Carter was still hammering away and appeared to reduce the opposition.

The second stick of D/Cs tumbled down and the Lib crew saw a great explosion which blasted pieces of the submarine into the air and then it heeled over. As the water subsided the boat had gone, leaving just oil and around 15 men in the water. After circling, Geoff Parker headed for home on three engines.

Diverted to Stornaway due to poor weather at their base at Tain, some of the crew later flew the Lib back to its base and when being stripped down for repair found that a flak shell had gone right through the main spar. The Lib should not have been flown at all until this had been attended to! Geoff Parker received the DFC for this attack and sinking. The boat had been on its first patrol and none of her 50-man crew survived either the attack or the cold waters of the North Sea.

F/L G W T Parker	Pilot	F/S A Hogan RAAF	WOP/AG
F/S S Norris	2nd pilot	F/S M Garrett RAAF	WOP/AG
F/S D Jones	1 Nav	Sgt A S Powell	WOM/AG
F/S D Carter RNZAF	2 Nav	P/O F S Hanlin	AG/
Sgt B J Hunt	Eng		passenger

* * *

On the last day of June, Oberleutnant Rudolf Rademacher's U-478 fought two aircraft in position 6327/0050, east-north-east of the Faeroes. The first was a Canso (9841 'A') from 162 Squadron, piloted by Flight Lieutenant R E MacBride RCAF, who had sunk U-477 on 3 June. The attack was met by flak which scored a hit in the flying boat's port wing. The D/Cs failed to release however, but MacBride remained near the boat, homing in E/86

Squadron (FL924) captained by Flying Officer N E M Smith.

The Liberator attacked at 2115 hours and was also met by flak fire. An accurate stick of D/Cs sank U-478 with all hands. Despite being hit in No.4 engine, the aircraft returned safely to base, as did the Canso. The U-boat gunners had scored hits on both aircraft but they had not proved fatal or sufficient to ward off the attacks. Norman Smith, who had won his DFC with 120 Squadron in 1943, was awarded a Bar to his decoration, Gazetted in August 1944. Robert MacBride's DFC for his earlier sinking was also Gazetted in August.

F/L R E MacBride RCAF	Pilot	P/O D G MacDonald	
F/O K J Gutternson		F/S G W King	
F/O W C Lawrence		Sgt C G White	
P/O G P McNulty		Sgt T C Harper	

F/O N E M Smith DFC	Pilot	Sgt F Chiltern	Eng
F/O G F Aspinall	2nd pilot	W/O J Hamilton	AG
F/L J D Symonds	Nav	W/O A A Tulip	WOP/AG
F/S E A Brown RAAF	2nd Nav	Sgt E A Horton	WOP/AG

CHAPTER TEN

THE LAST HOORAH

Action off South Africa
As we begin this last chapter in the U-boat versus aircraft war, we skip to the Indian Ocean in order to record two incidents there that need to be included in this story. German U-boats had been operating around South Africa and into the Indian Ocean since the early days of the war although encounters were far fewer than in the North Atlantic or the Bay of Biscay.

There were a number of squadrons operating out into the Indian Ocean, mainly flying Catalina flying-boats, one being 262 Squadron. On 5 July 1944 U-859, commanded by Kapitänleutnant Johann Jebsen, was sailing some way off the south-east coast of Africa. In position 3222/3458 she was sighted by the Catalina crew of Flight Lieutenant A M Fletcher (FP174 'L'). This aircraft had left St Lucia before dawn and was flying in fair weather, with 5/10ths cloud at 2,500 feet.

They were after a suspected U-boat as land-based radar fixes had picked up a D/F fix on a target some 300 miles south-west of Durban. A series of patrols had been organised to cover the area, the first two aircraft, 'L' and 'D', taking off before first light in order to be over the area by dawn. They commenced flying parallel track Creeping Line Ahead patrols to a depth of 100 miles.

Shortly after reaching the limit of his patrol, Fletcher had commenced a return to base but then, at 1311 hours, had the good fortune to observe the U-boat surfacing. He made an immediate attack but was met by an AA barrage – the U-boat crew quickly realising they had come up at the wrong time and in the wrong place! The boat took violent evasive action and the nearest of Fletcher's five D/Cs fell 10-15 feet from her port side, slightly forward of the conning tower; the sixth D/C hung-up.

The Catalina was hit several times on the run up, a series of hits on the port wing rendered the ASI u/s, another burst of fire tore a hole in the hull, forward of the port blister, while another gash was torn in the starboard wing. Four further attacks were made in attempts to drop the remaining D/C but in vain. By this time the boat crew were realising that the aircraft was now unable to inflict any real harm to them and went down, although she left a trail of oil.

In fact the boat had been damaged, including a punctured fuel tank, hence the oil slick. The boat's schnorkel elevating gear was also rendered inoperable. One crewman had been killed by machine-gun fire and three others wounded. These casualties had been inflicted by heavy fire from the Cat's port blister gun, and in fact, return fire from the U-boat had ceased after the second run. As far as can be ascertained, the Catalina crew had been:

F/L A M Fletcher	Pilot	F/S J W Jarrom
F/O R Williamson		F/S E A Hutcheson
F/O D G McCall *		F/S G K Gillman
W/O W D Winchester *		Cpl Bredt
Cpl Botes		Lt-Cdr Mackworth RN passenger

* Usually in F/L W R Wickson's crew.

The next day, with aircraft still searching for U-859, South African Air Force Venturas from No.23 Squadron SAAF, found another boat – Oberleutnant Heusinger von Waldegg's U-198. The first to attack was Ventura 'C', flown by Lieutenant E G Rosenberg. U-198 remained on the surface and scored hits on the bomber's bomb bay and tail as it came in. As a result of the damage, the D/Cs failed to release, but the aircraft and crew returned to base safely.

Within a few minutes Ventura 'B', Lieutenant J C White and crew, was on the scene. U-198 took the opportunity to crash-dive but the Ventura managed to get in an attack and the boat was shaken-up as six D/Cs followed her down. The subsequent oil slick and the fact that several life rafts appeared on the surface caused the SAAF to make a claim for a sinking, but in fact the boat was not seriously damaged. The rafts must have been lashed to the decking and been shaken loose in the attack.

These two attacks were the last carried out on U-boats by aircraft based in South Africa. The fact that neither U-859 nor U-198 returned from their patrols seems to have added considerable confusion as to the results of these air attacks. Both the Catalina and one Ventura had been damaged, however, attacking both boats respectively.

U-859, a type IXD2, was sunk off Penang on 23 September by HMS submarine *Trenchant*, the sub picking up ten of 18 survivors; the other eight were rescued by a Japanese submarine. Jebsen was not among those rescued. U-198 was caught by a hunter-killer group in the Indian Ocean on 12 August. Waldegg had reported to BdU his success in sinking two merchant ships and his lengthy signals led to his undoing. His position was picked up by British trackers and Force 66 found her on the 10th – or at least an aircraft from the escort carrier *Shah* did. Two days later she was sunk with the loss of all her crew.

Indian Ocean Actions
While the above action may have been the last by South African based

aircraft, it was not the last in the Indian Ocean. On 20 August 1944 U-862, under the command of Korvettenkapitän Heinrich Timm, was in the northern part of the Mozambique Channel – Grid LT5968.

Catalina FP104 'H' (call-sign Jig 4),of 265 Squadron, piloted by Flight Lieutenant W S 'Jock' Lough, was on a flight from Mombasa to Durban and in addition to the crew there were four maintenance crew passengers aboard. Although it was a transport flight, it also carried out a dual anti-submarine patrol *en route*. At about last light an 'SSS' (sighting report) signal was received from the aircraft – then that ominous, tell-tale silence.

U-862 was caught on the surface, but on board and on the bridge, was a photographer who captured the subsequent events on film. This must have taken a cool head as the Catalina, and possible imminent death, came roaring in towards him and the boat.

As the flying boat approached, its nose gun firing, it was hit in the starboard wing and engine by the 3.7 cannon and as the range narrowed the 20-mm gun scored hits on the cockpit. The machine passed over the boat and crashed into the sea just ten metres ahead of her, leaving just burning wreckage on the water.

The boat nosed through the wreckage but there was no sign of life. She had not been damaged nor had her bridge crew suffered any casualties. The crew, as listed in the Squadron Form 541 note the following:

F/L W S Lough	Pilot	F/S M S Popple	
F/O R A Willis	1 Nav	F/S F W A Bickmore	WOP/AG
F/S J Norton		F/S R R Baines	WOP/AG
F/S S Elliott AFM	Eng	F/S F C A Dow	WOP/AG
plus four passengers.			

However, Air Historical Branch, MoD, lists the crew as:

F/S W S Lough	Pilot	F/S R R Baines	WOP/AG
F/O J H L Watkins	2nd pilot	F/S F W A Bickmore	WOP/AG
F/O R A Willis	1 Nav	F/S C Glynn	WOP/AG
F/O G R Chaffe	2 Nav	F/S F C A Dow	WOP/AG
F/S S Surtees AFM	Eng		

With passengers: Sgt M S Popple and three fitters, Cpl P Hodoil, LAC A W Statham and LAC Halstead.

Norway Again

Back in northern waters, the first post-June loss of an aircraft to U-boat fire came on 15 July. Liberator 'E' (EV947) of 206 Squadron, departed base at 0550 hours, made no reports and failed to return. Circumstances lead to the conclusion that the aircraft and ten-man crew had a fatal encounter with U-319, commanded by Oberleutnant zur See Johann Clemens in about position 5740/0500. There were no survivors from either side.

U-319 had sailed from Stavanger on the 5th taking up station in Grid AN34 (off south-west Norway) on anti-invasion duty, but there were no further signals from the boat. On the 15th another 206 Squadron aircraft sighted a large oil slick and a man in a dinghy. The following day the body of Sergeant N Hilton was recovered from position 5742/0455, the area of U-319's sinking. Thus the conclusion was that aircraft and U-boat had annihilated each other.

F/O D W Thynne	Pilot	F/O A Forsyth RCAF
F/O A G Echlin RCAF		F/S C McRob
F/O L B Mollard RCAF		F/O A A Desilets RCAF
F/O J E Taylor RCAF		Sgt R Fitch
P/O W W Preston		Sgt N Hilton

Courage Under Fire

The next action resulted in the award of the Victoria Cross for the pilot of a 210 Squadron Catalina (JV928 'Y'), Flight Lieutenant J A Cruickshank. This famous action began on 17 July, following a radar contact which brought the Catalina to a surfaced U-boat in position 6835/0600 – west of the Lofoten Islands – at 2147 hours. John Cruickshank went straight in despite fierce gunfire from the boat. Near to the release point the flying boat was hit by a 37 mm shell which exploded beneath the bomb aimer's window position, killing the navigator and wounding four other crew members, including the pilot who received multiple shrapnel wounds to the chest and body.

The attack was continued, however, and the submarine destroyed. Then the second pilot headed home, while Cruickshank was taken to the rest bed and had his wounds attended to. Once they arrived at base, Sullom Voe, he insisted on taking over control again for the difficult landing with the damaged machine. He brought it down safely and because of the damage to the hull, ran the Cat up onto the beach.

Cruickshank was given a blood transfusion while still in his seat, then he and the other wounded men were taken to hospital. The second pilot, who was not fully experienced (and the third pilot was still under operational instruction) received the DFM but the gallant Cruickshank received Britain's highest award for bravery.

It has always been recorded and assumed that the U-boat involved was U-347, commanded by Oberleutnant zur See Johann de Buhr, and 210 Squadron is officially credited with its destruction. However, U-361 is listed as having been lost this same date to an attack by an 86 Squadron Liberator (Pilot Officer M G Moseley and crew) – position 6836/0833. An examination of the last signals from each boat reveals that in terms of time and position it is pretty certain the listing should be reversed. Therefore it is suggested here that Cruickshank's attack sank U-361, commanded by Kapitänleutnant Hans Seidel, while U/86 Squadron sank de Buhr's U-347.

Cruickshank's crew:

F/L J A Cruickshank	Pilot	W/O W C Jenkins	WOP
F/S J Garnett	2nd pilot	F/S H Gershenson	WOP
Sgt S I Fidler	3rd pilot	F/S F J Appleton	WOM/AG
F/O D C Dickson	Nav	Sgt R S C Proctor	WOP/AG
F/S S B Harbison	Eng	F/S A I Cregan	Rigger

* * *

By one of those strange coincidences, 210 Squadron was involved in an almost identical action the next day. Even the Catalina had the next serial number – JV929 and was 'Z' – which followed Cruickshank's alphabetical 'Y'. It was also in the same general area off Norway.

Flying Officer R W G Vaughan took off from Sullom Voe at 0635. At 1500 hours an object, thought to be a ship, was observed from 15 miles, but it then became a surfaced U-boat, position 6825/0951, Vaughan taking his flying boat into the attack.

Once again the U-boat made no attempt to submerge but instead opened fire while the aircraft was still three miles off. The flak was accurate and the flying boat was hit and two crewmen wounded, one, Flying Officer K S Freeman, seriously. The starboard engine was hit and the port fuel tank ruptured causing a 100-gallon an hour leak.

The attack was carried out from head-on, the stick of D/Cs seen to make a good straddle. On banking to port the submarine was observed to be sinking in a pool of oil while the crew were abandoning ship. Before leaving the scene, several yellow dinghies and 30-40 survivors and bodies were seen scattered across the sea's surface.

The Catalina returned on one engine but could not make base due mainly to the petrol leak. Vaughan landed and beached the machine at Heinkel Gap, by Sullom Voe. There is no doubt that the U-boat was U-742, commanded by Kapitänleutnant Heinz Schwassmann, which had begun this second and final patrol on 4 July. Her last message came from Grid AF23.

Flying Officer John Mills was the aircraft navigator on this occasion, and he later recalled:

> 'Flying Officer Vaughan's navigator was sick and I took over for this flight. Crews had trained together in the use of the low level bombsight, the height and air speed had to be fed in by the second pilot. As this was not my crew I did not use it, and the bombing was carried out visually by the captain. We left Sullom at 0635 to carry out a rectangular figure-8 patrol in a 30 by-40 mile rectangle off the Lofoten Islands.
>
> 'We arrived in the patrol area at 1147 at 600 feet. We had almost completed our first circuit of the area when we picked up a W/T

message reporting a U-boat sighting. Six minutes later we altered course for the position, arriving at 1442.

'The U-boat was sighted on the surface at 1458 and attacked immediately. The boat fired at us on the bomb-run and both the blister gunners were injured, one seriously. Because of the injury to the gunner, no photographs were taken of the subsequent wreckage. I have only a vague memory of looking out and seeing floating debris. We also received cannon shell damage to the hull, wing and the port engine. The citation for Vaughan's later DFC noted "... four hundred holes."

'Nine minutes after the sighting and attack we set out for home again and soon had to shut down the port engine because of loss of oil pressure. The question of landing in a Norwegian fjord and attempting to walk to Sweden was discussed but turned down because of the injured gunners. Fuel was being lost through holes in the wing tank but fortunately the holes were not in the bottom of the tank.

'It was difficult to maintain height on one engine so the guns, some radio equipment and all unnecessary gear were jettisoned. Four and a half hours after the attack and about 200 miles from home we were met by escorting aircraft. We finally landed at 2130 with very little fuel left and the aircraft was beached to prevent it sinking, hitting a telegraph pole as it came to rest. This was followed by a long intelligence de-briefing when we were in no state to appreciate the necessity for it.'

210 Squadron Crew List

F/O R W G Vaughan	Pilot	F/S J Maule	FE/AG
F/L J Sinclair	2nd Pilot	W/O C J Webster	1st WOP
F/O N Wheatley	3rd pilot	Sgt G Gibbons	2nd WOP
F/O J G Mills	NAV	F/O K S Freeman	WOM/AG
F/S P L Ludgate	FE	F/S S M Audifferen	Rigger

Lib Ditching – Catalina Rescue

This mid-July period was proving a busy time. Another incident on the 18th concerned Liberator 'F (FL907) of 86 Squadron which took off from Tain at 1402 hours. At 2231 Inverness (Scotland) picked up an SOS from the aircraft, position given as 6815/0846, but nothing else was heard.

The aircraft had been hit in the run-in, shells smashing into the starboard-inner engine, starboard mainplane and rear fuselage compartment which caught fire. The damaged engine was feathered by the second pilot while the engineer put out the fire in the fuselage. Course was set for base, the starboard wing still burning intensely. The flames burned through the structure and into the bomb bay, so obviously the two fuel tanks had been hit.

The pilot was left with little choice but to get down quickly before the burning wing came away and he did a great job although the Lib broke up on landing and sank within 30 seconds. Everyone escaped except the front gunner who may have been killed by the flak, or was unable to extricate himself and simply went down with the aircraft.

Luckily their SOS had been heard by a post at Inverness and the rest of the crew, who had successfully climbed into dinghies, were finally located and rescued on the 22nd by Catalina 'X' of 210 Squadron, although in the meantime, two more of the downed crew had died. However, it hadn't been easy. On the 19th, Catalina 'K' of 210 was searching for them and only found an upturned dinghy and some wreckage. On the 22nd, Squadron Leader F J French DFC and his crew in 'X'/210 located the three dinghies at 0730, which had been tied together, in position 6046/0953. French knew he would have difficulty in taking off again with the extra weight of the survivors so dumped all fuel, just leaving 500 gallons with which to fly home, and all excess gear. He then landed at 0817 and picked up the six survivors, including one injured and one wounded man. Frank French had sunk U-601 on 25 February 1944.

Squadron Leader Reginald Patrick Nelms RAF received the DFC. The crew members were:

S/L R P Nelms	Pilot	F/S J H E Contant	AG
F/O R M Sommerville	2nd pilot	RCAF	
RAAF		F/S W J Daly	WOP/AG
F/L K G Gray	1 Nav	Sgt R A C Gregory	WOP/AG
F/S G S Richardson	2 Nav	Sgt P Toner	FE
RNZAF			
Sgt D A Cossey	Eng		

Their antagonist had been U-968, commanded by Oberleutnant Otto Westphalen. He wrote in their KTB:

> "2203 hours, Grid AB8959. Liberator. Five bombs 100 metres to starboard. Flak. 2205 hours. Aircraft crosses over at 50 metres, strafing, flak hit on starboard inner motor. Two bombs fall to port side. Aircraft is burning, disappears into the fog."

Home on Three Engines

Liberator 'A' of 86 Squadron (FK225) also had an encounter on the 18th, way up between Norway and Greenland. The crew had left base at 0159 hours to patrol areas 6700/0900 and 6800/0600. They reached their patrol zone and at 1002 hours, in position 6838/0859, 100 miles west of the Lofoten Islands, they found a fully surfaced U-boat and attacked with six D/Cs which partially straddled the stern. In a follow-up attack the remaining two D/Cs were dropped accidentally during the run in. The Lib this time was hit in the nose and damaged, and her two navigators were both wounded. The No.3 engine was also hit and the pilot was ordered to head for home, being diverted to Scatsa, where they landed at 1748. When last seen the U-boat had lost speed and was down by the stern.

F/L J F Pettifer RAAF	Pilot	Sgt J L Riggs RAAF	WOP/AG
Sgt J S Jackson RAAF	2nd pilot	Sgt N J D Perry RAAF	WOP/AG
Sgt J C Warne RAAF	1 Nav	F/S R M Daniel	WOP/AG
Sgt W G Tarr	2 Nav	P/O G C Kent	FC
Sgt R Keppie	Eng		

Again an accurate account, if brief, is noted in a boat's KTB, this time that of Kapitänleutnant Rudolf Büchler's U-307:

> "1302 hours, Grid AF34 – Liberator attack. Six to eight bombs – flak and strafing. Probable hits on the aircraft were made."

Coastal Ace Hit

Terry Bulloch DSO DFC & Bar was famous in the annals of anti-submarine work with Coastal Command, and attacked more German subs than any other RAF pilot during the war. He seemed to have a knack of finding them whilst others went sometimes for a whole tour without seeing anything. He had already had successes against U-boats, but on 20 July another encounter ended with his aircraft damaged.

Their patrol began at 1755 hours on the 19th. After reaching the patrol area some time at around 0114 in the morning, the crew ran into sea fog but on coming out, found a fully surfaced U-boat as only Bulloch could find one. In fact the boat's bridge crew had heard the engines of the approaching bomber and had their guns trained on the sound. As the Lib emerged from the fog it was obvious by its movements that it had not seen the boat, and when someone did, it was too late. The submarine had then opened fire, causing damage to No.'s 3 and 4 engines, the starboard rudder, fuselage, rear turret and bomb bay. Bulloch was thus thwarted from the outset and had to turn and head for home without delay.

Bulloch had found Oberleutnant Eberhard Schendel's U-636, who wrote in his KTB:

> "Grid AB5885, 0310 hours. Liberator, distance 800 metres. Fly-over. Flak. Hits in starboard inner motor and rear of the hull. Aircraft disappears into the fog. Boat does not dive. 0315 hours, a distance of 500 metres and the aircraft breaks off and turns away. During the two attacks, no bombs and no strafing. 0318 hours, crash-dive."

Bulloch got 'B' of 86 Squadron (FK229) back to Tain on two engines although the crew had to jettison all guns, ammunition and depth-charges, as well as all spare equipment to do so. No.3 engine had to be shut down at once and after a short while the damaged No.4 was in danger of over-heating and catching fire, so this too had to be stopped and feathered. A large area of the starboard rudder had been shot away, making handling difficult, but Bulloch was no novice and made it back from the Norwegian coast.

S/L T M Bulloch DSO DFC AFC	Pilot	F/S D S Powell	WOP/AG
P/O N L Lord	2nd pilot	Sgt A G Dyer	WOP/AG
F/L F E H Durrant	Nav	Sgt S A Spicer	WOP/AG
F/O A E Hanson RAAF	2nd Nav	F/O A D Lewis	FC
W/O R J McColl	Eng		

Another "465" Followed by Silence

A Wellington XIV of 172 Squadron headed out for an anti-submarine patrol at 2203 hours on 29 July. At 0042, on the morning of the 30th, control received a '465' message from them, indicating an imminent attack on a U-boat. Nothing more was heard from the crew, and no position had been given. The latter was important, not only to show where a submarine was but in the event of having to come down in the sea, the RAF crew, if they survived, had a better chance of rescue if it was known approximately where they were.

U-618, commanded by Oberleutnant zur See Erich Faust, was making her way from St Nazaire to Brest, and in Grid BF5542, was attacked, but her gunners claimed hits on the aircraft which went into the sea. Faust's message to base reporting the encounter was timed at 0125 hours, and she safely made Brest later this day. J/172 and U-618 had made a fateful rendezvous.

F/L L H Such	Pilot	Sgt F J Barrett	WOP/AG
F/S A W Ashworth	2nd pilot	Sgt L G Cull	WOP/AG
Capt F E Brunschwig (FF)	Nav	Sgt J M Hewlett	WOP/AG

(Ashworth was not Such's usual co-pilot. He had arrived from 517 Squadron on 2 July)

August 1944

By this stage in the anti-U-boat war the DH Mosquito was ranging far and wide against all manner of maritime targets, not the least of which were German submarines. They could fly at will along the Norwegian coast or off the west coast of France, although with the Allied advance on the Continent the Bay ports were about to be put out of action for good.

On 2 August two Norwegian Mosquitoes of No.333 Squadron found and attacked U-771 and U-1163, commanded by Oberleutnants Helmut Block and Ernst-Ludwig Balduhn respectively. Ordinarily Mosquitoes posed quite a threat to whatever target they found, coming in low and fast spraying cannon and machine-gun fire ahead of them before releasing bombs or depth charges. On this occasion, however, it was very different.

The Mosquitoes were airborne from RAF Leuchars, Scotland, at 1220 hours and headed for their homeland coast. They first sighted a convoy of ships but were looking for better game – submarines. At 1330 the two U-boats were sighted, led by two armed trawlers in position 5827/0545. Aircraft 'E' (HP904) crewed by Lt-Commander H Jørgensen and Sub-Lieutenant G Helgedagsrud attacked first picking U-771 as their target. Coming in from astern of the boat, they let go their two D/Cs from 100 feet despite severe flak fire. They exploded close to the boat, which was covered by spray, while cannon strikes sparkled off the conning tower.

Aircraft 'S' (HR126), Sub-Lieutenant A R Eikemo and Petty Officer C Harr came in on the second U-boat. It too released D/Cs but was hit by flak and slewed into the mast of one of the escorting trawlers and plunged into the sea, disappearing instantly. Having expended his weapons, and experiencing feed trouble with a drop-tank, the first crew had no alternative but to head back to Scotland.

The two submarines were *en route* from Stavanger to Egersund, their escorting trawlers being UJ-1113 and UJ-1163. The KTB of U-1163 noted:

> "Grid AN3191, time 1328 hours. Alarm, two aircraft, opened fire at 4,500 metres on the first aircraft which attacked U-771. At 1331, opened fire on the second aircraft, type Mosquito, which is now attacking. Target height 80-100 metres. Approached from astern at 560-600 metres then banks hard to port. Two bombs fall 50-60 metres from the boat. All guns firing, no failures, targeting excellent. 1334 hours, shot down! Aircraft's port wing collapses and it plunges into the sea 80 metres in front of the boat."

Just over an hour later both submarines safely reached Egersund although U-771 had to sail to Bergen for repairs, which were not completed until late September. For 23-year-old Aksel Reidar Eikemo and 26-year-old Claus Harr this was their first sortie to the coast of their homeland – and their last.

Wilke Battles Through
Oberleutnant zur See Hans-Dietrich Wilke ran the gauntlet of the Bay during mid-August just sailing from Brest to La Pallice, and survived. She sailed on the 8th and on the 11th his U-766 was attacked by an unidentified aircraft. He recorded in the boat's KTB:

> "BF5526 – 2319 hours. Attack by Liberator, height 15 metres. Off the bows light flares; six bombs fall 100 metres astern of the boat. Strafing. Hits by 2 cm flak on aircraft. Crash-dive."

In point of fact it was not a Liberator but a Sunderland, aircraft 'P' of 201 Squadron (ML768) on a Rover 11 patrol, an area 50 miles west of Lorient. Flying at 1,800 feet in darkness, with slight haze, the moon having not yet risen, its crew had picked up two radar contacts at 2307 hours seven miles to port. There was also an aircraft blip on the radar which had to be avoided. Losing height while holding contact, the pilot, Flying Officer A H W Mold began his run from four miles and at $1/2$ a mile had ordered flares to be dropped. No sooner had the first one ignited than heavy flak fire – green, red and yellow tracer shells – came up from the sea. Initially this exploded behind and to starboard but the gunners corrected their aim and scored a hit, causing some damage and slightly wounding two of his crew.

Mold began evasive action and the front gunner began firing his .5 gun. With damage to the flare chute and camera hatch, the flares ceased, and as they passed over the target, flak was still coming from the second U-boat and another hit was scored on the Sunderland's wing root. Mold climbed away, and being just on PLE, began his flight home. The other aircraft at the scene was 'S' of 461 Squadron. The crew saw the attack but when they tracked over the area four minutes later, there were no contacts, the boats having gone below.

F/O A H W Mold	Pilot	F/S J K Gunman RNZAF
F/O S W Botting RNZAF		Sgt F L Evans
F/O J C Coffey RCAF		Sgt J W Pitt
W/O C Churm		Sgt R M Shuttlewood
F/S R M Hughes	Nav	Sgt J Turner
F/S G Downs		

The next afternoon came another attack.

"BF5529, 1430 hours. Attack by 2-engined aircraft, distance 6,000 metres. Passes U-boat on first approach then banks and attacks with six bombs. Strafing. Flak from 2 cm gun makes several hits, 3.7 cm fires semi-automatic. Aircraft flies away and stays outside flak range. At 1435 hours a second aircraft, Boeing Fortress. Circles the boat outside flak range. First aircraft departs. 1455 hours, crash-dive."

Again the aircraft can be identified. First was Wellington 'A' of 172 Squadron (NB833), flown by Pilot Officer D S Bielby. The crew were out on a Rover 11 patrol too, having taken off at 0807 hours that morning. Their radar contact was timed at 1429 at a range of ten miles. Five minutes later, in position 4706/0409, a U-boat was seen at three miles, and it was firing at them.

Bielby continued in and dropped six D/Cs from 30 feet. After the attack the boat began to turn in circles but at a decreased speed and an oil patch was clearly seen on the surface. The Wellington XIV had been hit, a hole blasted through the starboard wing, and while later they were to find the

starboard undercarrige tyre damaged, it had not been punctured. The RAF
crew began homing in other aircraft, and as the KTB noted, other aircraft
had started to arrive when the Captain decided to dive. In the event, three
Liberators, a Halifax and another Wellington were soon on the scene, but
the U-boat had gone.

P/O D S Bielby	Pilot	P/O R W Jenkins RAAF	WOP/AG
F/O B V Lott	2nd pilot	Sgt D H Evans	WOP/AG
F/O R Elyard RAAF	Nav	F/O F R Bean RAAF	WOP/AG

On the 14th Wilke's KTB records action at 0116 hours in Grid BF5537, an
attack by a twin-engined aircraft using a Leigh Light. The boat's gunners
once more opened up on their antagonist and hits were observed on the
machine's port engine. The aircraft began to burn and fell into the sea,
exploding 300 metres away, on the boat's starboard side.

This would appear to be Wellington 'E' of 407 Squadron RCAF (NB859)
which had departed RAF Chivenor at 2231 hours the previous evening and
failed to return with its six-man crew.

U-766 entered La Pallice on the 18th. However, she was unable to get
back to sea because of the Allied advance. She later served with the French
Navy as the *Laubie* until 1963.

F/O F A J Kemper	Pilot	W/O D L S Henderson	WOP/AG
F/S J M Richardson	2nd pilot	W/O B A Gauthier	WOP/AG
F/O A D Hoddinott	Nav	W/O A R Elliott	WOP/AG

However, there was a similar action in this area involving U-445. A
Wellington XIV from 172 Squadron had flown out at 2305 on the 13th to
fly in the same area as E/407 – Patrol 37 – and had also failed to return.
U-445 claimed a twin-engined aircraft (a Beaufighter) at 0414 hours in
Quadrant BF6721, during a trip from Brest to La Pallice. It seems certain
that the encounter was with K/172 which failed to return.

F/O D A Adams RCAF	Pilot	Sgt L R Trout	WOP/AG
Sgt R H Bloomfield	2nd pilot	Sgt W R O Matthews	WOP/AG
F/S T O'C Fitzgerald	Nav	Sgt G T Lewis	WOP/AG

Action off the Gironde
Returning from patrols, U-534 had met up with and was now part of a
group of three U-boats heading for the Gironde, having made rendezvous
with U-437 and U-857. As they neared the estuary, the group was located
by two RAF aircraft.

Ranger Patrols on 13 August by E/58 (JP301) and K/502 Squadrons
brought some excitement to the Halifax crews of Flight Lieutenant John
MacFadyen and Flying Officer D E Umpherson RCAF. MacFadyen found

three U-boats and four escort vessels in position 4538/0112 at 0630 hours and dropped four 600 lb bombs from 2,000 feet. However on the run-in a flak burst beneath the starboard wing at the crucial moment of bomb-release which threw the aircraft off track and the bomb explosions were not seen. They were then busy avoiding flak from all seven vessels as well as fire from nearby shore batteries.

Umpherson and crew had left base at 0200 hours and at 0640, in position 4535/0241, flying at 1,200 feet, sighted visually the three surfaced U-boats and a merchant vessel, possibly an M-class minesweeper, entering the Gironde estuary.

Umpherson climbed and increased speed as all vessels began to open fire on an unidentified twin-engined aircraft which was making a low level attack on the ships. The Halifax's rear gunner observed the bombs go down, but they were not on target. Umpherson made a diving turn and attacked from 5,000 feet with anti-submarine bombs, but how close they were could not be seen, as light flak and shore batteries began to open up on the aircraft which sustained damage to its starboard elevator, and extensive damage to the rear turret and rear fuselage, which also badly wounded the rear gunner. The starboard outer engine was hit, the CSU made u/s, and the intercom was shot out. U-857's KTB indicates the action:

"0414 hours – met by escort.
0500 hours – reached the Gironde, in convoy with U-Nollau and U-Lamby.
0641 hours – four-engined aircraft. Flak from all boats prevents a good bomb drop. They fall 300 metres from U-Nollau (U-534). Aircraft disappears in the fog." U-437's KTB confirms all this and also noted a smoke trail coming from one of the aeroplane's starboard motors. (This was MacFadyen's attack.)
"0656 hours – off Le Verdun, four-engined aircraft, height 800-1,000 metres, flak again prevents an accurate bombing. Bombs fall 500 metres behind U-857, aircraft banks off and disappears. One motor shows a smoke stream."

The KTB of U-437 claims two hits on the aircraft. (This was Umpherson's attack.)

Umpherson headed for home on three engines, jettisoning guns and loose equipment but managed to land at Predannack despite serious damage. The wounded signaller/air gunner, Flying Officer Davies, died the next day.

F/L J M MacFadyen	Pilot	F/S J J Scott	WOP/AG
F/O L B Davey	2nd pilot	W/O A E Moody	WOP/AG
F/O J M Wheeler RAAF	Nav	F/O W S Gibbons RCAF	WOP/AG
W/O A E B Darby	Eng	F/S J J E Scullion	WOP/AG

F/O W E Umpherson	Pilot	Sgt T H Veitch	Eng
RCAF		W/O A K Williams	WOP/AG
F/O C A McLennon	2nd pilot	W/O V H Smith	WOP/AG
RCAF		Sgt H A Pettett	WOP/AG
F/S D Durward	Nav	F/O C W Davies	Sig/AG

John Scott, MacFadyen's 1st WOP/AG, recalls:

> 'I was 1st WOP in Flight Lieutenant MacFadyen's crew for only a short period, from 28 July to 13 August 1944. The sortie was my 60th, and my last with 58 Squadron.
>
> 'The Bordeaux area was always a "hot-spot", and there was a lot of flak on this occasion. We attacked a group of three U-boats, four E-boats and two MVs. We were buffeted about on the bombing run, but I do not remember any serious damage to JP301, nor do I recall the identity of the other Halifax in the vicinity; all our concentration was on the attack. We returned to base and landed safely after nine hours, ten minutes airborne at 1040 am.
>
> 'A little anecdote: Arthur Moody (who died in 1997; we had previously flown in Tom Griffiths' crew until 1 January 1944, when I went into Toby Sladen's crew) and I would occasionally sally into Christchurch to a pub called the 'Black Horse'. He would cycle with me perched on the handlebars. On the outward journey we had to negotiate a wooden bridge over a wide stream. On the return trip, Arthur, having consumed a number of strong beers, or I obstructed his view, missed the bridge and we ended up in the stream, emerging as two very wet Senior NCOs. The 'erk' who checked out 1250's on the Station gate wisely said nothing!
>
> 'Paddy' Scullion, who was I believe an MA Dublin University, once wrote a vitriolic letter to Group Headquarters complaining about the poor armament in the Halifax turrets against the fire power of the Junkers 88. I can't remember what, if anything, Group replied.'

John MacFadyen was awarded the DFC in 1945.

Another Wellington Downed

Wellingtons had been well suited to anti-U-boat operations since the early days and in 1944 they were still operating successfully, especially at night. On 26 August, Wellington 'B' of 172 Squadron (NB798), piloted by Flying Officer G E Whiteley, was airborne at 1726 and headed for the Bay.

Fifteen minutes past midnight (27th) a '414' message was received and a position, but it was very weak. This led to a search by other Coastal Command aircraft. What had occurred was that the Wellington crew had found U-534 – Kapitänleutnant Herbert Nollau – outbound from Bordeaux and attacked. The boat's KTB recorded:

> "Grid BF9234, time 0009 hours. Aircraft attack with Leigh Light.

Flak, four bombs explode 1,000 metres astern of the boat. After a
few bursts of flak the 2-engined aircraft is seen to be hit and plunges
into the sea. Only heavy fire is seen at the crash scene."

Coming in low and fast, the Leigh Light was switched on and the aircraft
was met by heavy gunfire, and although D/Cs went down, the aeroplane
suffered mortal damage and crashed into the sea. Four of the crew survived
but Flying Officer R B Gray RCAF, died some hours before rescue arrived.

At 0234 on the morning of the 27th, the crew of another 172 aircraft,
spotted distress signals and went to investigate. They were certain there
was someone in the water and sent a position report. At 1428, in position
4528/0228, Sunderland 'P' of 461 Squadron RAAF found themselves
above a dinghy with three occupants, with another man in the water and
sent a message to base. The pilot was Flight Lieutenant W B Tilley, who
had sunk U-243 on 8 July 1944. After dumping his D/Cs, he brought his
flying boat in to a landing and pulled the three men from the sea, then flew
them back to Mount Batten.

The men had been through quite an ordeal. The Wellington's port engine
had been hit and set on fire, then the aircraft went into the sea, sinking
immediately, leaving burning petrol on the surface. Warrant Officer G H
Bulley found himself going down with the machine, and was several feet
below the surface by the time he broke clear through the astrodome. On the
surface he swam round, flashing a torch until he found other survivors,
helping Whiteley and Ford, who had both been injured, into the dinghy.
The injured Whiteley and the badly wounded Ford were in a small dinghy,
while Gray and Bulley remained in the water, holding onto the dinghy rope.
Gray, so it was thought, had a severe leg wound (he may even have lost the
lower part of the limb) but had helped keep everyone's spirits up and
refused to swop places with either of the other two wounded men in the
dinghy. He eventually succumbed to the cold and his injury, and although
Whiteley tried to hold on to him, once they knew he had died, eventually
he had to be left. Bulley remained in the water for the whole 15 hours until
they were rescued at 1510.

Whiteley was later awarded the DSO, Gordon Henry Bulley the DFC
and Sergeant John William Cecil Ford the DFM. For his self sacrifice,
Roderick Borden Gray was awarded a posthumous George Cross. The crew
had been:

F/O G E Whiteley	Pilot	Sgt D Rowell	WOP/AG+
F/O T G Robb RCAF	2nd pilot +	Sgt J W C Ford	WOP/AG
F/O R B Gray RCAF	Nav +	W/O G H Bulley RCAF	WOP/AG
+ Lost.			

This was not the last aircraft/U-boat action but it was the last recorded RAF
aircraft lost to submarine gunfire until the final weeks of the war. These

actions were mainly fought against U-boats in and around the Kattegat, several trying to escape from northern Germany to Norway or Denmark.

Mosquito Down

On 24 March 1945, ranging Mosquito aircraft located U-249, commanded by Kapitänleutnant Uwe Koch. She had sailed from Bergen for British waters on the 21st, but was found off the Norwegian coast. Mosquito VI 'Q' (HR434) of 235 Squadron made an attack but in the exchange the Mossie was hit and dived into the sea. U-249 recorded the action in Quadrant AN2412 at 1324 hours. It is assumed the U-boat was damaged or perhaps had suffered injuries to her bridge crew as she put back into Bergen later that day. Joseph Richard Williams and John Thomas Flower did not survive.

F/L J R Williams   Pilot   A/F/L J T Flower   Nav

Debris or Flak?

One loss, while not directly attributable to U-boat flak, was caused by an attack on two U-boats on 9 April 1945. U-84 (OL Herbert Meyer) and U-1065 (OL Johannes Panitz) were attacked – or rather swamped – by 34 Mosquitoes from Coastal Command's Banff Strike Wing, led by Squadron Leader H H Gunnis DFC. It comprised aircraft from 143, 235 and 248 Squadrons.

Finding the boats in position 5805/1110 (Skagerrak, north-east of the Skaw, Denmark), which were *en route* from Norway to Kiel, at 1722 hours, 'Alec' Gunnis detailed 143 to attack the first, followed by 235. It was all over in a few minutes.

Both U-boats were covered by numerous hits from rockets, cannon and machine-gun fire, both wet and dry (below and above the water-line). The leading boat was seen to submerge following the attacks, then resurface seconds later, only to begin to settle again stern first – then it blew up.

The second sub disappeared after the attacks by all three squadrons, leaving a pool of debris, oil and some survivors. Some of the attacking crews also mentioned an explosion. Flak was only encountered from the leading boat, but following the explosion of this target, an accompanying Banff Wing PRU Mosquito which was being used to photograph the attack (DZ592) was seen to flip onto its back and crash into the sea. Flight Lieutenant W M O Jones and Flying Officer A J Newell were both killed.

Almost certainly they were victims of the flying debris which also damaged at least four other Mosquitoes, two of which were forced to head for Sweden.

Mustang Mayhem

In the late afternoon of 4 May 1945, three U-boats were found by attack aircraft, searching for all manner of ships located north of Flensburg Fjord, position 5455/1007. Records are sketchy at best for this period but one group of submarines, U-155 (OL Friedrich Altemeier), U-680 (OL Max

Ulber) and U-1233 (OL Heinrich Niemeyer) were attacked while making for Fredericia, Denmark. They reported being attacked by aircraft during passage on this day and all three opened fire and the crewmen aboard U-155 later reported that they had shot down an aircraft.

It seems more than probable that their victim was a single-engined Mustang of 126 Squadron RAF, piloted by the unit's CO, Major A Austeen DFC, killed on this operation. Arne Austeen was a distinguished Norwegian fighter pilot. Having escaped from Norway early in the war he had flown fighter operations since 1942; he was aged over 30.

On 4 May 1945 his Mustang Squadron was supplying escort for the Beaufighters of the North Coates Strike Wing. Amongst vessels attacked and sunk were U-236, U-393 and U-2338, while 126 also attacked a Sperrbrecher north of the Fjord. Austeen was flying a Mustang III serial number KH478.

Finalé

The next day came the last of the blood-letting. Liberators were ranging over the Kattegat region, attacking and sinking several U-boats. Aircraft 'E' of 547 Squadron (KK299) was hit by flak as it attacked one of three U-boats and crashed into the sea with one engine on fire. There was apparently only one survivor and he was picked up by a rescue boat from a nearby lighthouse. However, if true he does not appear to have survived, the whole crew being listing as lost.

F/L G W Hill	Pilot	W/O A J Dale
F/O J L Howatson RAAF		W/O H Parks
F/L R J Allen		Sgt A E Tyrer
P/O V D Sweeney RCAF		F/S R J McLean RCAF
Sgt P D Phelan		F/S C A Keown RCAF
F/S W Devins		

One of the boats involved was Herbert Nollau's U-534, the same boat which had shot down Flying Officer Whiteley's 172 Squadron Wellington back on 27 August 1944. This was attacked and sunk by Warrant Officer J D Nicol and crew of 86 Squadron. (Another was U-3503 – OL Hugo Deiring.) U-534 remained on the bottom of the sea bed until located in 1986 and raised in August 1993.

In 1996 she was taken to Liverpool, England, to be restored and opened to the public as a permanent memorial to all who died in the Battle of the Atlantic. The men of the Royal Navy, Merchant Navy, German Navy, Luftwaffe, and Royal Air Force Coastal Command, plus all those attached for temporary duty to the latter force. They had fought their bitter war above, on and below the grey, often cruel Atlantic. Courage above all survives in the memories, and those that did not get home must be honoured, and never forgotten.

SELECT BIBLIOGRAPHY

Alwyn, Jay	*Endurance*, Banner Books, 1996.
Banks, Arthur	*Wings of the Dawning*, Images Publishing, 1996.
Bolitho, Hector	*A Penguin in the Eyrie*, Hutchinson, 1955.
Bowyer, Chaz	*The Short Sunderland*, Aston Publications, 1984.
	Men of Coastal Command, Wm Kimber, 1985.
Clouston, A/Cdr A E	*The Dangerous Skies*, Cassell & Co, 1954.
Creed, Roscoe	*PBY, The Catalina Flying Boat*, US Naval Institute Press, 1985.
Cremer, Peter	*U-333*, Triad Grafton Books, 1986.
Douglas W A B	*The Creation of a National Air Force*, Official History of the RCAF, Vol II, University of Toronto Press, 1986.
Franks, Norman	*Search, Find and Kill*, Revised Edition, Grub Street, 1995.
	Dark Sky, Deep Water, Grub Street, 1997.
	Conflict over the Bay, Wm Kimber, 1986.
Goss, Chris	*Bloody Biscay*, Crécy Books, 1997.
Grenhous, Brereton *et al.*	*The Crucible of War*, Official History of the RCAF, Vol III, University of Toronto Press, 1986.
Hendrie, Andrew	*Flying Cats*, Airlife, 1988.
	Short Sunderland, Airlife, 1994
	Canadian Squadrons in Coastal Command, Vanwell Publishing Ltd, 1997.
Herington, John	*Air War Against Germany & Italy 1939-45,* 2 Vols.
Herzog, Bodo	*U-boats in Action 1939-1945*, Ian Allan, 1970.
Hessler, Günter	*The U-boat War in the Atlantic*, MoD
Jones, Geoffrey	*Autumn of the U-boats*, Wm Kimber, 1984.
	Death of the Wolf Packs, Wm Kimber, 1986.
Kelshall, Gaylord	*The U-boat War in the Caribbean*, US Naval Institute Press, 1994.
Martin, H J and Orpen, N D	*South Africa at War*, Vols VI & VII, Purnell
Merrick, K A	*The Handley-Page Halifax*, Aston Publications.
Morrison, S E	*The Atlantic Battle Won, May 1943-May 1945*, History of US Naval Operations in WWII, Vol X, Little, Brown and Co, 1956.
Nesbit, Roy C	*The Strike Wings*, Wm Kimber, 1984.
Niestlé, Dr Axel	*German U-boat losses During WWII*, US Naval Institute Press, 1998.
Poolman, Kenneth	*Allied Escort Carriers of WWII*, Blandford Press, 1988.
	Escort Carrier, HMS Vindex at War, Leo Cooper, 1983.
Price, Alfred	*Aircraft versus Submarine*, Wm Kimber, 1973.
Quinn, John and Reilly, Alan	*Covering the Approaches*, Impact Printing, 1996.
Rohwer, Prof Dr Jürgan Hümmelchen, Gerhard	*Chronology of the War at Sea, 1939-1945*, Rev Ed. US Naval Institute Press, 1992.
Roskill, Stephen W	*The War at Sea, 1939-1945*, 3 vols, HMSO, 1954-61.
Schoenfeld, Max	*Stalking the U-boats*, Smithsonian Institution Press, 1995.
Spooner, Tony	*Coastal Ace*, Wm Kimber, 1986.
Spring, Ivan	*Flying Boat*, Spring Air, 1995.
Sturtivant, Ray	*The Swordfish Story*, Arms & Armour, 1993.
	Fleet Air Arm Aircraft, 1939-1945, Air Britain, 1995.
Syrett, David	*The Defeat of the German U-boats,* University of South Carolina Press, 1994.
Turner, L C F, *et al.*	*War in the Southern Oceans, 1939-1945,* Oxford University Press, 1961.
Werner, Herbert	*Iron Coffins*, Bantam Books, 1969.
Woodman, Richard	*Artic Convoys, 1941-1945*, John Murray, 1994.
Wynn, Kenneth	*U-boat Operations of the Second World War*, 2 Vols, Chatham Publishing, 1998.
Y'blood, William T	*Hunter-Killer*, US Naval Institute Press, 1983.

APPENDIX

Over the years a number of suspected aeroplane casualties have been listed, especially where a U-boat may have thought an action resulted in one being shot down. Often the encounter did not cause any hurt to the aircraft, just as some claims by aircraft crews did not inflict any damage on a submarine. The incidents listed here are those where it was thought an aircraft was shot down or at least hit, but where either this proved untrue or where no corresponding loss has been found in surviving records. If nothing else, this list can be used as a starting point for anyone wishing to research these queries.

1942
12 August: Two attacks on the Italian submarine *Giada* in the Western Mediterranean, 70 miles north-west of Algiers, one in the morning and one in the afternoon, both by Sunderland flying boats, one being shot down. No loss found.

1943
4 February: Still under active investigation is the loss of Wellington 'L' of 172 Squadron. It is thought possible that this machine encountered U-519, which originally had been thought to have been attacked by a USAAF Liberator, but this is now believed to have been a damaging attack on U-752. The possibility is that L/172 (HX653) was lost attacking – and sinking – U-519. The crew was F/O J N Myers, Sgts S T Pollard, E Francis, F Whitwell, E E Paul and J G Faux.

16 February: U-755 was attacked by an unidentified Swordfish, west-north-west of Algiers at 1940 hours (Grid CH8352). It suddenly disappeared at sea level and the boat's KTB noted that it presumably hit the sea. No loss found.

5 April: U-438 claimed to have shot down an aircraft. No obvious loss found.

8 April: U-168 was attacked by Sunderland 'E' of 423 Squadron RCAF south of Iceland and the flying boat was claimed as damaged. D/Cs were unarmed when released although one did explode. The Sunderland did not suffer any damage.

12 May: U-180 was found by a SAAF Anson of No.44 Air School south-east of Port Elizabeth, South Africa at 0915 hours (Grid KZ4155). The Anson was unarmed but as it investigated the U-boat, its gunners opened fire, claiming the 'Hampden' as possibly shot down. It wasn't.

23 May: Attacks by Swordfish on U-468 occurred in fact on the 22nd, by 819 Squadron from HMS *Archer*, in the mid-Atlantic, and an Avenger of VC-9 of USS Bogue. Flak was encountered but neither aircraft suffered any damage.

28 May: A Halifax of 502 Squadron encountered U-594 that had been attacked the previous day (see Chapter Two). Again the U-boat claimed hits on her attacker, but on this occasion was not hit and returned to base unscathed.

29 May: U-662 is listed as having a success over an aircraft on this date, but the boat was in port at St Nazaire between 19 May and 26 June and it is assumed the listing refers to U-667 which encountered a 190 Squadron Catalina on the 29th.

13 June: An action by U-653 refers to the exchange between U-564 and U/228 Squadron.

20 June: An action by U-558 refers to 20 *July* 1943.

24 June: U-271 shot down an unidentified aircraft at 0850 hours in Grid AK7253, south-east of Cape Farewell. The machine was seen to crash on fire and later the boat passed through the wreckage looking for survivors. No RAF aircraft were lost this date and no others appear missing either. Still investigating.

8 July: U-228 was returning from a patrol started on 4 May and had survived an attack by 58 Squadron on 7 May. On 8 July she was attacked by a Catalina from Gibraltar, G/210 Squadron (F/O D H Clarke). This aircraft had used its D/Cs attacking a submarine at 1745 hours, so when it found U-228 at 1943 hours, it could only exchange gunfire with it. Her gunners claimed hits on the bow and stern, and unsure if another attack was coming, the boat crash-dived at 1945 hours. The Catalina suffered no damage. (see also Chapter 3)

13 July: Attack on U-333 off the coast of West Africa. The boat crew claimed hits on a Hudson but this aircraft has yet to be identified.

22 July: U-571 was attacked by an aircraft of No.26 Squadron SAAF flying from Takoradi, West Africa, and claimed hits on it. The Squadron's diary makes no mention of this event.

22 July: Two Beaufighters encountered U-664 in the Bay of Biscay and while aircraft and boat exchanged fire, the claim by the boat of scoring hits and possibly shooting one Beau down were over-optimistic. Neither were hit.

30 July: Attack on U-604 by a Ventura of VB-129 USN (Lt Cdr T D Davies) off the Brazilian coast. Flak did not inflict any damage on the aircraft, but the action started a chain of events that led to the boat's loss.

5/6 September: The listing of an action on this date is in error. There were no air actions on the boat until attacked by Wellingtons of 179 Squadron on 11/12 September.

22 September: U-270 was attacked and damaged by Liberator L/10 RCAF (W/O J Billings) in action around convoy ON-202/ONS-18. The aircraft was also seriously shot-up.

1944

7 February: Many sources credit U-238 with shooting down Wellington W/407 Squadron RCAF (F/O O G Campbell). W/407 did indeed encounter this boat and in the same action, U-256, but no claims were made by either of the German crews and 'W' returned safely to base.

5 May: Claim by U-955 to have shot down a Liberator south of Iceland, Grid AL2449, at 0420 hours. Aircraft is unidentified.

24 May: When U-476 was sunk on 24 May by 210 Squadron it was assumed the boat had shot down its attacker because when U-476 arrived at the scene they reported seeing aircraft wreckage on the water. Based on this, credit was given to U-476 for a kill.

6/7 June: U-981 attacked by U/502 Squadron and after it crash-dived her crew thought their earlier flak fire might have hit and damaged their attacker. This was not the case.

14 Jun: U-290 claimed hits and possible downing of an attacking aircraft. In fact the boat was attacked by Mosquito H/333 Norwegian Squadron which was not hit.

5/6 July: U-859 and/or U-198 is often credited with shooting down a Ventura aircraft, variously listed as SAAF or USN. (see Chapter Ten for full details of the actual action.)

9 July: 210 Squadron had Catalina 'T' (JX574) piloted by F/O C L Hodsman fail to return from a patrol north of the Shetlands. The Squadron ORB notes it was presumed shot down by a U-boat which it had sighted, but there is no recorded evidence of a claim by a U-boat.

18 July: U-286 reported an attack and the possible downing of an attacking Stirling off south Norway. In fact the attacking aircraft was a Mosquito, K/333 Norwegian Squadron, which suffered no damage.

20 August: 58 Squadron (W/C Grant) lost an aircraft during encounter with U-boats although our best evidence indicates that a U-boat was probably not responsible. The explosion that destroyed the Halifax may well have been caused by flak but it is more probable that a surface vessel or even a land battery was the cause.

30 September: A mystery surrounds the loss of a Swordfish of 813 Squadron (NR986), off HMS *Campania*, it failing to return from an anti-submarine search over the Barents Sea. There is a possibility that it ran into an action with U-921 but this is still under review. The crew had been Lt-Commander Cyril Arthur Allen RNVR, Lieutenant Keith H Tilley RNVR and Lieutenant Charles R Russ RNVR. In addition to U-921, submarines U-310, U-636 and U-968 were all attacked by aircraft and fought back with flak fire, any one of which could have caused the Swordfish's loss.

14 November: Liberator A/224 Squadron failed to return from a patrol off Norway and is sometimes presumed to have been lost to U-boat flak. Her crew's last transmission, north-west of Bergen, indicated attacks by German fighters and not a U-boat.

May 1945: There is a report that U-862 shot down a USAAF P-38 fighter during an air raid on Singapore Harbour.

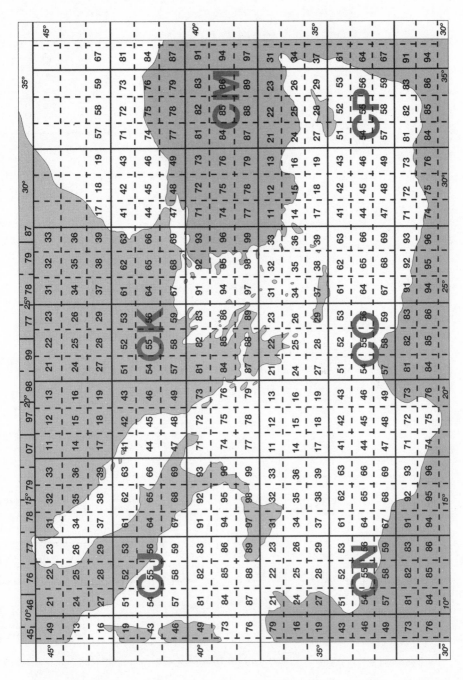

Close-up of the Mediterranean area showing both German Quadrant Grid letters and the numbers within each Grid reference.

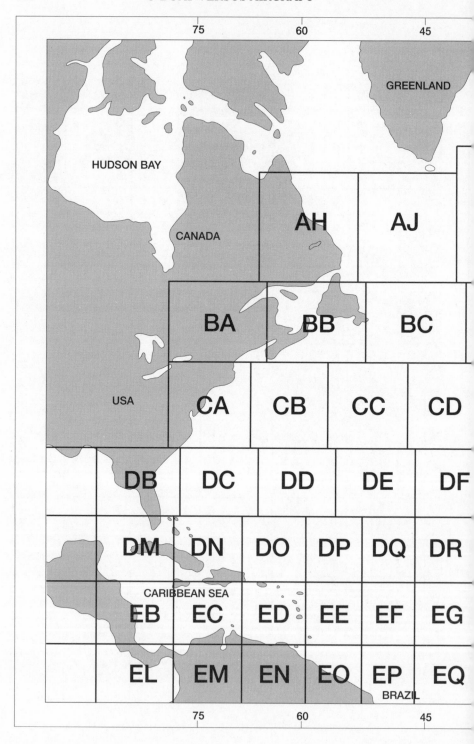

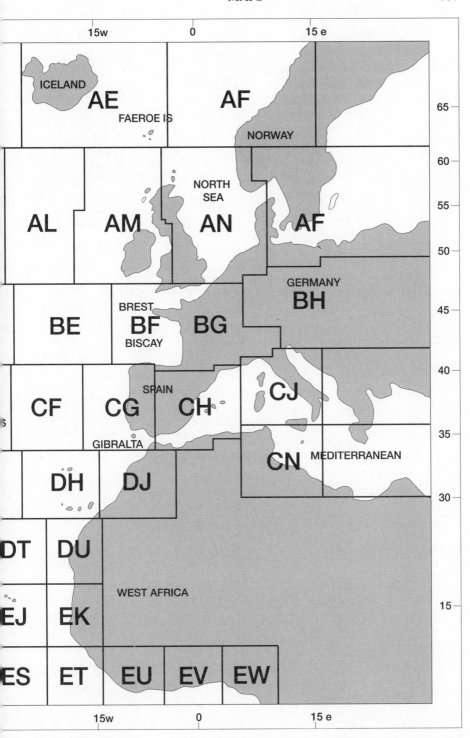

Map of the Atlantic showing the German Grid Quadrant letters, and the international longitude and latitude.

INDEX